PLAYWORK

NVQ/SVQ

LEVEL **3**

Candidate Handbook

2nd edition

Tina Farrow

Geraldine Chaffe

Penny Tassoni

www.heinemann.co.uk

✓ Free online support
✓ Useful weblinks
✓ 24 hour online ordering

01865 888058

D0493434

Heinemann is an imprint of Pearson Education Limited, a company incorporated
in England and Wales, having its registered office at Edinburgh Gate, Harlow, Essex,
CM20 2JE. Registered company number: 872828

www.heinemann.co.uk

Heinemann is a registered trademark of Pearson Education Ltd.

© Tina Farrow, Geraldine Chaffe, Penny Tassoni, 2006

First published 2006

10
10 9 8 7 6 5

British Library Cataloguing in Publication Data is available
from the British Library on request.

ISBN: 978 0 435449 24 7

Edited by Phebe Kynaston
Typeset and illustrated by Tek-Art
Original illustrations © Harcourt Education Limited, 2005
Cover design by Wooden Ark
Printed in China (CTPSC/05)
Cover photo: © Getty Images/Digital Vision

Websites

Please note that the examples of websites suggested in this book were up to date at the time of writing.
It is essential for tutors to preview each site before using it to ensure that the URL is still accurate and the
content is appropriate. We suggest that tutors bookmark useful sites and consider enabling students to
access them through the school or college intranet.

Acknowledgements

The author and publisher would like to thank the following individuals and organisations for permission
to reproduce photographs:
Student book: ©Ariel Skelley/CORBIS p**275**; ©Bob Rowan, Progressive Image/CORBIS p**314**;
Corbis p**280**; educationphotos.co.uk/walmsley p**187**; Gedling Play Forum pp**54**, **158**, **297**, **310**, **320**;
Harcourt Ltd/Gareth Boden p**94**; Harcourt Ltd/Haddon Davies p**299**; Harcourt Ltd/Jules Selmes pp**44**, **64**,
216; Harcourt Ltd/Keith Gibson p**147**; Harcourt Ltd/Tudor Photography pp**12**, **28**, **114**, **238**, **252**, **287**,
322; ©Joseph Sohm, ChromoSohm Inc./CORBIS p**220**; Lauren Shear/Science Photo Library p**304**;
Taxi/Getty Images p**149**. **Web units:** Gedling Play Forum pp**7**, **18**(A320), **22**(B227); Harcourt Ltd/Tudor
Photography p **5**(A320); Richard Smith p**27**(A319).

Every effort has been made to contact copyright holders of material reproduced in this book. Any omissions
will be rectified in subsequent printings if notice is given to the publishers.

Acknowledgements

Geraldine would like to thank the staff at the Nottingham City Early Years & Childcare Unit for their support and for keeping her up to date with information. She would particularly like to thank Kathryn Bouchlaghem who has encouraged and inspired her and has urged her to keep going when inspiration failed her, and her Service Manager Paulette Thompson-Omenka for her forbearance when the going got tough.

Tina would like to thank the NVQ team at Nottingham City Council for their encouragement, and her colleague Anne Volbracht for her assistance throughout the time it took to rewrite this book. She would also like to mention her family, and Janice Rushton of Phoenix Training for her support and encouragement.

We would both like to thank the following people:

Ann Partington for allowing us to use her information on the Common Assessment Framework (CAF)

Fiona McManus, Out of School Co-ordinator for Gedling and Gedling Play Forum, for allowing us to use a selection of photographs, and Esther Cumberpatch for the use of some of her policies and procedures from her Out-of-School provision

Phebe Kynaston and Catherine Turner for their patience and guidance in the editing process and for never showing their frustration in our delays

Finally we would like to thank Ali Wood and Meynell Walters for the information given on their training days.

Tina Farrow and Geraldine Chaffe

About the authors

Tina Farrow has many years' experience of working with young people in disadvantaged inner city areas. She is a qualified level 3 playworker, assessor and verifier for playwork and other childcare-related S/NVQs. Tina has particular expertise in working with young people with complex needs which ensures she remains fully aware of the many challenges faced by playworkers on a daily basis.

Geraldine Chaffe has long been involved in the field of play and play development. She is a qualified assessor and verifier and has a passionate commitment to the importance of play, particularly in the outdoor environment. In her present role as an LA Workforce Development Officer she uses every opportunity to promote and support the value of play and playworkers.

Penny Tassoni is an educational consultant, trainer and well-known author. Over 20 years, she has had a wide ranging career which includes monitoring play schemes as well as looking at ways of enhancing play provision for children of all ages. Penny is an experienced tutor and has taught on a variety of courses. She is also an examiner and reviser for CACHE.

Contents

*Three additional optional units are available to download **for free** from
www.heinemann.co.uk/vocational. Click on *Childcare* on the subject list, then *Free Resources*
under the Resource Centre at the top right of the screen. The units available are:

A319 Recruit, select and keep colleagues
A320 Allocate and monitor the progress and quality of work in your area of responsibility
B227 Contribute to evaluating, developing and promoting services.

Introduction

Welcome to this revised handbook for the National Vocational Qualification (NVQ) or Scottish Vocational Qualification (SVQ) Level 3 in Playwork. The original handbook, written by Penny Tassoni, has been revised to meet the requirements of the new National Occupational Standards (NOS). This handbook is designed to give you guidance and help you identify good practice in working with children and young people aged from 4–15 years. It is particularly focused towards those who are embarking on an S/NVQ Level 3 in Playwork award.

To be an effective and competent playworker it is important not only to gain knowledge, skills and understanding about children and young people, but also to continually update and improve your practice. This book provides ideas and suggestions to aid you in this role.

It can be difficult to keep up to date with current thinking in these ever-changing times. In the light of the Every Child Matters: Change for Children agenda, and the five outcomes for children – Being Healthy, Staying Safe, Enjoy and Achieve, Make a Positive Contribution and Achieve Economic Well-being – the demands on all those who work with children and young people have increased.

These five outcomes are universal ambitions for every child and young person whatever their background or circumstances, and playworkers will be expected to work much more closely with other professionals such as childcare workers, teachers and youth workers to ensure the best possible outcomes for children and young people.

All local authorities will have now created a new department focused on children's services. This department will be an amalgamation of the old education, social services (children's department), play and youth services. This merger should ensure that local children's services reflect the needs of children and young people and that the professionals who work with them recognise the need for, and benefits of, partnership working.

There are increasing opportunities for qualified playworkers and we are now just a short step away from the emergence of the new Qualifications Framework and the transitional modules that will enable workers with a childcare or playwork qualification to move easily from sector to sector. This means that the opportunities for playworkers have never been greater and quality, well-trained playworkers will be in great demand.

How the standards work

To achieve an award at Level 3 you will need to complete nine units, five of which are mandatory and four of which are optional. In this book we have covered the five mandatory units and a selection of five from the twelve optional units. You will need to collect and provide evidence to demonstrate that you are competent in working with children and young people.

Each unit has an introduction which should be read carefully. This will give a brief summary of the content of the unit and the target group i.e. the type of work you need to be doing to achieve that unit.

This summary will be followed by a breakdown of the Playwork values and applicable Ofsted National Standards which are relevant to that unit.

Finally, you will see a section entitled **What you must know and understand**. This section contains the knowledge that underpins the unit and will need to be demonstrated to enable you to achieve the aims of the unit.

Using this book to help you with your S/NVQ

This book gives unit by unit coverage of each of the mandatory units and a selection of optional units. It provides information and advice to help you examine your practice and provide evidence for your units. It will give you options and ideas to help you with your S/NVQ, but remember to confer with your assessor who will give you guidance and support.

At the end of each chapter there is a short **End of Unit Knowledge Check**. These contain questions that will help you check your knowledge and understanding. They can be used in your portfolio to provide evidence of your knowledge.

Within each of the units there are features such as '**Keys to good practice**', '**Consolidation**' and '**Active knowledge**'. These features will help you to reflect upon your learning and can also be used as evidence in your portfolio.

Three additional optional units are available for you to download **for free** from www.heinemann.co.uk/vocational. Click on *Childcare* on the subject list, then *Free Resources* under the Resource Centre at the top right of the screen. The units available are:

- A319 Recruit, select and keep colleagues
- A320 Allocate and monitor the progress and quality of work in your area of responsibility
- B227 Contribute to evaluating, developing and promoting services.

Remember!

Play enables children to create, explore, discover and sometimes take risks. It is an essential part of a child's life and vital to their development. Playworkers need to provide a wide range of opportunities that extend children's choices and allow them the freedom to play in their own way. Achieving the S/NVQ Level 3 in Playwork award will go some way towards creating that type of playworker but it doesn't stop there.

Assumptions and values

Playworkers have a special role in working with children as they are able to create safe and exciting opportunities for children to play. This is reflected in the assumptions and values of this sector and in turn underpins the occupational standards for S/NVQs. It is important to make sure that you have read and understood the value statement before starting your course of study.

Assumptions

The first assumption is that:

- children's play is freely chosen, personally directed behaviour, motivated from within; through play, the child explores the world and her or his relationship with it, elaborating all the while a flexible range of responses to the challenges she or he encounters; by playing, the child learns and develops as an individual.

The second is that:

- whereas children may play without encouragement or help, adults can, through the provision of an appropriate human and physical environment, significantly enhance opportunities for the child to play creatively and thus develop through play.

In this way the component playworker always aims to provide opportunities for the individual child to achieve her or his full potential while being careful not to control the child's direction or choice.

Values

Play opportunities are provided in a number of settings (for example, Local Authority, Voluntary or Commercial) for children with a variety of needs, in a complex society diverse in culture and belief; nevertheless, competent playwork always has the following underlying values.

- The child must be at the centre of the process; the opportunities provided and the organisation which supports, co-ordinates and manages these should always start with the child's needs and offer sufficient flexibility to meet these.

- Play should empower children, affirm and support their right to make choices, to discover their own solutions, to play and develop at their own pace and in their own way.

- Whereas play may sometimes be enriched by the playworker's participation, adults should always be sensitive to children's needs and never try to control a child's play so long as it remains within safe and acceptable boundaries.

- Every child has the right to a play environment which stimulates and provides opportunities for risk, challenge and the growth of confidence and self-esteem.

- The contemporary environment in which many children grow up does not lend itself to safe and creative play; all children have the right to a play environment which is free from hazard, one which ensures physical and personal safety, a setting within which the child ultimately feels physically and personally safe.

- Every child is an individual and has the right to be respected as such: each child should feel confident that individuality and diversity are valued by the adults who work and play with them.

- A considerate and caring attitude to individual children and their families is essential to competent playwork and should be displayed at all times.

- Prejudice against people with disabilities or who suffer social and economic disadvantage, racism and sexism have no place in an environment which seeks to enhance development through play. Adults involved in Play should always promote equality of opportunity and access for all children, and seek to develop anti-discriminatory practice and positive attitudes to those who are disadvantaged.

- Play should offer the child opportunities to extend her or his exploration and understanding of the wider world and therefore physical, social and cultural settings beyond their immediate experience.

- Play is essentially a co-operative activity for children both individually and in groups. Playworkers should always encourage children to be sensitive to the needs of others; in providing play opportunities, they should always seek to work together with children, their parents, colleagues and other professionals and, where possible, make their own expertise available to the wider community.

- Play opportunities should always be provided within the current legislative framework relevant to children's rights, health, safety and well-being.

- Every child has a right to an environment for play, and such environments must be made accessible to children.

Note for Scottish Vocational Qualification (SVQ) candidates

Throughout this candidate handbook, the following notes apply:

- For National Standards or National Day Care Standards, please refer to the Scottish National Care Standards produced by the Scottish Executive.

- For Ofsted, please refer to the Scottish Commission for the Regulation of Care (also known as the Care Commission).

- For the DfES (Department for Education and Skills), please refer to the Scottish Executive Education Department.

- For The Children Act (1989), please refer to The Children (Scotland) Act (1995).

- For Every Child Matters (2003) and The Protection of Children Act (1999), please refer to The Charter Protecting Children and Young People.

Contribute to an organisational framework that reflects the needs and protects the rights of children and young people

Unit PW6

Play is a vital element in the lives of children and young people. Experiences gained through play enrich all areas of development. Playworkers are in the unique position of being able to build trusting relationships, give information and advice about diversity and help empower children and young people to assert their rights. One way you can achieve this is by providing children and young people with opportunities for freely chosen, self-directed play within the context of an inclusive play setting.

This unit focuses on how playworkers can develop and implement the policies and procedures that:

- support children and young people
- meet their needs, preferences and wishes
- ensure that their rights are known and understood
- help them to assert their rights.

The unit also looks at how to promote diversity and inclusion in the play setting and contribute to child protection issues.

This unit is divided into four sections:

- PW6.1 Investigate and consult on children's and young people's rights
- PW6.2 Contribute to policies and procedures that reflect children's and young people's needs and rights
- PW6.3 Promote a diverse and inclusive environment
- PW6.4 Contribute to the protection of children and young people from abuse.

Playwork values

The playwork values relating to this unit are shown in the following table.

Value	Details
1	The child must be at the centre of the process; the opportunities provided and the organisation which supports, co-ordinates and manages these should always start with the child's needs and offer sufficient flexibility to meet these.
2	Play should empower children, affirm and support their right to make choices, to discover their own solutions, to play and develop at their own pace and in their own way.
3	Whereas play may sometimes be enriched by the playworker's participation, adults should always be sensitive to children's needs and never try to control a child's play so long as it remains within safe and acceptable boundaries.
4	Every child has a right to a play environment which stimulates and provides opportunities for risk, challenge and the growth of confidence and self-esteem.
5	The contemporary environment in which many children grow up does not lend itself to safe and creative play; all children have the right to a play environment which is free from hazard, one which ensures physical and personal safety, a setting within which the child ultimately feels physical and personally safe.
6	Every child is an individual and has the right to be respected as such: each child should feel confident that individuality and diversity are valued by the adults who work and play with them.
7	A considerate and caring attitude to individual children and their families is essential to competent playwork and should be displayed at all times.
8	Prejudice against people with disabilities or who suffer social and economic disadvantage, racism and sexism have no place in an environment which seeks to enhance development through play. Adults involved in play should always promote equality of opportunity and access for all children, and seek to develop anti-discriminatory practice and positive attitudes to those who are disadvantaged.
9	Play should offer the child opportunities to extend his or her exploration and understanding of the wider world and therefore physical, social and cultural settings beyond their immediate experience.
10	Play is essentially a co-operative activity for children both individually and in groups. Playworkers should always encourage children to be sensitive to the needs of others; in providing play opportunities, they should always seek to work together with children, their parents, colleagues and other professionals and, where possible, make their own expertise available to the wider community. [The new standards are not mapped completely to this value as playwork practice is not comfortable with the first sentence.]
11	Play opportunities should always be provided within the current legislative framework relevant to children's rights, health, safety and well-being.
12	Every child has a right to an environment for play, and such environments must be made accessible to children.

Ofsted national standards

The Out of School Care: Guidance to the National Standards, published by the DfES (2001, Annesley, Nottingham), provides guidelines to the 14 national standards. The guidelines include a set of 'outcomes' that providers (who operate for more than 2 hours and have children under 8 years old in attendance) should aim to achieve. They acknowledge that providers will reach these outcomes in different ways depending upon the particular circumstances they operate in.

Ofsted will expect providers to demonstrate how they achieve each of these standards. The guidelines explain how Ofsted childcare inspectors will register and inspect against the national standards. They aim to help providers and development workers 'ensure good quality provision'.

All of the national standards relate to this unit.

What you must know and understand

For the whole unit
K1: The assumptions and values of playwork that are relevant to this unit
K2: Basic requirements under the United Nations Convention on the Rights of the Child
K3: Basic requirements of national legislation on the rights of children and young people
K4: Basic requirements of legislation covering Equal Opportunities and Disability Discrimination
K5: The basic stages of child development and their implications for children's and young people's needs and rights in a playwork context
K6: The importance of the setting having policies and procedures that reflect children's and young people's rights
K7: The importance of children and young people being consulted and involved in decision making
K8: The importance of diversity and inclusion in the play setting
K9: Current theories and good practice to do with inclusion
K10: How to identify good inclusive practice in the play setting
K11: How to recognise attitudinal, environmental and institutional barriers to inclusion in the play setting
K12: Ways to overcome these barriers to inclusion
K13: The difference between separate, segregated, integrated and inclusive play provision
K14: The social and medical models of disability and the differences between them

For PW6.1
K15: How to carry out research on children's and young people's rights and identify the implications for your setting
K16: Your organisation's strategies and policies that have an impact on children's and young people's rights and how to evaluate these
K17: How to consult effectively with children and young people
K18: How to promote and advocate children's and young people's rights in the setting

For PW6.2

K19: The importance of developing group agreements with children and young people and how to do so

K20: How to develop policies and procedures for your setting covering:
- play and social activities
- health and safety
- anti-discriminatory practice
- child protection and bullying
- responding to behaviour

K21: How to ensure that policies and procedures are put into practice

K22: The importance of constantly reviewing policies and procedures and how to do so

For PW6.3

K23: How to judge whether a setting is inclusive and supportive of diversity

K24: How to show that you support inclusion and diversity through your words, actions and behaviour in the setting

K25: Why it is important to promote the setting to children who may experience barriers to participation

K26: Types of support that children may need to access and make best use of the setting

K27: How to support children and young people in valuing inclusion and diversity

K28: How to challenge and deal with words and behaviour that are not consistent with inclusion and diversity

For PW6.4

K29: The basic stages of child development and the implications of these for helping children to protect themselves

K30: Types of inappropriate behaviour by others that a child may experience

K31: Situations that may put a child's personal safety at risk and advice on how children can avoid or deal with these situations

K32: The importance of children having a strong sense of self-esteem and factors that may make them more vulnerable to abuse

K33: Strategies to encourage children to understand their rights and assert these

K34: Strategies that children can use to deal with abusive or potentially abusive situations

K35: How to respond when there are suspicions of abuse

K36: Why it is important to collect, assess and share information about possible abuse

K37: Reporting procedures relating to abuse

K38: Types of support that you or your colleagues may need and how to access such support

K39: The rules and guidelines covering the confidentiality of information relating to abuse

The legal framework

The United Nations Convention on the Rights of the Child

Everyone in the United Kingdom, including children and young people, have rights that are recognised and protected. These rights are granted by legislation, for example, human rights legislation, the Children Act, etc., which have evolved from a variety of sources. One of these sources is the United Nations Convention on the Rights of the Child. Before this was adopted any laws relating to the care and protection of children gave all rights to the child's parents to do as they felt fit.

The Convention on the Rights of the Child is an international treaty which has been adopted by the UK. It was approved by the general assembly of the United Nations on 20 November 1989 and it set out principles relating to children (this includes all children and young people under 18). The UK government agreed to be bound by the convention in 1991 and it underpins all childcare practice. The convention is made up of a series of articles on rights. The wording of these articles is at times dated and so the terminology, in some cases, is now not appropriate. However, the principles are still important. The articles are divided into three groups:

- basic principles which apply to all rights: these cover non-discrimination on grounds of gender, religion, disability, language, other opinion, ethnic or social origin. The best interests of the child are always to be considered by adults and organisations when making decisions about children. The child's view is to be heard and taken seriously
- civil and political rights: these include rights to a name and nationality, access to information and protection from abuse, neglect, torture or the deprivation of liberty
- economic, social, cultural and protective rights: these include rights to life and opportunities, a decent standard of living, day to day care, health care and a healthy environment, education and protection from exploitation.

The declaration of the 'rights of the child' (article 31) from the UN convention states that children are especially vulnerable and need protection, and also that their human rights should be respected. Playworkers need to work in a manner which protects these rights and empowers children and young people to assert them. Within this comprehensive set of rights it was identified that a child has a right to play, rest and have leisure. It was internationally agreed that these were of vital importance and even essential to the development and well-being of a child.

The requirements of national legislation on the rights of children and young people

The legal aspects of your role as a playworker are important. To be an efficient and effective playworker you need to be aware of the content of relevant legislation, ensure implementation and understand that legislation is constantly being updated to reflect current issues. You need to keep abreast of the changes and adapt as necessary to include these in your practice.

The Children Act

The Children Act (1989) covered a wide range of topics and set out the duties of local authorities. It was established to form a balance between the rights and responsibilities of the parents and the rights and well-being of the child. The Act covered all aspects relating to the well-being and protection of the child. The Children Act 2004 provides a framework for the wider strategy for improving children's lives. It covers the services which every child accesses as well as those services which children and young people with additional needs access.

Every Child Matters (2003)

The green paper entitled Every Child Matters (2003) called for radical improvements in opportunities and outcomes for children.

It identified five outcomes for children:

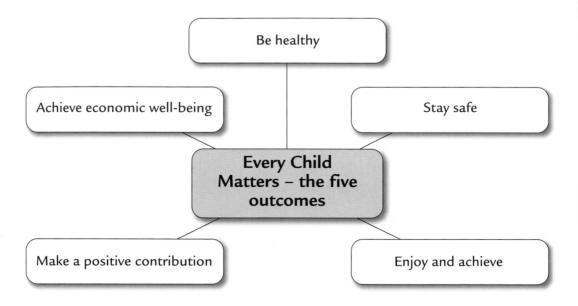

Common Assessment Framework (2005)

The Common Assessment Framework (CAF) is being implemented nationally in response to recent pieces of legislation and government guidance.

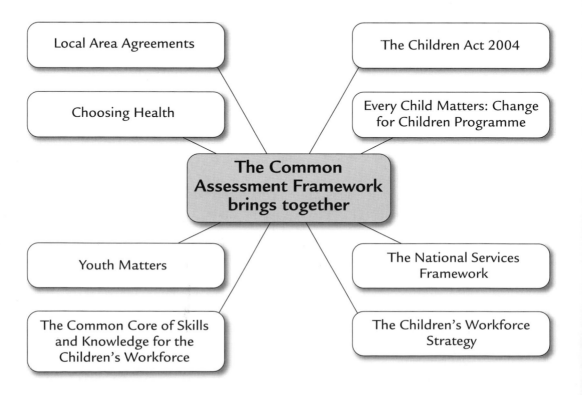

The aim is to protect children and ensure joint responsibility in the safeguarding process. The wider picture focuses on all children achieving their full potential, particularly in relation to the five outcomes mentioned above.

As part of the integrated children's services the CAF will promote:

- early intervention and prevention of potential problems
- a shared assessment tool
- information sharing
- multi-agency working.

The CAF is not designed to be used in cases where a practitioner, including a playworker, has immediate child protection concerns. In this situation the local LSCB (Local Safeguarding Children Board) child protection procedures should be followed as before and a referral made to social services. The CAF is to be used when a child has additional needs that require an integrated package of support from a number of agencies, and it may help in the identification of early concerns about a child.

An assessment using the CAF can be undertaken by any agency, including a playwork setting. It will provide a holistic view of a child by assessing three areas:

- child development
- parents and carers
- family/environmental factors.

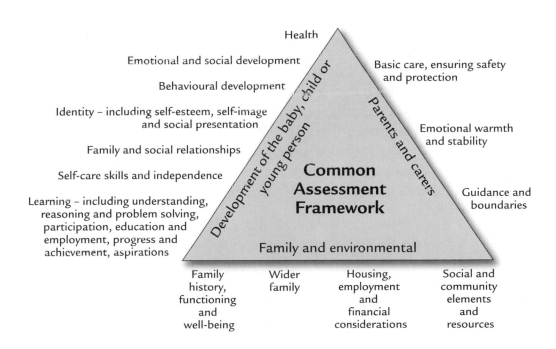

The Common Assessment Framework triangle

This is a simple tool to use and should be empowering for children, young people and their families. It should be completed in partnership with them. There is clear guidance to the process that gives three steps to follow:

- step one: preparation
- step two: discussion
- step three: service delivery.

Guidance on the CAF and its implementation can be found at the following websites: www.everychildmatters.gov.uk and www.dfes.gov.uk.

Local authorities have been directed to set up teams to train all childcare workers to ensure that individual agencies include the CAF within their work practices and that the strategy is implemented.

The Human Rights Act (1989)

The Human Rights Act was established in conjunction with the European Convention of Human Rights. Part of the Act lists the organisations that are subject to the Act, for example, charities, voluntary services, public services, etc. Anyone who feels that their rights have been infringed can seek help from the courts to pursue the matter.

The Act sets out a list of rights, similar to those of the UN Convention on the Rights of the Child but relating to adults and childcare.

The Protection of Children Act (1999)

This Act relates to the child's right to protection. The Act sets stringent measures for those wishing to work and those already working in the childcare sector. It has set up a body to check into the criminal records of people who apply to work with children and/or young people to ensure they are suitable to work with children. These are called CRB checks.

The Data Protection Act (1989)

The Data Protection Act protects the rights of people with regard to confidentiality of information. It sets out clear, legally enforceable guidelines about the storage and sharing of information. It states the rules of:

- confidentiality, including when and how it can be broken
- how records should be written, stored and accessed
- what personal information can be kept, for how long and in what manner.

The Freedom of Information Act (2000)

This Act enables people to access information held by public authorities in Great Britain. It also gives greater access to information about how decisions are taken in government and how public services are developed and delivered. It operates alongside the Data Protection Act. Further information on the Act can be found in a leaflet published by the Department of Constitutional Affairs or via the internet on www.foi.gov.uk.

Health and safety legislation

There is a range of legislation and regulations on the health and safety aspects of your role as a playworker. You need to be aware of these as they could also affect the rights of the child in regard to safe practice. The legislation includes:

- the Health and Safety at Work Act (1974)
- Manual Handling/Lifting and Handling
- the Management of Health and Safety at Work Regulations
- Reporting of Injuries, Diseases and Dangerous Occurrences Regulations (RIDDOR)
- Control of Substances Hazardous to Health regulations (COSHH).

Legislation covering equal opportunities, disability and discrimination

Respect for children's and young people's rights with regard to equality of opportunity, diversity, disability and discrimination should be part of your practice as a playworker. Your knowledge of the legislation and your responsibilities within this should encompass everything you say and do. It is vital that you update your knowledge to meet the changes in legislation as well as the introduction of new regulations and legislation.

The previous section on legislation includes and integrates aspects of diversity. However, there is specific legislation covering discrimination:

- the Sex Discrimination Act 1975 (amended 1986)
- the Race Relations Act 1976 (amended 2000)
- the Disability Discrimination Act and the Disability Rights Commission Act 1999.

The Sex Discrimination Act 1975 (amended 1986)

This act makes it unlawful to discriminate between men and women in respect of employment, goods and facilities. To ensure that people's rights are protected the Equal Opportunities Commission was established to advise, monitor and provide information on people's rights.

The Race Relations Act 1976 (amended 2000)

This law makes it unlawful to discriminate on 'racial grounds' in services, housing and employment. It includes discrimination due to colour, race, nationality and ethnic or national origins. It also makes it an offence to encourage or incite racial hatred. The Commission for Racial Equity was established to investigate and give advice to those who feel that they are being discriminated against.

The Disability Discrimination Act (1995)

The main aim of this Act is to prevent discrimination against people (including children and young people) in employment, access to education and transport, housing, and obtaining goods and services. All services must ensure that disabled people can access and use them.

The Disability Rights Commission Act established the Disability Rights Commission to investigate and take action against anyone breaching this Act. The Commission also gives help and advice to anyone who feels that they have been or are being discriminated against.

Keys to good practice: Keeping up to date with legislation

✓ Attend any courses or training on new and updated legislation and then pass on the relevant details to your team.
✓ Regularly review your policies and procedures to ensure that they fulfil the requirements of the law.
✓ Ensure your playwork team is aware of the importance of following legislation.
✓ Cut out articles and information on relevant legislation and keep them in a resources file for you and your team to access.

ACTIVE KNOWLEDGE

Research legislation on the internet and prepare a true/false quiz to use at your next team meeting. Alternatively you could use the one below.

True or false?

1 The Children Act was established to protect the well-being and rights of children.
2 Children only have rights when they are with an adult.
3 Your records should be kept secure.
4 Young people are not allowed to express their opinions and rights.
5 You can share personal information with anyone in your setting.
6 You should challenge racial comments.
7 If a stranger walks in and asks to see the records you keep you must show them to him/her.
8 You must ensure that those with a disability have access to your provision.
9 You cannot have anyone who has a criminal record helping in your setting.
10 CRB stands for Criminal Records Bureau.

The basic stages of child development and their implications for children's and young people's needs and rights in playwork

As a playworker you will be in a unique position to observe and assess the developmental levels and needs of the children and young people in your care. Although you are not expected to be an expert in all aspects of child development, it is important to understand the children and young people that you work with. Knowledge relating to their development could be crucial in helping you and others support children and young people in key areas of their lives.

The relationships that you form with them are of a very different nature to their relationships with other professionals with whom they come in contact. Your views and opinions of the children and young people will undoubtedly be unique and it is good practice to involve them in some self assessment.

Remember that if you are requesting information that you have been asked to provide from the children and young people, it is important that the children and young people are aware of the reason for the request. It is also good practice to share reports and information with them, unless child protection regulations prevent this.

The legislation relating to this which you should be aware of is the Data Protection Act, the Children Act and the Freedom of Information Act. It will all be in line with the UN Convention on the Rights of the Child.

If you are unsure of the areas you could assess, the main areas of development are included in the CAF guidelines (see www.everychildmatters.gov.uk).

Area	Examples of issues to assess
Health	Do they appear healthy and well? Are they progressing through the developmental milestones with regard to physical development, speech, language and communication? Are you aware that they access any health services?
Emotional and social development	How well do they cope with everyday life? What about their attitudes, disposition and temperament? Are there any psychological difficulties that you have become aware of?
Behaviour development	Comment on their general behavioural difficulties – any antisocial behaviour or aggression that you are concerned about.
Identity	Include in this self-esteem and self-image. How confident and self-assured are they? Do they have a sense of belonging?
Family and social relationships	How good are they at developing relationships with their peers? Are the relationships that you are aware of secure and stable?
Self-care and independence	How independent are they in relation to their age? Can they and are they willing to take on responsibilities? Have they had the opportunity to meet challenges and do things for themselves?
Learning	Do they actively participate in discussions, debates and other communication methods? Are they thirsty for knowledge relating to their play experiences?

Assessing areas of development

ACTIVE KNOWLEDGE

Think about and record how the areas of development in the table above could form the basis of an imaginary report in relation to a child or young person in your setting. When you have cause for concern in the future, refer to your notes and record your thoughts in the same way.

ACTIVE KNOWLEDGE

Produce a chart to show the different play provisions available in your local community. Think about the type of play they provide and any access restrictions. Look at the section about separate, segregated and integrated play on page 29 and use these headings when listing the provisions.

Evaluate policies and procedures to ensure children's rights are met

Your organisation will have set policies and procedures that relate to and include the rights of the children and young people in your setting. You may find that these have been in place for quite a while and that recent changes in legislation and thinking mean that they are now in need of reviewing and updating – or you may have recently updated them to bring them in line with national and local initiatives and changes. Whichever applies to your setting there is always scope for evaluating these policies to ensure they include the points in the diagram below.

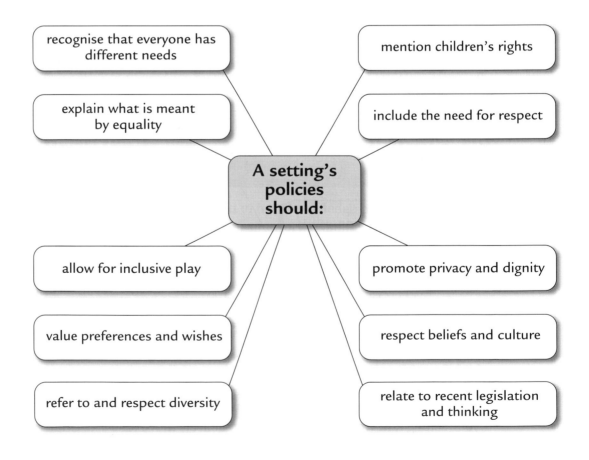

A setting's policies should:
- recognise that everyone has different needs
- explain what is meant by equality
- allow for inclusive play
- value preferences and wishes
- refer to and respect diversity
- mention children's rights
- include the need for respect
- promote privacy and dignity
- respect beliefs and culture
- relate to recent legislation and thinking

By evaluating your policies and procedures you will be able to judge the impact they have on children's rights. This will help you as a team to ensure the rights of children and young people in your setting are being met.

Consult with children and young people on the most effective way the setting can meet their rights

The children and young people in your setting should be the main focus of your work so you need to find ways to involve them in making decisions about all aspects of their play and care and also about aspects relating to the setting.

The UN Convention on the Rights of the Child (Section 12) states that any child 'who is capable of forming his or her views' should have the right to express them freely in all matters affecting them. The importance of listening to children's wishes and feelings is also a major principle of the Children Act.

Consulting children and young people will help you to become aware of their needs, opinions and ideas and will assist you in being objective when analysing the strengths and weaknesses of the provision. To be able to offer views and opinions, the children and young people will need to feel comfortable with the adults around them. They will need to feel confident that the adults will respect them, listen to their ideas and take them forward.

To empower the children and young people to offer their views and opinions, playworkers need to have interpersonal skills which include communication techniques that show open-mindedness and respect. Once you have an atmosphere where the children and young people feel free to express their thoughts, feelings and opinions safely without fear of ridicule or of being ignored, you will be able to ensure that their rights are upheld by consulting them and involving them in decision making.

In Unit PW8 you will find information about building, developing and maintaining positive relationships with children and young people (see pages 92–100). You will be able to try out and use some of the techniques suggested when you consult with the children and young people.

CASE STUDY

You have been approached by a local school teacher who sees the need for children and young people at her school to have a homework club. She wants you to provide this in your setting. You have your own strong views on the value of play and the benefits of the play provision that you provide.

1 What would you do in these circumstances?
2 Who would you involve?
3 How would you introduce the topic in a non-biased way?

Keys to good practice: Consulting effectively with children

✓ Remember that developing a positive relationship will involve a number of different skills as well as knowledge of theories underpinning child development.

✓ Ensure that your communication methods are clear and that they take into account the children's level of understanding.

✓ Respond to suggestions and ideas by acting upon them or explaining why you have decided not to take them up.

✓ Acknowledge opinions and be open to criticism.

Promote children's and young people's rights to adults

One of the best things a playworker can do for children is to always 'be there for them'. By developing a trusting and respectful relationship, the children and young people in your care will recognise that you care about them and their well-being. Not only will they know that you care, but also that you will advocate ('stick up') for them in a manner that promotes their rights, allows for their views and opinions to be heard and ensures that they are not discriminated against.

There will be many times when you have felt that you need to be a child's 'campaigner' or 'champion'. This could be in relation to your own setting, to other children or young people, or to adults (including other team members, your line manager, their parents, other parents and visitors). The children need to feel confident that whatever the situation you will challenge discrimination and promote equality of opportunity. It is important that you know how to promote the children's and young people's rights in your setting. This could be on an individual basis or on a small or large group basis.

Keys to good practice: Promoting children's rights

✓ Include the children and young people in decision making.

✓ Challenge discriminatory remarks.

✓ Correct misunderstandings that could disadvantage them.

✓ Ensure that they have the time to offer their opinion and their side of the story.

✓ Do not jump to conclusions.

✓ Adopt a non-discriminatory manner.

✓ Be open-minded to different attitudes and opinions.

Sometimes you will need to promote the rights of the children and young people to others outside the setting. This could be for a variety of reasons and using various communication methods, both formal and informal.

Sometimes this will involve working in partnership with other professionals and at these times it is important that you ensure that they understand and listen to the child's point of view. As a playworker you will have a unique relationship with the children and young people in your setting and this could put you in a good position to support them and promote their rights. At times you may have to represent their views and opinions, even if you do not necessarily agree with them, in a non-judgemental and professional way.

Medical services (GP, health visitor, ambulance crews, paramedics, psychologists, etc.)

School staff (teachers, exclusion team, education welfare officers, midday supervisors, estates people etc.)

Local community people (local shop owners and workers, community wardens, neighbours, etc.)

Funding bodies (lottery bids, ESF funding bids, local initiatives, etc.)

Outside people to whom you may have to promote children's rights

Police (community police officers, arresting officers)

Social Services (social workers, family support workers, child protection officers, etc.)

Other community services (youth offending team, youth workers, advocacy workers, etc.)

Playwork personnel (play development workers, local play forums, Ofsted, etc.)

Evaluate feedback on meeting children's rights

If you promote inclusive play and operate or wish to operate a setting where children and young people can freely express their thoughts, suggestions and opinions, a major role will be working in partnership with them to evaluate, discuss and develop their suggestions, opinions and wishes with regard to how their needs can be best met. If you ask for opinions and then do not act upon them, it will give the impression that you do not consider the suggestion worthy of comment and will show that you do not respect the opinion or the child. Children and young people can be very sensitive and if they were to offer a suggestion that was not seen as acceptable their self-esteem could be damaged. It is also likely that they will not bother to even comment the next time. Some suggestions may not be appropriate, but as an effective playworker you should be able to develop ideas around the initial suggestion to either make it acceptable or give a valid reason why you feel that the suggestion is not acceptable.

To meet regularly with the children and young people and to act on and develop their suggestions shows that you are operating in a manner that promotes their rights.

CASE STUDY

Shanika works in an inner city play setting. She decides to go out and speak to children in the area about what they would like in a play setting. She goes to the local park and sees a group of children aged 9 to 12 years. Shanika explains that she is thinking of setting up a project and asks for their ideas and opinions on what they would like if they came.

These are a few of the suggestions:
- Sianne, aged 9 years, says she would really like to be able to make jewellery
- Rebecca, aged 12, says she would like to listen to music and dance
- Jawad, aged 12, says he only likes to play on computers
- Joel says he likes food. He thinks he should be allowed choices of food when he has a snack as he is fed up with school where they now have to 'eat rabbit food'
- Sasha suggests that a drama group should visit so they can put on plays
- Amy thinks the setting should have pets and Rosie thinks it should have a horse as she wants to learn to ride.

1 Remembering that it is important to acknowledge suggestions, how would you reply to the suggestions above?
2 Are there any suggestions you would definitely say no to?
3 How could you help to meet the ideas suggested?

PORTFOLIO EVIDENCE

Actively research or recall a research project that you have undertaken in your local community regarding the play and different play facilities that are available. (You may have done this already for a funding application and you could use this as an example.) Explain how you shared this by involving the children and young people and how their rights were promoted and acknowledged – you may, for example, have carried out research similar to that in the case study above. You could use this as portfolio evidence, especially if you have it witnessed or hold a professional discussion with your assessor.

CONSOLIDATION

Think of a policy or procedure in your setting which you feel does not fully respect children's rights. Outline the steps you would take to amend the procedure. Mention whom you would consult and why.

Contribute to policies and procedures that reflect children's and young people's needs and rights

Your playwork setting will have its own policies and procedures. These may be solely related to the specific setting and may focus on the ethos of the setting when it was established and developed. Some settings may belong to an organisation, agency or local authority department. These settings may have organisational policies that follow the organisation's ethos or they may have developed their own policies in line with the organisation's procedures.

Whatever the source, the policies need to be in line with recent legislation and cover the areas required by the law. If you have children in the younger age bracket and meet the inspection requirements regarding the length of time you are open, you will need to follow the Ofsted guidelines and will be inspected regularly. This will include the checking of policies and procedures.

A good playwork setting will base all of its policies and procedures around the rights and well-being of the child and ensure they reflect the five outcomes from the government's green paper, Every Child Matters (see page 6).

It is not expected that every playworker has the power to change every policy in the setting. However, to change or update one or more policies would be a positive way to respect the rights of the child. One important thing to check is whether your play setting has a play policy. If it does not, this would be a good place to begin.

What you need to demonstrate you can do

- Develop group agreements with children and young people on ways of meeting their needs and rights
- Contribute to, consult on and agree procedures that are based on these ways of meeting needs and rights
- Provide information and guidance on these procedures to children, young people and adults in the setting
- Observe, collect feedback and evaluate how well the procedures are working
- Negotiate ways of improving the procedures with children, young people and adults

Develop group agreements with children and young people

Current playwork practice promotes the use of group agreements as a means of ensuring that current policies and procedures are formed by the children for the children. For example, settings used to have behaviour policies that included rules for the children and young people about ways that they were expected to behave. It has now been realised that it is more effective to talk to the children and young people about their behaviour, their needs and their rights in order to develop and draw up agreements. The advantages of this are that their needs, wishes and opinions can be integrated into the agreement which will mean they have ownership of the agreement and are more likely to adhere to the conditions.

It is important to keep group agreements short and focused on the suggestions of the children and young people, who should all sign the agreement. Below is an example of a group agreement.

Stansville Play Project

Group Agreement

We, the members of Stansville Play Project, agree to:

- treat each other with respect
- listen to what each person has to say
- sort out arguments without fighting
- make sure that we all get a chance to play with the computer
- help to put away the equipment when we have finished playing.

Signed:

Group agreements are a useful tool for all policies and procedures in your setting. It is also important to understand that these agreements will be constantly changing to keep abreast of the needs, rights and wishes of both individual children and the group. Group agreements could be described as organic – they grow within the group and they then become a flexible working document. For example, the agreement above could be revisited with the group approximately every three months, or when an incident arises during which the agreement is broken or challenged.

More information on developing agreements can be found in Unit PW8, page 112.

ACTIVE KNOWLEDGE

Think of all the policies and procedures that you already have in place and cluster the different topics into a logical order for your setting. Then look at the following range of statements in the S/NVQ standards for PW6.1 and see if you came up with the same or similar topic areas:

- for play and social activities
- for care and safety
- for emotional well-being
- for inclusion
- for acknowledging identity
- for information
- for consultation and decision making.

Agree procedures based on ways of meeting children's rights

If you are in a position where you are able to address all the policies and procedures and change them accordingly, it would be advantageous to use the techniques and methods of developing group agreements mentioned above. If, at present, you are not in such a position, it would be good practice to set about introducing the concept of group agreements into policies and procedures. You could do this by providing information with reasons and evidence of the potential benefits to your line manager, your management committee, your team, the children and their parent and carers.

Policies will be required to cover the following procedures:

- play and social activities
- inclusion and anti-discriminatory practice
- child protection and dealing with bullying
- health and safety
- responding to behaviour
- assisting children and young people to make transitions
- inter-agency working.

For example, if you choose to focus on the health and safety policy you may first of all discuss your current policy with the relevant parties:

- the parents and carers by asking for their views and opinions
- the children and young people by asking them to work on a group agreement
- the playwork team, who could draw up a group agreement in line with the updating of the policy after consulting with the parents, carers and children.

The policy can then be presented to the committee or the owners with an explanation of the input from the various parties.

ACTIVE KNOWLEDGE

Check through your policies and procedures to see whether they are in line with current thinking. If they are, you could consider whether any need updating. If they are not, you could start by developing a play policy using the prompts that follow and then adding your own ideas.

Play agreement

In our setting children and young people:

- will be involved in …
- enjoy …
- will be encouraged to …
- are given choices about …
- are empowered in play by …

Keys to good practice: Checking your setting's policies and procedures

✓ Ensure your setting's policies cover all relevant aspects relating to the children's and young people's well-being and rights.
✓ Ensure the policies are implemented by the whole of the playwork team.
✓ Review and update the procedures on a regular basis so they comply with current regulations and legislation.
✓ Ensure every child has the opportunity to contribute to the agreements and be included in the consultation process.

Provide information and guidance on these procedures

Once you have developed agreements and integrated these into your policies and procedures you will then need to promote them to:

- the children and young people
- the playwork team
- the parents and carers
- the management or management committee
- the inspecting and funding bodies
- the agencies you work with
- anyone else who may be associated with and interested in your setting.

There are many different ways to promote your policies and procedures (see the table below). You should ensure the method you choose suits the diverse needs of the children and young people as well as their families.

Who to provide information to	How and when
The children and young people	Involvement in the developing, implementing and constant updating
The playwork team	Involvement in the developing, implementing and constant updating
The parents and carers	Individually as and when, also at the initial visit to the setting In written form in a range of languages and forms, e.g. email/internet site At open evenings and events
The management or management committee	Initially and then at appropriate times during the developing and updating
The inspecting and funding bodies	In report form
The agencies you work with	At meetings and individual interviews, also in written form as a promotion

Ways of providing information on procedures

Collect feedback, evaluate and improve the procedures

Being an effective playworker will require you to monitor your policies, agreements and procedures to ensure that they are meeting the current needs, wishes and preferences of the children and young people in your setting. This will probably be encompassed into your role as a playworker so it is important to recognise that you still have the skills and opportunity to do this within your role. Observational skills will enable you to see if the policies are still empowering the children and young people. You will also be in a good position to receive honest feedback from them, which will enable you to assess, either individually or as a team, whether the policies are still effective for the children.

Observing children and young people will help you to:

- see how they respond to situations
- gain a broader picture of their actions and behaviour
- gain an understanding of any issues or behaviour that they are unable to communicate to you
- decide if their individual needs are being met
- assess if they are confident and able to express themselves, especially with regard to their needs and preferences
- choose an appropriate time to discuss issues and agreements with them.

CASE STUDY

Sianne and Jas are making a model and are trying to cut a large box with a very small pair of scissors. They are experiencing some difficulties and eventually Sianne says to Jas, 'Go and ask for a knife.' Jas tells her that it will be no good as they will not give her one due to health and safety.
Jas and Sianne then move on to the imaginative play box and Sianne puts on a Spanish dress and starts to dance. Jas says, 'I would dance with you if they had another dress, or better still an Asian dance costume.'
Along comes Jade who is older. She demands that Sianne takes off the dress and gives it to her. Sianne looks frightened and starts to take off the dress. Jas looks around for support but the playworkers just walk away.

1 Which of the following procedures would apply to these situations: health and safety procedures, play and social activities procedures, procedures for responding to behaviour and maybe bullying (you would only look at bullying procedures if this had happened on several occasions)?
2 What would you suggest at the next team meeting?

Think about it

Spend about thirty minutes observing the children at play and then consider whether:

- the materials and equipment provided were of sufficient interest, quality and use to enable the children to play effectively
- the behaviour agreement was used by the children appropriately
- the children were confident enough to voice their opinions and assert their rights.

If you find that your policies, agreements and procedures meet the needs of the children and young people and are empowering them to assert their rights, it is still important to ask for their opinion as to whether they feel that they are effective.

If, on the other hand, you feel that your policies, agreements and procedures could do with a fuller evaluation, you could encourage the children and young people to become involved in the evaluation and engage them in negotiation to ensure that all their needs are met. Constant reviewing is essential if you are to meet individual and group needs. Formal reviewing should take place on a regular basis, for example, at your monthly team meetings.

CONSOLIDATION

Think of a time when you developed a group agreement with children in your setting. (If you have not yet done so, you could develop one now.)

1 Write down:

- how you involved the children in developing the agreement
- how you reflected the agreement in your setting's procedures
- how you set up and evaluated the resulting changes.

2 Can you think of any ways in which you could improve on this for next time?

Element PW6.3 | **Promote a diverse and inclusive environment**

If the play setting is going to attract a wide range of children and young people the playwork team will need to actively promote a diverse and inclusive environment.

What you need to demonstrate you can do

- Make sure the environment reflects and promotes diversity and inclusion
- Make sure the resources are accessible to all children
- Promote the environment to children and young people who may experience barriers to participation and provide them with appropriate forms of support
- Provide a positive role model for issues to do with diversity and inclusion
- Provide opportunities for children and young people to understand and value diversity and inclusion
- Promote diversity and inclusion to colleagues and other relevant adults and, where necessary, provide them with relevant support
- Deal with words and behaviour that challenge diversity and inclusion in a way that is appropriate to the people involved

Current theories about inclusion

Current theories about inclusive play revolve around the idea that play is important for life and that all playworkers should be committed to creating play environments that are inclusive and that offer multi-sensory experiences for all children. Play environments should ensure children can become involved in imaginary play and can develop motor activity. They should also allow interaction in a safe environment.

Play is seen as the language that can bring children of different abilities together. All children have the same basic needs and go through the same developmental stages, even though they may not all go through them at the same pace: some go through some stages more quickly than most while others may become static in their development for a while. None of this should prevent access to any setting. Through play with other children they develop social skills and learn about behaviour, communication and friendship. Play is the tool for practical learning so the opportunity to engage in meaningful play is important. If a child is prevented from playing it diminishes the play experience for all the children involved.

All children and young people should feel included and integrated to give them a feeling of belonging. Play should be accessible without discrimination and without playworkers being overcautious. All children need and want to take on challenges, especially those with an element of risk. In this way they can explore limits, gain new experiences and develop their own capabilities from a young age. Children and young people with disabilities have an equal if not greater need for these opportunities.

Playworkers need to support play between children of diverse abilities. They should remember that this means making sure that the setting is suitable for the child, and not seeing if the child is suitable for the setting.

Further information about inclusive play, reports and examples of good practice from inclusive play projects can be found on the internet by inputting 'inclusive play' into a search engine. Using the information above you will be able to identify good inclusive practice in the play setting.

ACTIVE KNOWLEDGE

Use the internet to research an inclusive play project. Recall one good idea that you think you could introduce into your setting and discuss this at your next team meeting.

The social and medical models of disability

As an inclusive play setting it is likely that you will have children and young people who have a disability, and it is important to be able to understand the models that you may come across. Models are a way of explaining how the ability of a child or young person affects their experience of life. They will help you to look at things from other people's points of view. When working in an integrated way with other professionals, for example, using the CAF guidelines, you will probably hear this terminology from the medical professional. It is useful to be able to understand the terminology so you can contribute to such discussions.

The medical model of disability focuses on a person's medical diagnosis (the pathology of an individual), or what the body is capable of doing. This is then seen as the cause of someone's disability, hence the term 'medical model'.

The social model of disability sees that the lack of appropriate facilities, access, provision, etc. can restrict and limit some people's ability to participate in society. The focus is on the society which has created these barriers and not on the individual disability.

Make sure the environment reflects and promotes diversity and inclusion

It is important that you ensure that your setting reflects and promotes diversity and inclusion. Diversity is about recognising individuals and that everyone will make different choices and have different needs. Inclusion is about ensuring that the play provision is open and accessible to all and provides for individual needs. Each of these should be reflected within your setting.

Diversity is essential in any playwork setting. Just as you should be valuing and encouraging social and cultural diversity, you should also understand that the children, their families and the people you work with will bring to the setting their own ideas and values. You need to accept that other playworkers will work and relate to children and young people in their own ways, and that this is a huge bonus to the setting as long as they operate within the policies regarding equality of opportunity. It allows the children to see that teamwork means working alongside people who have different styles. It also means that the team is more likely to be able to meet the needs of all those with whom you work, as different children and parents will be able to identify with the styles of different team members. All children are unique and their interests, needs and experiences differ. Within your setting each child will have different needs and so will respond in different ways to play opportunities and experiences.

Inclusion is about open access to all children and young people to enable them to participate fully and reach their full potential. Playworkers must be able meet the needs and interests of all the children at the setting as well as those who may wish to attend. This will include providing for children individually as well as in groups. It is important to acknowledge that this may mean that some children and young people require more help, care and supervision than others, but that this should be offered in an unobtrusive and willing manner to enable them to feel included in the setting.

Promoting understanding between children and young people

Every family operates differently; it has its own rules, values and personalities. This is a good starting point when working with children as once children understand this, they are more likely to be tolerant of culture, religion and ways of life that are different to their own.

Children need to take pride in their own family and traditions in order that they can grow in confidence and feel positive about themselves. It is interesting to note that some people who show discriminatory behaviour and prejudices are insecure and lacking in confidence, and that is why they find it difficult to cope with things that are different. Helping children and young people to be confident and secure is therefore one way in which playworkers can foster respect and tolerance. In addition, children need to learn that different lifestyles from their own are to be valued. This can be encouraged by helping them to find out about a range of cultures, traditions and religions other than their own.

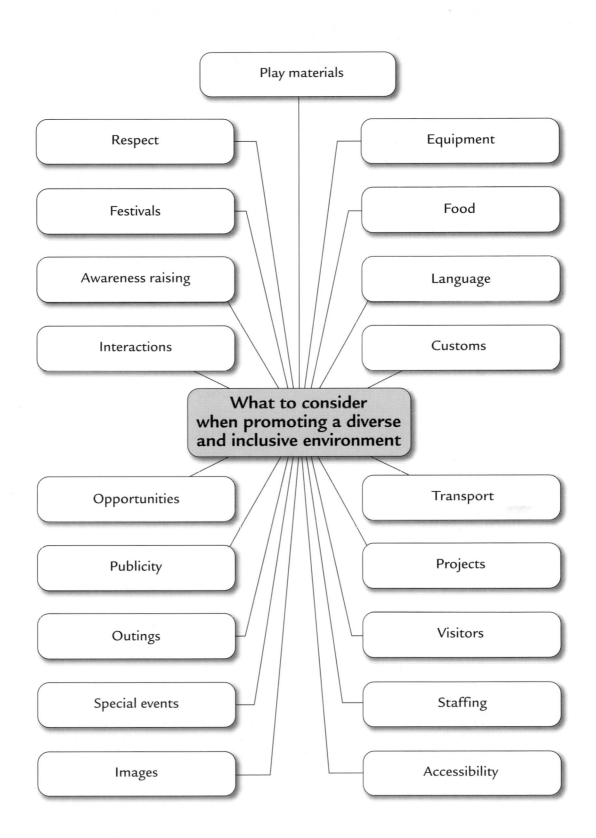

ACTIVE KNOWLEDGE

Look at the chart below which shows ways of promoting positive images in the setting. See if you can complete another set of boxes by choosing some of the topics in the previous diagram.

	Examples of resources
Play materials	Paint/crayons that reflect skin types Imaginative play items such as dressing-up clothes, cooking pots, eating implements, jewellery, etc. that reflect a variety of cultures
Equipment	Books in a range of languages and medias Games equipment for right- and left-handed children with hand grips for those with limited muscle control and in all sizes and shapes
Food	Information on a variety of cultural foods in books, posters, magazines, etc. Different types of food and drinks on the menu (if you provide food and drinks) Opportunities to taste and learn about different foods
Outings	Visits to different places of interest and opportunities to take part in different types of activities

Costumes, jewellery and musical instruments from a variety of cultures could be used by young people in drama activities

How to judge whether a setting is inclusive and supportive of diversity

The introduction to this section looks at inclusive play and where you can access information about good practice (see page 9). As a responsible playworker you will need to constantly review the provision you have, to ensure that it offers inclusive play.

✓ **ACTIVE KNOWLEDGE**

Visit another play setting which promotes inclusion and then compare it to your own setting.

1 Did you gain any new ideas?
2 Did you see resources that you would like to buy for your setting?
3 Were there any opportunities or activities you could adopt or adapt?
4 Would it help to bring your playwork team to visit the other setting?

Other types of play provision

Early in this chapter you will have found information about inclusive play provision and will recall that the most important thing is that there are no barriers to participation (see page 9).

Within local communities you may find a variety of settings offering some form of play. These may differ in the type of play offered and the restrictions to access. The three main types of provision are:

- separate
- segregated
- integrated.

The difference between separate, segregated and integrated play provision can be seen in the table below.

Explanation	Example
Separate This is a play provision for a specific group. If you do not belong to that group you cannot gain access.	Play provision for the Jewish faith
Segregated This is play within a provision that is separated for a reason.	Age differences Muslim swimming
Integrated This is a provision where two or more groups are deliberately brought together.	Two age ranges Different settings for a visit

Reflecting on the way you promote diversity and inclusion

You may say that your setting is inclusive, but unless this is tested and challenged you will not be fully aware of all the different aspects you need to consider to meet individual needs and preferences.

To be able to offer access to children and young people with different needs may mean that there are some aspects you are striving to provide. For example, you may have children with English as their second (or in some cases third) language. While you might like to have staff with the language skills to be able to communicate fully with these children in their first language, you may not have the capacity to employ more workers on a full-time basis. This may mean that you 'buy' in or access staff when necessary. However, you may be aiming to have permanent staff who speak a range of languages other than English.

You may have some aspect you think that, at the present time, you fully meet. For example, you may have different materials and equipment that reflect a wide range of cultures and social backgrounds. It is important to keep abreast of changes and new information and resources to aid the promotion of diversity and inclusion.

ACTIVE KNOWLEDGE

At a team meeting bring in some catalogues that offer materials and equipment to promote diversity and ask the team to comment on the ideas they see. Hopefully you will provoke an active discussion that will challenge and question some pieces of equipment and promote others.

It would also be useful to bring to the team's attention that not all play materials need to be bought from catalogues. Items such as lengths of material often have more play value if they are bought from local traders and suppliers. You could then set aside a working party to research local providers.

Make sure the resources are accessible to all children

Although you may have a good range and variety of resources, they will only be of value if they are readily available and accessible to the children and young people. As well as having accessible resources it is important that the team positively promotes them.

CASE STUDY

● During a play session you see Gerard with some CDs in his hand. He goes over to one of your team members and you overhear him asking if he could have the stereo out to play some of the CDs he has found in a box of dressing-up clothes. Your colleague looks at the CDs and replies that they are not his type of music and it is too near the end of the session to get out any other big equipment.

- Atifa and her friend Daisy are dressing up and they start to dance. Atifa is showing Daisy some Asian dance moves and Daisy is copying Atifa. Daisy asks Atifa if they could dance to music. Atifa goes over to the stereo and chooses a CD and places it in the disk drive. Asian music drifts across the room and both girls continue to dance.
- Jerome's uncle is a rapper and he takes Jerome to the recording studios at the weekends. Jerome is really interested in rap music, and he and his friends have made up some lyrics about how they are going to spend their money this weekend. They are using the karaoke machine and are having a great time rapping, laughing and loudly discussing the content of this rap. You see another playworker go over and ask them to 'keep the noise down'. This disturbs the group for a while but their enthusiasm takes over and they soon become loud again. This time the playworker goes over to them and threatens to turn off the machine if they do not stop the noise.

1 Which of these case studies shows access to the resources?
2 How could the playworker in the first case study have responded to promote the use of resources?
3 What words did the playworker in the last case study use that showed he had a low opinion of what the group were doing?

Promote the environment to children and young people who may experience barriers to participation

Barriers to participation can be:

- physical
- psychological
- social
- cultural
- environmental.

Often two or more of the barriers mentioned above can be present at the same time. In an inclusive setting the barriers should be removed and positive steps taken to support access.

There are many children within communities who access very little play provision because of the barriers mentioned above. To promote your facility in the local community using a range of different but appropriate methods will help remove these barriers. Local organisations and agencies will be able to offer you the chance to promote your setting at their meetings and will often refer children and young people to you once they are aware of the opportunities and facilities you offer.

Once you have promoted the environment to the children and young people who may experience barriers to participation, you will need to provide them with appropriate forms of support.

Barrier to participation	What groups might be affected?	How can you help remove the barriers?
Physical	Children and young people with physical difficulties	Ensure the setting has disabled access Provide aids such as grips for brushes/pens/pencils, tables that can be accessed by wheelchairs, balls that can be easily gripped, etc.
Psychological	Children with emotional difficulties, those who have been abused or neglected	Have a welcoming and friendly atmosphere where they can relax and feel safe Provide a range of equipment that they can relate to
Social	Children who have had little guidance on how to interact due to poor parenting skills	Help them to join in group agreements and to realise the importance of respecting others
Cultural	Children who have English as a second, third or fourth language	Have staff who can speak their language Provide dual language books and information
Environmental	Children from inner city homes without gardens and open spaces Children who are not allowed to play outside	Provide an outside area that is environmentally friendly and has space to experiment and learn about nature

How you can help to remove barriers to participation

Types of support that children may need to access the setting

You may find that it is easy to support children and young people who can tell you clearly what they want and when they want something. However, you may work with young children or children and young people with sensory needs, learning difficulties or medical disabilities who are unable to express themselves in an articulate manner. Some children may be withdrawn or unable to communicate due to trauma or lack of confidence. In these instances you will need to adapt your method of communication to meet their needs (see Unit PW8, page 101, for different methods of communication) and have a range of resources available, some of which will need to be tailor made for individuals (for example, memory boards, computerised voice programmes, pictures or flash cards).

As a playworker, you will need to pay particular attention to supporting the cultural and spiritual needs and preferences of the children and young people. Children and young people may not always find it easy to talk about these aspects of their lives, particularly if they are in the minority or have no positive role models to identify with. You will be able to understand their needs more fully if you have taken part in training or researched into the different aspects of culture and religion.

Some children and young people will require physical help with access, participation and/or personal care. Whatever support you provide, the child's needs, dignity and preferences should be considered and steps taken to provide for these.

Provide a positive role model for diversity and inclusion

Part of your role will be that of providing a positive role model so you must show that you support inclusion and diversity through your words, actions and behaviour in the setting. To treat children, young people and adults with respect is one aspect that should underpin all your practice.

The way that very young children initially learn is by copying. Playworkers who are open-minded and respect other people will be positive role models. This can enhance the learning and accepting process for all children and young people. This is also the key way that children learn how to co-operate and respect each other. Playworkers need to show that they are interested in finding out more about others' traditions and ways of life. Comments such as, 'I don't know if I would like that much,' should be avoided, as should words such as 'strange' and 'funny' when talking about diverse issues. Playworkers can also demonstrate by example that though they may have different views and beliefs they can still work together.

It is vital that you avoid making assumptions and remain open-minded about the families you work with. If you take the trouble to find out about the personal beliefs and values of each of the families you will find that you are able to build and maintain respectful relationships.

You may find that their values and beliefs are different from your own and you must remember that you must not impose your beliefs on others, especially on to children. As a professional worker there may be times when you promote or advocate their beliefs, for example, if a Muslim girl needs specific space to change for swimming and has different swim wear.

To recognise your own prejudices is very hard to do but it is necessary as they affect what you do. Work situation conflict often arises as a result of your own beliefs and values. While everyone has different values and beliefs, you need to be aware of any that could or do affect your work. For example, you may have been brought up to have 'good table manners' and so may expect that everyone else should do the same, whereas different cultures have different traditions at the table and these should be approached with respect. In Unit PW10 there is more information and exercises for you about your personal values and beliefs (see page 176). To reflect on and evaluate your behaviour is always difficult but constructive criticism will help your practice.

Once you have recognised and acknowledged that your values and beliefs are important to you, you will be able to accept the beliefs and values of others.

Your work practice should never discriminate against anyone. The way that you behave and your attitude are important. Finding out about other cultures, religions, lifestyles, etc. will help you meet the individual needs of the children and young people and will ultimately give you job satisfaction.

Using appropriate language

It is important to understand the meaning of words about equality of opportunity and diversity as well as being aware of:

- the way that you talk
- the expressions you use
- the language you speak.

An effective playworker should always maintain an anti-discriminatory approach. You should avoid language that suggests assumptions and stereotypes and use correct terminology. It is easy to offend people so it is important that you keep up to date with the correct wording for the different groups in society.

ACTIVE KNOWLEDGE

Look at the chart below and cover over the definitions. See how many words you can define in three minutes.

Word	Definition
Equality	Being equal or identical in value
To respect	To treat with consideration and regard
To value	To regard highly, with worth and merit
Diversity	When people have a variety of different beliefs
Preferences	Things people choose or favour above other things
Rights	A legal entitlement to have or do something
To discriminate	To treat differently or unfavourably due to prejudice
Assumption	Something taken for granted, often without proof
Prejudice	Judgement or opinion made without adequate knowledge
Stereotype	A fixed, general image of a person or group
Labelling	A term of generalised classification

There are also phrases that relate to anti-discriminatory practice and an understanding of these will aid your practice.

ACTIVE KNOWLEDGE

Look at the chart below and see if you can think of examples to complete the boxes.

Phrase	Meaning	Example
Equality of opportunity	Treating people according to individual needs to gain the same result	
Anti-discriminatory practice	Taking positive action against discrimination; not treating people differently or having prejudices	
Respecting diversity	Recognising that everyone is different and will make different choices; being open-minded	Not insisting that children use a knife and fork if at home and in their culture they use other eating implements (or fingers)
Inclusion	Ensuring a setting is open and accessible to all and that positive steps are taken to remove barriers so all can participate	Having information in a range of different medias and languages

There may be times when you say or do the wrong thing and it is important that you acknowledge this and use these instances as a learning opportunity. To address these situations and learn from them will enhance your future practice.

Provide opportunities for children and young people to understand and value diversity and inclusion

Children and young people may need support to help them value inclusion and diversity. Some children may have been subjected to discrimination and prejudice throughout their lives and will find it difficult to adopt and change their attitudes, especially if this means they are different from their friends' and family's attitudes. Other children and young people will come from backgrounds where diversity and equality are an integral part of family life. These children will act as good role models and help you support the ones without such an understanding.

If you provide opportunities for children and young people to understand and value diversity, act as a good role model and promote inclusion, your setting will be an important flagship in the community.

Promote diversity and inclusion to colleagues and provide them with support

There may be times when you need to support your team members in promoting diversity and challenging discrimination to ensure a consistent approach by all members of the team. As a senior playworker you will be in a position to help them address issues related to their practice and to their own personal views and opinions. You could support them informally, for example, by talking through things that they find difficult to accept, and more formally, for example, through training and work on policies and procedures.

Deal with words and behaviour that challenge diversity and inclusion

It is important that the whole team adopts a consistent approach to challenging words and actions that may offend or hurt others who hold specific values or beliefs. If one person in the team ignores a discriminatory comment, it will undermine the efforts of the rest of the team.

Although your team members will adopt a consistent approach, the way that they challenge discriminatory words and actions may differ according to the age, the stage of development and the understanding of the child, young person or adult who has shown such behaviour.

To deal with words and behaviour that challenge diversity and inclusion in a way that is appropriate to the people involved will require good communication skills. A useful technique would be to state the point you are making and back this up with an explanation as to why you are challenging the behaviour and the effects that such behaviour can have on the person concerned. If the comment or behaviour is aimed at a specific child or adult, it is important that you support that person in an appropriate manner to show that you are actively promoting diversity and inclusion and not siding with the perpetrator.

Part of the group agreement of the setting, which all the children and young people will have participated in, should revolve around diversity and inclusion. The agreement is also a good tool to use when challenging and discussing discriminatory behaviour.

There is a range of excellent materials available that promote diversity and these can be used to aid understanding and support diversity (for example, Incentive Plus produce a range of resources which can be accessed at www.incentiveplus.co.uk).

CASE STUDY

You are a senior female playworker and are outside in the grounds supervising the young people. David, who took early retirement from his job in industry and has been taken on as a relief driver and handyperson at the setting, is also outside attending the garden. You see him talking to one of the young people (Josh, aged 12). They seem to be sharing a joke as David is laughing and Josh is looking confused but is still laughing. Later in the day you are talking to Josh and you mention the conversation that you saw he had with David. Josh looks uncomfortable and says it was just a joke that David told him. You ask if he wants to share it with you. He looks away and then says, 'No, it's not for women's ears.'

1 What might you say to Josh?
2 Would you demand to hear the joke?
3 Would you challenge David?
4 Would you automatically give David a verbal warning?

CONSOLIDATION

Choose one of your setting's policies that promotes diversity and inclusion. Discuss with your colleagues how you can strengthen the policy. You should take into account any new ideas or information that you need to keep abreast of.

ement PW6.4 Contribute to the protection of children and young people from abuse

This section aims to give a brief overview of how to help protect children and young people from abuse and the measures to take if you suspect abuse. This topic is covered in more detail in Unit PW12 which looks at:

- the definitions of the different types of abuse
- the signs and symptoms of abuse
- techniques to use when a child discloses to you
- the reporting procedures you need to abide by.

What you need to demonstrate you can do

- Make sure you and your colleagues have relevant information about child protection policies and procedures
- Give children clear and relevant information about potentially risky situations and how to keep themselves safe from abuse

- Help children to feel confident in asserting themselves and their rights
- Provide children with guidance on what they can do if they or others experience abuse
- Promptly identify when there are suspicions that children and young people are experiencing abuse
- Sensitively collect and assess as much information as possible about suspected abuse
- Promptly follow the correct procedures for reporting the information you have collected and assessed
- Ensure that you and other staff involved receive support
- Maintain confidentiality of information

Make sure you have relevant information about child protection policies and procedures

Each setting will have a set of policies and procedures about safeguarding children. These will include the actions that they should take if they suspect that a child or young person is in danger or is experiencing abuse. Each setting should have a designated person whose role it is to take forward allegations and suspicions with regard to child protection issues. This may be a senior playworker, a supervisor, a co-ordinator or the owner of the setting. If you are concerned about a child or young person but do not suspect abuse at this stage, it is a good idea to begin to implement the common assessment framework and to start to monitor the child or young person and record information under the headings on the framework triangle (see page 7).

It is important to ensure that you and your colleagues have relevant information about child protection policies and procedures. You should all be aware of what to do, what paperwork you will be requested to complete and the support you will receive throughout the process. Further information can be obtained from your local children's service or LSCB.

ACTIVE KNOWLEDGE

Check that your policies and procedures have been updated to include the current wording and procedures for safeguarding children. These can be found at www.dfes.gov.uk. Also check that there is information in the policy about the common assessment framework. If you find that you need to update your policies, research current thinking and update your policies accordingly. Take the updated policy to your next team meeting and spend some time looking at and explaining the guidelines.

Give children clear information about potentially risky situations and how to keep themselves safe

You and your colleagues can make sure that while the children and young people are with you, they are in a safe environment. You also need to think about how you can help them to keep themselves safe when they are not with you. This means looking at ways in which you can teach children and young people to be confident about themselves, to know where they can go for help and advice and how to avoid potentially dangerous situations.

Children and young people will need information on the following in order to keep themselves safe from abuse:

- knowing how to cope with bullying
- knowing how to deal with strangers
- understanding that they have a right to privacy
- trusting their own feelings and instincts
- valuing and respecting their bodies
- being aware of good and bad secrets
- knowing what they should do if they are or someone else is being bullied or abused
- knowing that it is all right to say no to adults.

To develop these skills and knowledge, and to use them, children and young people need to be confident and assertive.

Some children will have very little awareness of personal safety. They may:

- not understand privacy and respect for their bodies
- have a family background where there are few if any boundaries
- lack self-worth
- like to please adults and crave adult attention of any kind
- have no understanding of appropriate touch
- spend time with older family members who are poor role models
- lack understanding due to their age or personal circumstances.

These children may need particular help in developing the skills to keep themselves safe from abuse. This will include understanding that they need to avoid dangerous situations such as walking home alone in the dark. They will also need explanations as to why the caring adults around them introduce specific measures to protect them, such as not leaving them alone in the house.

As a playworker you will be aware of 'all round child development' relating to the ages and stages of development of the children and young people in your care. It is important to remember that all children, regardless of their age or stage of development, will need to be taught about and reminded about the need to protect themselves. This can begin at a very early age, for example, explaining why people cover certain parts of their bodies in public, the importance of closing the toilet door in public places, etc. Children often forget things, especially when they are deeply involved in play, so there may be times when it is appropriate to remind them about the importance of protecting themselves.

Your knowledge of the developmental stages of the children you are working with will help you to explain in an appropriate manner the risks involved in potentially risky situations.

When deciding how to explain risks to children, it is important to choose a method that is appropriate to the type of situation and the individual child or young person. Some possible methods are shown in the diagram below.

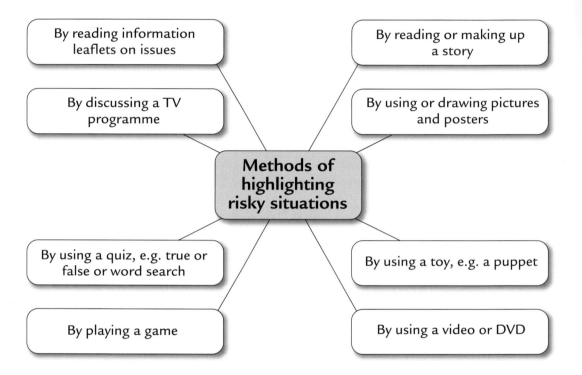

By reading information leaflets on issues

By discussing a TV programme

By reading or making up a story

By using or drawing pictures and posters

Methods of highlighting risky situations

By using a quiz, e.g. true or false or word search

By using a toy, e.g. a puppet

By playing a game

By using a video or DVD

Helping children to understand about secrets

One of the ways in which some abusers gain control over children is by telling them that the abuse is a secret, and that they should never tell anyone about this secret. In some cases children are also told that if they break the secret, terrible things will happen to them or their families, or that they will not be believed by others.

You can help children keep safe from abuse by making it clear that it is all right to break a secret if it is making them unhappy. Sometimes children are taught to think of secrets as 'good' and 'bad'. *Bad* secrets are ones that make them unhappy in any way; whereas *good* secrets are ones that make them happy and that they know that they can break.

The following case study shows how one playworker helps children to think about secrets.

It is Farah's birthday next week and one of the children has asked Jo, the playworker, if they can plan a party for her. This seems like a good idea, and Jo asks the children what they would like to do. One of the older children says that everyone must keep the party a secret from Farah, and that no one is allowed to talk about it. One of the younger children looks a little concerned and Jo quickly decides to take this as an opportunity to talk about secrets.

Jo: 'I can see that it would be nice if this turns out to be a real surprise for Farah, but perhaps we should remember that this is a *good* secret. That means that if you want to tell your parents or someone else about what we are doing, you can. *Good* secrets always make us feel happy and excited in this way; but remember that if you are keeping a secret that makes you feel uncomfortable or unhappy, you can always tell someone. It'll be good if we can make this party a surprise for Farah – do you know what kind of games you might want to play?'

1 How has Jo managed to make a point about secrets without scaring the children?
2 Why is it important that the word 'surprises' rather than 'secrets' is used when planning this type of activity with children?

Helping children to feel good about and respect their bodies

In order for children to feel confident, they also need to value their bodies and reach an understanding about 'ownership' of their bodies. You can help children learn that they can protest or seek help if an adult or another child touches them in a way that makes them feel uncomfortable. Children also need to acquire a sense of personal space and privacy – in some cases the children themselves do not realise that the way they are being treated is not appropriate.

Below is an outline of some of the ways in which you might help children to develop a sense of 'ownership' over their bodies, and the right to privacy and personal space.

Touching and gestures

Children need to develop an awareness of what are and are not appropriate touches from adults and others. For example, a pat on the arm in a situation where a child needs a little encouragement would generally be considered to be appropriate, but stroking the arm is likely to be an *inappropriate* gesture.

Most children have a natural instinct about being touched, but they need to learn to trust their instinct and to be confident enough to say 'no' if someone is touching them in a way that makes them feel uncomfortable.

This is a sensitive area to approach with children and there are some structured materials that have been produced by organisations such as Kidscape which can be used to help discussions.

Children eventually need to learn that they have control over their bodies and that if someone touches them in a way that makes them feel uncomfortable, they can say so. It is, of course, essential that you act as a good role model and are consciously aware that you do not touch children inappropriately.

Touching children – being a good role model

Playworkers should make sure that they only touch children in appropriate ways, according to their ages and needs. For example, a young child might wish to hold your hand for reassurance, but this might not be an appropriate gesture with a 14-year-old unless there were special circumstances.

This does not mean that you should make *no* physical contact, just that you should be sure that it is appropriate. In some situations it may be a good idea to check that the child is happy with the contact, and feels in control. Look at the case study below.

CASE STUDY

- Michael is 12 years old and has suddenly burst into tears while talking about his father, who died recently. The playworker feels that some physical reassurance would be helpful and says, 'I think you need a hug – would that help?' Michael nods his head and, arms outstretched, he reaches out for a firm hug. He then releases the playworker.
- Simone is 10 years old and is next to the playworker as they are crossing a busy road. The playworker says, 'This is a busy road – I think it might be a good idea if you grab either my elbow or my hand as we cross. What do you think?' Simone holds on to the playworker's elbow as they cross the road.

1 How in each of these cases has the playworker helped the child to remain in control?

Respecting privacy

As children develop, they tend naturally to wish for more privacy when they change and go to the toilet. This should be encouraged and respected. If children need to change out of clothes, therefore – for example, if they have got wet – they should always be given access to a safe changing area. If for some reason you need to give some assistance, always knock on the door, or find a way of making the child feel comfortable about your presence and in control of the situation.

Helping children value their bodies

From around the age of 10 years, many children begin to develop a strong awareness of their bodies as the process of puberty begins. In some cases, children also develop low self-esteem about their bodies, believing themselves to be too thin or too fat. This means in practical terms that you should avoid making remarks about children's weight, height or size, and make sure that you act as a good role model by taking good care of your own body – for example, by not smoking in front of the children.

Help children to feel confident in asserting themselves and their rights

In order to help children and young people to feel confident enough to speak out about potential abuse and abusive situations and issues playworkers can give them enough confidence and strength to 'find a voice' and become assertive.

In order for children to become assertive they first need to be confident about themselves. Inner confidence is often referred to as self-esteem. Children who have high self-esteem value themselves and therefore have, in most cases, enough confidence to put their ideas forward, or in the case of child protection issues, to challenge the abuser and/or seek help.

Children with low self-esteem are more easily bullied and controlled because they lack the confidence to speak out. Victims of bullying or child abuse often have very low self-esteem. They are made to feel responsible or guilty for what is happening to them. By helping children and young people to feel more confident, you can help protect them from abuse. You can also help children who are being abused to seek help.

Building confidence and self-esteem takes time. Children gather signals about themselves from a variety of sources including their families, friends, teachers, playworkers and others around them. These signals are often hidden ones:

- do people listen to them when they are talking?
- are they praised?
- do they have plenty of friends?

Signals such as these lead children to judge themselves and contribute either positively or negatively to their confidence. Children and young people may judge themselves according to their achievements, often in comparison with their peers, siblings or friends.

As children are always taking in information about themselves it is essential that you and your fellow playworkers help them feel confident.

Ways of raising children's self-esteem

You can help children's self-esteem by showing them that you value them for who they are, not what they do or how they behave. This can be referred to as *unconditional positive regard*. In practical terms this means actively welcoming children, listening to their ideas, and showing them through your facial expressions and body language that you enjoy being with them. The signals that you send out in this way must be sincere: children are quick to sense when people do not really mean what they are saying.

Helping children with low self-esteem

Showing children unconditional positive regard is not always easy, as in many cases the children who really need to experience this are the ones who are most difficult to work with. Previous experience may have left them with low self-esteem, and as a consequence they may at times show attention-seeking or unwanted behaviour. You need to deal with their behaviour, but at the same time you need to show them that you still value them as people. You could look for particular ways of making them feel special and wanted – examples might include asking them if they would like to help set up a game, or asking for their advice or opinion.

ACTIVE KNOWLEDGE

A child in your setting seems to be lacking in confidence. She seems unsure, and tends to wait for other children or adults to make decisions for her, such as which games to play. The child often makes remarks such as 'I don't mind'.

Think of five ways in which you could help to build up this child's self-esteem.

Keys to good practice: Helping children and young people become more confident and gain self-esteem

✓ Offer a range of opportunities where they play without fear of criticism.
✓ Encourage them to take on appropriate responsibilities.
✓ Actively listen to them and help implement their ideas.
✓ Never show favouritism.
✓ Encourage them to value their own background, culture and beliefs.
✓ Demonstrate that you value their ideas and opinions.
✓ Involve them in decision making.
✓ Remain open-minded and non-judgemental.
✓ Do not make assumptions about their needs and requirements.
✓ Explain things in an appropriate manner for their stage of development without patronising them.
✓ Give opportunities for them to experiment in different roles.
✓ Keep on their side – do not presume they are wrong.
✓ Encourage them to discuss their feelings and fears.

Actively listening to children can help them gain self-esteem

ACTIVE KNOWLEDGE

During your next play session, look around the room(s) to see how many opportunities are available that will help children and young people become more confident and build up their self-esteem.

Provide children with guidance on what they can do if they or others experience abuse

Unit PW8 looks at the importance of developing relationships with children and young people (see page 92) and this will help them to approach you and trust you when they talk about difficult situations. They will want to talk to someone who will listen to their views, take their opinions seriously and support them with interactions with other adults and professionals. You will probably be the person that they feel secure with so will feel able to talk to you about their fears or anxieties, including details relating to child protection issues. Research has shown that children often do not believe that adults will take them seriously so are less likely to tell someone about abuse.

It is always a good idea to have information available to children and young people in the form of posters, stories, books and quizzes that relate to what to do if they experience abuse or are put into abusive situations. It is also useful to display a ChildLine poster with the telephone number.

Promptly identify when there are suspicions that children and young people are experiencing abuse

Professionals working with children and young people must put the child's welfare and protection first. If you have any doubts or niggles about a child's behaviour, you should take them seriously and start evaluating whether abuse is the cause. Think carefully about what has made you suspect abuse, then share these concerns with the designated person at your setting. This person may also have had some concerns about the child.

In some cases you may be able to probe the child carefully for a little more information, for example, if the child comes in with a bruised eye, you might gently ask the child what happened. Or if the child seemed particularly depressed, you might make a comment such as, 'You look a little down today – what's up?' Most children will be ready enough to give you an answer to this type of question in an open, natural way. If you get negative and surprising reactions or if the child's reply is unconvincing, you should start to follow your setting's procedures.

You might also gain some information about the child from the parents. Most parents put their child's welfare first, so a comment such as 'he seems a little down lately' is generally taken positively as a sign that the play setting team care about the child. If parents seem particularly anxious, defensive or even aggressive about your general comments or questions, this might be a sign that there may be an underlying problem. Further information on identifying abuse can be found in Unit PW12 (see page 238).

Your role as a playworker will mean that you are in a position where children and young people may disclose information to you, which may include harm or abuse that they have been subjected to. Information on how to respond to disclosure of abuse can also be found in Unit PW12 (page 252).

Sensitively collect and assess information about suspected abuse

It is important to collect, assess and share information about possible abuse and promptly follow the correct procedure for reporting the information you have collected and assessed.

If you suspect that a child or young person is being abused, you should keep a note of the signs that have caused the suspicion. Be accurate in your recording, use the correct documentation and note down only what you have either seen or heard. Be aware that the notes may be used as evidence in a criminal court. You should write clearly in pen and sign and date the paper. If you are unsure about what to write, refer to your setting's procedures. The note should be stored in a secure place.

If you suspect abuse, you should always consult your designated person or, if you do not have a designated person, your supervisor, and follow the procedures for the setting. Most settings follow their local authority guidelines and build these into their procedures. By following these procedures you will be helping the child; you will also be protecting yourself against accusations of maliciousness. In cases where procedures have not been followed, abusers have sometimes not been convicted because of contamination of evidence or have escaped conviction on a technicality. In other cases parents have been angered because cases have been handled badly, and it has emerged afterwards that no abuse had been evident.

Further guidance on collecting and reporting information can be found in Unit PW12 (see pages 257–264).

Ensure that you and other staff involved receive support

Many professionals working with children and young people find that reporting and being involved in child abuse cases is emotionally draining and potentially disturbing. Child abuse exposes people to a side of life that many would prefer not to see. If you are involved in a child abuse case you might need to talk to someone else about what has happened. In some cases a supervisor or colleague who is also involved may be able to offer you some support.

If you feel that you need more professional help, many child protection teams will be able to offer support directly or they may be able to point you in the direction of a counselling service. It is important to remember, however, that if you are talking to someone who is not directly involved you must respect confidentiality. You should not mention the child's name or the name of the abuser, or indicate where you work.

Maintain confidentiality of information

In some cases of suspected abuse, children are showing signs of stress not caused by abuse but by family upheaval or changes at school. People's lives can be ruined by gossip and false accusations. At every step of a suspected abuse case confidentiality must be maintained as victims of abuse have the right not only to protection, but also to their privacy. If you have needed to report a case of suspected abuse, do not talk about it to anyone, including colleagues, unless called upon to do so. The confidentiality must be maintained permanently, even after the case has been resolved. Any documents that are linked to the case should be securely handled and kept in a place where only those directly involved have access to them.

Legislation such as the Data Protection Act sets out clear guidelines regarding the sharing and storing of information and it is your responsibility to adhere to these guidelines (see page 8).

CONSOLIDATION

Review your setting's policies with regard to safeguarding children from abuse. Consider whether they need updating, or whether any changes need to be made to make them more effective.

END OF UNIT KNOWLEDGE CHECK

1 List the legislation relating to the protection of children and young people.

2 What does CAF stand for and what is its aim?

3 Why is it important to involve children and young people in decision making?

4 What are the differences between the social and medical models of disability?

5 Give an example of how a setting can be inclusive.

6 State two advantages of having group agreements.

7 List four ways in which you can promote diversity in the setting.

8 Why is it important to challenge discriminatory comments and remarks?

9 Give an example of how you can help children and young people protect themselves.

10 What are the steps you should take if you suspect abuse?

Useful resources

NSPCC

The National Society for the Prevention of Cruelty to Children (NSPCC) specialises in child protection. It employs its own social workers and child protection officers. It also has a helpline for people to use if they suspect that abuse is taking place. More information can be found at www.nspcc.org.uk.

Childline

This is a charity which runs a freephone line for children to use. The freephone line takes about 3000 calls a day from children who need someone to listen to them. Children know that they can talk in confidence to an adult and remain anonymous, although the specially trained counsellors encourage children to seek further help from people in their home area. More information can be found at www.childline.org.uk. For Scotland, please refer to www.childline.org.uk/Scotland.

Kidscape

This organisation was founded to help children learn the skills of keeping safe. It produces many resources aimed at schools, parents and organisations caring for children to help them teach children strategies for protecting themselves. Kidscape also runs training programmes and a bullying helpline. More information can be found at www.kidscape.org.uk.

Develop and maintain a healthy, safe and secure environment for children

This unit looks at how to provide an environment in a playwork setting that promotes children's health, safety and protection. It also covers outings that form part of work activities. The unit is appropriate for all settings and services where children and young people are present.

This unit is divided into three sections:

- PW7.1 Establish a healthy, safe and secure environment for children
- PW7.2 Maintain a healthy, safe and secure environment for children
- PW7.3 Implement procedures for accidents, injuries, illnesses and other emergencies.

Playwork values

The playwork values relating to this unit are shown in the table below.

Value	Details
5	The contemporary environment in which many children grow up does not lend itself to safe and creative play; all children have the right to a play environment which is free from hazard, one which ensures physical and personal safety, a setting within which the child ultimately feels physically and personally safe.
11	Play opportunities should always be provided within the current legislative framework relevant to children's rights, health, safety and well-being.

Ofsted national standards

Standard 6: Safety

The focus:

The safety of children is paramount at all times. An awareness of children's constantly developing abilities helps to ensure appropriate safety measures are applied to avoid dangerous situations. (Scottish National Care Standard 2; see page 344.)

Standard 7: Health

The focus:

High standards of hygiene and the prevention of the spread of infection are essential to children's good health. Where the registered person and staff have a secure knowledge of the setting's policies and arrangements for health and hygiene and a commitment to adhering to their agreed procedures, they are likely to promote children's good health. (Scottish National Care Standard 3; see page 344.)

What you must know and understand

For the whole unit

K1: Statutory and regulatory arrangements covering health and safety for the children, workers, families and visitors in your setting

K2: The basic stages of child development and the implications these have for health, safety and security arrangements

K3: Regulations covering manual handling and the risks associated with lifting and carrying children

For PW7.1

K4: Safety checking of the children's indoor and outdoor environment before and during work activities to include facilities and equipment, toilet and washing areas, and movement and activity of children

K5: Security arrangements to include children's arrival at the setting and children's departure from the setting

K6: Regulations and procedures for the storage and administration of medicines

For PW7.2

K7: Principles and models of risk assessment that are applied in your setting to cover the environment for children and workers both indoors, outdoors and on outings

K8: Differences between formal and informal risk assessments

K9: Why it is important to allow children to assess and manage risk according to their stage of development and how this can be done

For PW7.3

K10: How to record accidents and incidents

K11: The appropriate contents of a first aid kit

K12: The correct responses to situations involving accidents and injuries taking into account the ages of the children and the procedures of the setting

K13: Signs and symptoms of common childhood illnesses and allergies and appropriate responses according to established procedures

K14: Good hygiene practice including
- Principles of cross-infection
- Appropriate systems to dispose of different types of waste
- Food handling
- Handling bodily fluids
- Issues concerning spread of HIV and the AIDS virus and hepatitis

K15: Emergency procedures in your setting covering fire, missing children, evacuation

---

Element PW7.1 | # Establish a healthy, safe and secure environment for children

All staff should have an understanding of health, safety and security procedures and know their responsibilities for each other, the premises and the children. There is a legal duty to ensure children's health, safety and security while they are in the care of the play setting.

What you need to demonstrate you can do

- Have up-to-date and accurate information about the health, safety and security requirements for your setting
- Check all areas of your setting and identify and record hazards
- Identify and remove those hazards that can be eliminated
- Assess and record the levels of risk for all other hazards and establish procedures for managing these risks to an acceptable level
- Make sure that all children and adults using the setting have information about the health, safety and security procedures relevant to them
- Review and revise your health, safety and security procedures in line with changing circumstances and requirements, and to make improvements

Have up-to-date and accurate information about the health, safety and security requirements

All adults working with children have a responsibility to keep them healthy and safe. In playwork settings this means that you have to:

- be aware of potential hazards
- develop emergency and health and safety policies
- be able to respond appropriately in the event of an accident or emergency.

Playworkers also have a role to play in helping children to maintain their own health and safety. There is a legal duty on playworkers to ensure children's health and safety at all times.

Legislation relating to health and safety

The Health and Safety at Work Act 1974

The main piece of legislation that affects the day-to-day provision of health and safety in workplaces is the Health and Safety at Work Act 1974. Settings have a duty to comply with this Act, as well as any further regulations that have been added. Work settings cannot plead that they did not know about the regulations: it is essential that senior staff keep their knowledge of this Act up to date. You can check current regulations by contacting the government agency responsible: the Health and Safety Executive.

According to the Act the duties of employers and employees are as follows.

- **Duties of employers:** Essentially the Act requires employers to ensure that they are providing a safe work environment. They must provide training and equipment, and produce health and safety policies. Employers employing more than five people must carry out a risk assessment on their premises. They must also write a safety policy that explains how the risks are to be minimised.
- **Duties of employees:** The Act makes it clear that employees must follow the setting's health and safety policies and use the safety equipment and protection provided. It also makes it clear that employees must not place either themselves or others at risk of harm as a result of their actions.

Manual handling

Adults must be conscious of the regulations covering manual handling and be aware of the risks associated with lifting and carrying children. Permanent damage can be done to your body if you lift incorrectly or carry too heavy a load. It is recommended that all staff have specific training to help them care for themselves. This can usually be accessed through your local children's services training plan.

Other legislation

The table below shows other regulations that affect the provision of health and safety in settings.

Regulation	Duty of the setting
Control of Substances Hazardous to Health Regulations (COSHH) 1994	Many settings use chemicals or materials that are potentially hazardous, such as bleach and cleaning materials. The COSHH regulations require settings to list the hazards and consider how they will minimise the risks. For example, cleaning materials should be stored in a locked cupboard.
Reporting of Injuries, Diseases and Dangerous Occurrences Regulations (RIDDOR) 1995	Workplaces must provide an accident report book. All accidents must be recorded in this. Most settings keep separate books for staff and children. Any injury to an employee that means that he or she cannot work for three or more days must be reported to the Health and Safety Executive.
Fire Precautions (Workplace) Regulations 1997	Settings should have plans for evacuation and procedures in the event of a fire. Alarm systems should be in place and fire drills should be carried out regularly. Signs showing what to do in the event of a fire should be placed in every room.
Health and Safety (First Aid) Regulations 1981	There is a legal duty for employers to keep a first aid box and to appoint at least one person to be responsible in the event of an accident.
Children Act 1989 (amended 2004)	This Act was wide-ranging and gave several duties to local authorities. Under the Act, settings that care for children under 8 years old for more than 2 hours must be registered and inspected. As part of the inspection, health and safety arrangements will be examined.

Keys to good practice: Keeping up to date with health and safety requirements

✓ Include health, safety and security issues in induction and on-the-job training.
✓ Check the setting has as a minimum a health and safety policy, an evacuation policy, a named first-aider, a session register, accident records and medication records.
✓ Check Standard 14 of the Daycare Standards for a comprehensive list of all documentation that your Ofsted Inspector will expect to examine.
✓ Incorporate responsibilities into job descriptions.
✓ Delegate responsibilities to suitably qualified and named staff.
✓ Use professional trainers to help staff (local children's services training plan).
✓ Prepare a manual for staff, students, trainees and volunteers.
✓ Regularly include health, safety and security issues on staff meeting agendas.

Check all areas of your setting and identify and record hazards

Hazards and risks

A hazard is a situation which creates a 'real' risk. For example, a hole in the floor is a hazard, which creates the risk of a fall. Most hazards need managing immediately – in this case, the floor will have to be mended.

A risk is a potential danger which might or might not happen. There are different levels of risk: for example, the risk of falling through a hole in the floor is high, but the risk of an aircraft falling on to the setting is low.

Playworkers need to be able to identify hazards and deal with them while children are playing. They also need to look at the way in which children are playing and consider the risks.

What hazards can you spot here?

Anticipating potential problems

There are many different types of hazard that you need to be aware of in the play environment. Some hazards are visible, such as broken equipment; others are less obvious, such as a blocked fire exit or the risk of food poisoning from food that is not stored properly. Although you can carry out some checks at the start of sessions, many hazards and dangers emerge as sessions proceed, so you need to pay constant attention to possible hazards.

Accidents and incidents of unwanted behaviour can happen very quickly: you must be able to identify hazards rapidly. In many cases this means being able to predict the likely outcome of a situation. For example, if you can see that a group of children are shouting encouragement to a child who is climbing over a fence to collect a ball, you might predict that the child might fall, run into the road or damage the fence. In some cases, you may also recognise that the use of certain pieces of equipment, if not carefully supervised, might be hazardous, including paddling pools, skipping ropes and bats.

Hazards can also come from the environment. In order to spot these types of hazards promptly, it is useful if you have a good understanding of the risks unique to your setting. Is there a main road nearby? Are there dustbins? Is there an access gate? Be aware also of the general state of the equipment being used.

Public places can pose potential risks too, for example, in a public park there might be danger from dogs or from litter that has been dropped, as well as from strangers.

Hazards should be recorded when carrying out a risk assessment and should be kept for inspection by Ofsted.

If not carefully supervised, some activities might be hazardous

Identify and remove those hazards that can be eliminated

Dealing with hazards

Once a hazard has been identified, it is essential that quick action is taken. This might mean stopping the children's play temporarily while you deal with the hazard. If individual children's behaviour is putting either himself/herself or others in danger, you might need to talk to him or her about the risk they are posing.

The table below shows some of the main dangers that might be present in play environments and looks at ways of preventing them.

Danger	Causes	Ways of prevention
Falls	Falling off equipment Slipping on floors, mats or off equipment	Keep the setting tidy Make sure children are aware of behavioural agreements before using equipment Check that equipment is safe and secure
Cuts and bruises	Broken equipment Overcrowding in areas Children engaged in unsuitable activities	Regularly check equipment for faults Supervise children well
Poisoning	Cleaning fluids or other chemicals being left out Children experimenting with drugs and other substances	Store cleaning materials and other hazardous substances correctly Supervise children well Help children to be aware of ways to keep themselves safe
Food poisoning	Food being served at incorrect temperature Poor hygiene when preparing food Incorrect storage of food	Make sure that staff who handle food have been on food-handling courses Ensure good overall cleanliness in all areas of the setting, especially in kitchen and toilet areas
Burns and scalds	Temperature of water in taps too high Poor supervision in kitchen areas Children experimenting with lighters or matches	Ensure regular maintenance of central heating and water systems Supervise children well Help children to be aware of ways to keep themselves safe
Infection	Poor hygiene procedures, especially in the toilets or the kitchen Lack of ventilation	Use posters to remind children and others to wash their hands Help children to become aware of ways to keep themselves healthy Dispose of tissues and other products safely Use disposable gloves when handling bodily fluids Check ventilation in the setting

Keys to good practice: Carrying out a risk assessment

✓ Identify risks and hazards both indoors and out paying attention to equipment, materials and procedures.

✓ Evaluate the risk or hazard and identify whom will be put at risk.

✓ Identify what action needs to be taken to eliminate or minimise the risk or hazard and include a timescale.

✓ Identify who will be responsible for taking the necessary action.

✓ Keep a record of the risk assessment for inspection by Ofsted.

Assess and record the levels of risk for all other hazards and establish procedures for managing these risks

No environment will ever be risk-free. You need to strike a balance between the needs of the children to play and their right to be safe.

When thinking about the activities that you provide and that the children choose, you should consider the risks and decide how these can be minimised. Children will inevitably be taking some risks in order to be able to explore and play freely. For example, climbing up a tree has an element of risk: the child might fall. A playworker needs therefore to be able to assess the risks and provide a safe environment, without being over-protective. This allows the children to learn to take 'safe risks', and to gain confidence and independence.

Playworkers need to be able to assess the risk of allowing children to play freely

Taking action to deal with hazards

Although you should always try to look out for hazards before children arrive in the play environment, there may still be times when you need to deal promptly with an unexpected hazard, for example, a glass might break on the floor.

Once a hazard has been recognised, quick action must be taken. In working quickly, you might be able either to prevent an accident or incident, or to limit the extent of it. In some cases, you will need to move children away from the area; in others, you will need to remove the hazard.

Hazard	Action that may be needed	Timescale	Who is responsible
Broken equipment	Remove the piece of equipment if possible, or 'section off' the area or equipment	Immediate	All playworkers
Child's behaviour	Intervene quickly but sensitively, using strategies outlined on page 118	Immediate	All adults in vicinity
Suspicious stranger	Evaluate the risk Consider moving the children away, or stay with the children	Ongoing, depending on how the situation develops	Senior staff member
Weather	Move children to shelter or shade Avoid children being exposed to extreme temperatures or being soaked (Never shelter under a tree in a storm)	May be for a short time or longer, depending on weather conditions	Playworker in charge
Dangerous item	Steer children away If it is within the setting, arrange for it to be cleared away (always wear appropriate protection, wrap dangerous items up and dispose of them appropriately)	Immediate	Playworker
Fire	Evacuate the building according to your setting's procedures	Immediate	Playworker or any adult in vicinity
Accident	Follow the procedures of your setting	As quickly as is practical	Playworker/First-aider

Dealing with hazards

Once you have assessed and recorded the levels of risk, you need to follow the procedures of your setting for managing these risks (see PW7.3).

Security arrangements

In order to reduce the risk to children, the door of the setting should be locked so that unauthorised people cannot just wander into the setting. Staff, parents and children should be fully aware of arrangements for answering the door.

It is essential to develop an effective system for managing access to the setting. As a minimum there should be a visitors' book in which the name of the visitor, the purpose of the visit and details of arrival and departure times are recorded. The identity of visitors should be checked and verified to ensure the safety of the children in your care.

Clear arrival and departure procedures for staff, children, parents and any visitors will include a signing in and out system so that staff can see at a glance who is in the building. If a child is to be picked up by another adult, written permission must be obtained from the parent. If there is any issue about who has legal access to a child it is important that full details are recorded about who can and cannot collect the child.

CASE STUDY

It has been noted by staff that on a number of occasions parents are letting other people enter the premises when the automatic entry system has been released to allow them to collect their child.

1 How would you address this with parents?
2 How would you address this with staff?
3 How would you avoid the situation arising in the future?

Formal and informal risk assessments

It is important to understand the differences between formal and informal risk assessments. Formal risk assessments are carried out regularly and the results are kept on record for inspection by Ofsted. Informal risk assessments are carried out before, during and after a play session by all adults as they observe and supervise the children in their care. Informal assessments are not usually documented but any risks or hazards identified are dealt with there and then.

Make sure that all children and adults have information about health, safety and security procedures

Health, safety and security procedures should be readily available and prominently displayed so that both adults and children are aware of them. Posters informing the children about the procedures could be illustrated to assist the youngest children and those who are not confident readers. An example of an illustrated poster showing a fire evacuation procedure is shown below. These posters could be created as a fun activity by staff and children together, which will help to reinforce the messages for children.

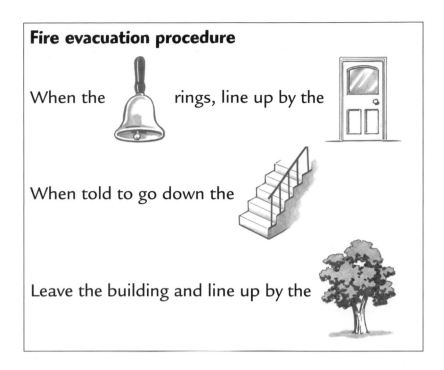

Fire evacuation procedure

When the [bell] rings, line up by the [door]

When told to go down the [stairs]

Leave the building and line up by the [tree]

The leader should consider giving every new parent a copy of these procedures in their welcome pack to reinforce how important the procedures are and how seriously they are adhered to within the setting.

Review and revise your health, safety and security procedures

Reviews should happen at least annually and the whole staff team should be involved. There may be changes in circumstances, that would necessitate more regular revisions, for instance, if the age group of children catered for changes or your setting starts to offer cooked meals.

You may want to consult with another play setting to compare the ways you work. This would give you the opportunity to share procedures and examples of good practice.

It is very important to review and revise your health, safety and security procedures on a regular basis to ensure your setting follows current regulations. Consult the children's services section of your local authority for the most up-to-date information to assist you with the review and revision.

Changes to managing medicines policies (March 2005)

An example of having to revise policies in line with changing circumstances was in March 2005 when the Department of Health issued new guidance about managing medicines in early years. New regulations require that parents give their consent to medicines being administered to their child and that the provider keeps written records. This is now the standard that Ofsted use when inspecting settings, thus ensuring that settings amend their policies to reflect the changes.

ACTIVE KNOWLEDGE

Review the last Ofsted inspection report for your setting. It will highlight good practice and any concerns and issues which should have been addressed.

CONSOLIDATION

Think about a recent time when you checked for hazards.

1 Write an account of this.

2 Why did you need to check for hazards?

3 How did you deal with any hazards that you found?

Element PW7.2 | # Maintain a healthy, safe and secure environment for children

Playworkers have a responsibility to keep children safe and secure, and to help them learn how to keep themselves healthy. As children grow, adults should help them to learn to manage risks for themselves and teach them to take responsibility for their own and others' safety.

What you need to demonstrate you can do

- Assess the health, safety and security of the setting before starting, during and at the end of work activities
- Make sure children and adults in the setting are following health, safety and security procedures, providing them with help and support when necessary
- Maintain supervision of children appropriate to the risk and their stages of development
- Encourage children to help manage risks for themselves
- Encourage children's awareness of their own and others' safety and their personal responsibility

Assess the health, safety and security of the setting

One way in which you can minimise unacceptable risks is by carrying out regular checks on the environment and the equipment. This should also include looking at the cleanliness of areas such as the toilets and the kitchen. Some settings devise checklists in order to help staff remember what areas in particular they should be concentrating on.

Outdoor checks

Any outdoor play area should be checked before it is used, on a session by session basis. It is often harder to maintain cleanliness and safety outside; for example, animals such as dogs and birds can easily enter such areas and foul them. Some settings also have problems with vandalism or misuse of property, so will need to be checked with this in mind.

The table below shows the types of checks that might need to be carried out.

Area	Checks to be made
Grass areas	Look out for evidence of animal faeces, litter and broken glass, and for areas of the grass that might be slippery.
Concrete areas	Look out for litter, and uneven areas which might cause children to fall over.
Large equipment	Check for signs of rusting, metal fatigue or cracking plastic. Make sure that the equipment is stable, especially climbing frames.
Bikes and other equipment that moves	Check brakes, steering and overall condition. Make sure that protection such as knee and elbow pads and protective headgear is available for activities such as rollerblading or skateboards.
Litter bins	Make sure that these are not overflowing, and that there is no litter dropped around them. Empty them if necessary. In summer, look out for wasps.
Fencing	Consider whether there are any gaps which might pose problems, either by children leaving the site or by strangers entering. Check that fencing is secure as children are likely to lean against it.

Indoor checks

The indoor setting should be carefully checked at the start of each session. In most settings, all staff take equal responsibility for making sure the environment is suitable for children's play. Some settings are able to pay cleaners and caretakers, which means that the routine cleaning and maintenance is done for them.

While checks before the children arrive are essential, checks should also be carried out during and after the play session. Areas such as toilet and hand washing facilities need regular checks to replenish supplies and verify cleanliness.

The following table shows the checks that will need to be carried out in indoor settings.

Area	Checks to be made
Flooring	Make sure that floors are clean. Look out for rugs or carpets that are not firmly attached to the floor.
Electrical appliances	Make sure that these are checked annually. Look out for overloaded sockets and for trailing flexes – these might cause children and others to fall over.
Kitchen areas	Kitchens should be clean. Check regularly that the temperature is correct inside fridges and freezers. Throw away any food that has been incorrectly stored.
Toilet areas	These should be cleaned and checked regularly during sessions. Make sure that soap and paper towels are provided. Make sure that waste bins are provided and are regularly emptied. Check that there are bags and bins for the disposal of sanitary towels.
First aid kits	A first aid kit should be placed in the kitchen, and another in an area such as the staff room or the office. Check the first aid kits regularly.
Temperature, ventilation and lighting	Check that the room is well ventilated. Never block ventilation vents: they prevent the potentially dangerous build-up of gases. Check the lighting and temperature of the room. Acceptable temperatures are between 17° C and 22° C.
Equipment	Ensure that equipment is clean and in good repair. Store equipment carefully at the end of sessions.

Make sure children and adults in the setting are following health, safety and security procedures

All members of staff are responsible for the health, safety and security both of the premises and of children and other staff. Staff should be aware of the local and national health and safety requirements and may need the support of a senior member of staff who will be familiar with the requirements. All staff should be involved in drawing up and reviewing health, safety and security policies.

To ensure that both children and adults are following health, safety and security procedures, regular reminders are necessary. For adults, health, safety and security should be regular agenda items at team meetings.

Children will need regular reminders which can be given in a variety of ways and you will want children to remain as safe as possible without frightening them. Regular procedures, such as fire drills and other evacuation procedures, should be carried out as often as possible. Both children and adults will then know exactly what they should do and will be able to carry out the procedure quickly and safely. Other reminders should include reinforcing the message that children should not talk to strangers and should not leave the premises without letting an adult know.

Reporting incidents

It is always a good idea to report incidents to colleagues or in some cases to your line manager. They will then know about the incident if it needs following up later or there is a possibility of the hazard recurring. For example, there might be several wasps around a waste bin in the park, or a particular child might be acting rather aggressively. When reporting incidents, say how you dealt with the situation and if any further action is needed. Minor incidents can be reported verbally, but major incidents must be recorded.

You should always report and record accidents, and the setting should keep an accident book. Other incidents that need noting down might be kept in a log, or in a way that has been agreed by the setting. Writing down incidents provides a record for the future, which may later prove very useful.

Maintain supervision of children

Supervising children during play

One important way in which you can help children to be safe and ensure they are following the health, safety and security procedures is by supervising them as they play. This is a way of preventing accidents and incidents that might be potentially dangerous. There are different ways of supervising children, depending on the play situation; these might be seen as levels of supervision.

A further factor in deciding on the appropriate level of supervision is the child's stage of development. This is often linked to the child's chronological age. However, this can be a dangerous link to make as two children with the same chronological age can have very different levels of skills, confidence and abilities.

It is the playworker's responsibility to get to know the stage each individual child in their care has reached and to plan each child's need for supervision appropriately.

General supervision

This tends to be low-key, and in some ways could be thought of as monitoring rather than supervising. Children remain free to explore their environment, take 'safe risks' and be active in their play.

Close supervision

This type of supervision is more focused as the playworker is nearer to the children. Most playworkers find that if they are not involved themselves in an activity, they can walk around and talk to children as they play. This allows them to assess the potential risks and hazards, while still allowing children to control their play.

There are different ways of agreeing appropriate behaviour with children, including:

- discussion in small groups
- discussion with all the children in the setting.

There are also different stages at which appropriate behaviour may be agreed:

- at the start of an activity
- during an activity, if children are playing in unexpected ways
- after an incident
- when new children join the activity
- when new children come into the setting.

CASE STUDY

The children at a holiday playscheme ask if they can make a water slide as the weather is hot. Look at these two different responses from playworkers.

- Response A: Well, I suppose you can, but I warn you that if you are not playing safely, I will have to ask you to stop. That means no messing around, no pushing and no waving the hosepipe around. If I see any of that, I will turn the water off and you will have to go inside. Is that agreed?
- Response B: That sounds like a good idea, but before we can get out the equipment, we will have to think about how we can make this a safe activity. I have known children get quite bad bruises and knocks unless there are some rules. If I tell you what the main dangers are, can you think about how we can manage these fairly?

1 Which response is more likely to help children take responsibility for their safety and actions?
2 Why is it important to explain the potential safety hazards to children before an activity starts?

CONSOLIDATION

Think about a time recently when you were involved in a play activity that did not go well due to inappropriate supervision.

1 What type of supervision were you using?
2 On reflection, how would you change the way you supervised the children?
3 Explain why you would make these changes.

Implement procedures for accidents, injuries, illnesses and other emergencies

All settings need procedures to be used in emergencies. Procedures help everyone in the setting to react calmly and efficiently in the event of an emergency. In some cases, being able to follow procedures quickly might be life-saving. It is important that everyone in the setting is aware of procedures, and that the procedures are practised from time to time.

What you need to demonstrate you can do

- Make sure that accidents, injuries, signs of illness and other emergencies are promptly identified
- Follow the correct procedures to deal with accidents, injuries, signs of illness and other emergencies calmly and safely
- Make sure that you and others are not put at unnecessary risk
- Provide comfort and reassurance to those involved
- Make sure that first aid and medication are provided according to the correct procedures
- Follow the correct procedures for recording and reporting accidents, injuries, signs of illness and other emergencies

Make sure that accidents, injuries, signs of illness and other emergencies are promptly identified

As well as knowing how to avoid potential dangers and accidents, playworkers need to be able to respond if children do have accidents or feel unwell. As you never know where or when a child may need first aid treatment, it is a good idea for all adults working with children to attend a basic first aid course and then keep their skills up to date. Ofsted require a minimum 12-hour course, which includes an element relating specifically to children.

Prompt identification of accidents, injuries, signs of illness and other emergencies is essential to enable everyone involved to react calmly and efficiently. The following table gives details of some common illnesses.

Contacting the emergency services

The emergency services have specially trained operators who guide callers through a series of questions in order to provide the right type of assistance quickly. They also want to establish the identity and location of the caller. The quickest way of getting help is to listen to the questions you are being asked and to respond to them carefully.

Details that are usually asked for include:

- your location
- your phone number
- your name
- the type of service required – police, ambulance, fire service, mountain rescue, coastguard, etc.
- the location of the incident
- what has happened.

Reporting a fire

When reporting a fire, in addition to the general questions that will be asked, you should also be ready to tell the operator more about the fire and its location, and whether there are still any people who have not been accounted for.

This information will help the fire service to know how they should approach the incident. For example, if chemicals were involved, the crew would use breathing apparatus. It is also helpful if you are able to tell the operator about the type of building, such as how many storeys it has, and where the fire has broken out. This will help the fire crew attack the fire efficiently.

Reporting a security incident

A security incident may need some form of police assistance, although the police may also bring in back-up support such as an ambulance or the fire service. In addition to the general questions, the emergency operators might also ask for further information. For example, if the incident involved an intruder, you might be asked to provide a description of the person and details of this person's behaviour. If you have received a bomb threat, you might be asked to provide details about the call or message that you have received.

Reporting missing persons

An incident involving missing persons might require the assistance of the police or a specific service such as mountain rescue, the coastguard or the river police. In addition to the general information, you will need to provide details about the person who is missing, including a description of his or her clothing, age and general appearance. You will also be asked when this person was last seen and what information had been given to other people about the missing person's plans before she or he went missing.

Contacting colleagues in the setting

During an emergency you might also have to summon help from or warn colleagues. This might mean using a telephone or simply calling out for help. In either case, you must be able to pass on information accurately. This is harder than reporting to the emergency operators as your colleagues will not be trained in handling emergency information. Speak clearly and check that they are taking in the information you are giving them

You might also need to give colleagues clear instructions, so that they know what they need to do. For example, you might need a trained first-aider to stay with an injured child while you phone for the ambulance, or you might need someone to look after the other children while you look for a missing child.

Following instructions in an emergency

You too will need to be able to follow instructions carefully. Those to whom you report the emergency may ask you to do something specific. For example, in the event of an intruder on the premises, you might be asked to observe the intruder at a distance, in order to report the intruder's current location. Similarly, in the event of a fire, you might be asked to move the children to a different evacuation zone.

Listening to instructions is not always easy when you are under stress. One way of helping yourself to remember instructions is to repeat them back; another is to write them down.

Treating injuries

The following table shows the types of common injuries that children might sustain, and the suggested treatment for these. Wherever possible, always get a qualified first-aider's assistance. If you are concerned that the injury might be serious, seek emergency help.

Injury	Treatment	What to check for
Bump to the head	Apply cotton wool squeezed in cold water. If the bump is bad, apply wrapped, crushed ice.	Drowsiness, vomiting or headaches might indicate concussion. Seek emergency help immediately.
Nosebleed	Tip the head forward. Pinch the nose at the base of the bone to close off the nostrils and apply a wet or cold tissue.	Check for continued bleeding or blood mixed with clear fluid. Seek emergency help immediately.
Grazed skin	Rinse the wound with cold running water. Allow it to heal in the open air.	Check for any debris, such as broken glass. Seek medical help if the debris is difficult to remove.
Bruises and trapped fingers	Apply cotton wool squeezed in cold water.	Gently feel the area to check for bumps that might indicate a fracture. If necessary seek emergency help. If a child feels unwell and shows you bruises, consider whether this could be meningitis. Test bruises by putting a glass on top of them: if the marks still show under the glass, seek emergency help urgently.
Vomiting	Do not leave the child unattended. Try to work out the cause of vomiting. Give small sips of water.	Get help if the vomiting is persistent or if it occurs after a bump to the head. If there is any blood in the vomit, seek help.
Insect stings	Reassure the child. Do not squeeze the sting. Seek help to remove the sting.	If the sting is in the mouth or if the child starts to have difficulty in breathing, seek urgent emergency help. Some children are allergic to stings.

Common injuries and suggested treatment

Make sure that you and others are not put at unnecessary risk

Throughout an emergency, you need to maintain the safety of yourself, the children and others while you are dealing with the incident. If a child has gone missing, for example, you still need to consider how to keep the rest of the children safe. If there is a fire in the building, you need to consider how to ensure that once outside, the children will not be in any further danger during the arrival of police, ambulance and fire vehicles.

You need to think clearly about how to keep others safe while managing the incident. In most cases, you will have another adult with you, so one adult can supervise the children while the other manages the incident, for example, reporting the fire or finding a colleague.

If you are alone in an emergency situation, making sure that the children are out of danger must be your first priority however tempting it might be to try to deal directly with the incident.

Good hygiene practices

In order to minimise the risk of illness, staff need to be aware of the principles of cross-infection. Hand washing is the main line of defence against cross-infection. However, developing appropriate systems to dispose of different types of waste is very important if you are to safeguard children from potential infections and illnesses. Where possible gloves should be worn when dealing with bodily fluids and staff should have training and full information on good hygiene practices. The table below shows how to dispose of different types of waste.

Type of waste	Method of waste
Nose wiping tissues	Flush down toilet or put in bin with lid
Sanitary products	Put in sanitary disposal bin or tie in bag and put in outdoor bin with lid
Dressings from cuts	Put in bin with lid
Soiled toilet paper	Flush down toilet
Soiled clothing	If no laundry facilities available, rinse if possible and put in sealed plastic bag to give to parent

Issues concerning the spread of HIV and the AIDS virus must not be avoided and discussions about how these issues should be addressed in your setting are essential. If you do not feel confident dealing with these subjects, you could consider training (the local children's services department may provide this or you could contact the Terrence Higgins Trust, who will inform you about where you can get support locally).

Provide comfort and reassurance to those involved

When children are feeling unwell or have had an accident, you can help by giving them plenty of reassurance and by providing a calm atmosphere for them. Remember that other children in the setting who have witnessed the accident, or who have noticed that the child is ill, will also be worried. They too need reassurance, and praise for remaining calm.

It may be helpful to explain to the casualty and the other children what exactly is going to happen. For example: 'What we have to do now is just wait for a minute or so, to see whether you are going to be sick again. Sometimes being sick is nature's way of telling you that you need to slow down or that you have eaten something that doesn't agree with you.' Explaining in a positive way helps children understand the situation, which can make it less frightening.

Young children may also need some physical comfort: you can offer this by holding their hands or sitting near them. If possible, you should stay with the casualty or the child who is feeling unwell, so that she or he feels less frightened.

Make sure that first aid and medication are provided according to the correct procedures

Providing first aid

There should be at least one member of staff who has attended a recognised first aid course within the last three years on duty at all times.

Every setting should have at least one first aid kit. There is no mandatory ruling of the items that should be in the kit as this will depend, among other things, on the size of the setting. As a guide, the following diagram shows the items that could be included in your first aid kit.

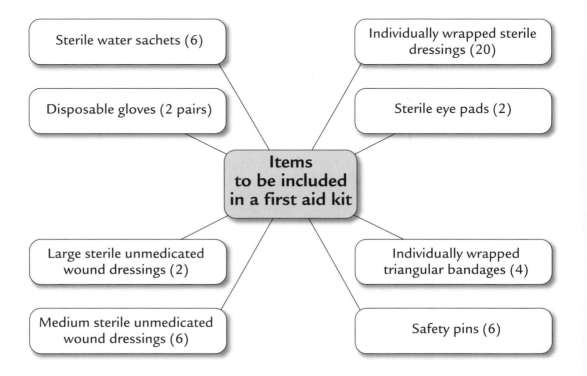

The numbers in brackets are suggested quantities only and your kit should be tailored to the size and needs of your setting. Contents should be checked regularly and replenished as soon as items are used. Expiry dates should be checked, such as those on sterile water sachets, and items should not be used after that date.

Your setting should have a monitoring book to show who checked the kit, when and what was added.

(See also the table on page 78 on common injuries and suggested treatments.)

Administering medication

Medications should be stored in a locked cupboard away from areas where children have access.

A written record must be kept of each time medicines are given. Where possible the administration of medicines should be witnessed by a second adult. Record keeping is paramount and written details should include the name of the child, name of the medicine, dose, method and frequency of administration, any side effects and the expiry date.

Items should be clearly labelled with the name of the child they are intended for.

Non-prescribed medicines should never be administered to a child unless there is specific prior written permission from parents.

Some medicines need to be refrigerated. These can be stored in a refrigerator containing food but should be in an airtight container and clearly labelled. There should be restricted access to a fridge containing medicines.

Staff should not dispose of medicines. Parents are responsible for ensuring that date-expired medicines are returned to the pharmacy for safe disposal. They should also collect all medicines at the end of each session.

Follow the correct procedures for recording and reporting accidents, injuries, signs of illness and other emergencies

As well as it being good practice to keep parents and carers informed about the health of their children, most children in emergencies want to see their parents or carers. This shows how important it is that emergency contact numbers for all the children you work with are accurate and up to date.

When telephoning parents or carers, it is important to stay calm. Tell them carefully about what is happening to their child and what they need to do. Tell them where their child is and the telephone number either of the setting or the place to which the child has been taken.

Minor injuries also need to be reported to parents and carers. Most settings do this at the end of the day. Many settings have standard slips which tell the parents and carers briefly about the incident and the treatment, if any, that has been given (see the example on the next page). Giving parents and carers this information is essential in case the child's state of health deteriorates later on, for example, a bump on the head could later bring on concussion.

How to record accidents and incidents

Whatever the illness or injury, the procedures and policies of your setting should be followed. All types of accidents and incidents must be logged in the accident/incident book. This is a legal requirement and conforms with the Health and Safety Act 1974 and also the requirements of the Children Act Regulations, which state: 'You must keep a signed record of all accidents to children and notify Ofsted of any serious injury or death of any child in your care or adult on the premises.'

The Guidance for the National Day Care Standards suggests accident records could contain:

● details of any existing injuries when a child arrives
● the time, date and nature of any accident
● details of the child(ren) affected
● the type and location of any injury
● the action taken and any subsequent action and by whom
● the circumstances of the accident, any adults and children involved and any witnesses
● the signature of the staff member who dealt with the incident and any witnesses as well as the signature of the parent or carer when the child is collected.

In addition you may consider recording all injuries and incidents when no wound is visible.

It is a good idea to look at the accident book regularly, in case a pattern of accidents can be detected. It might be that accidents tend to occur around the same time of day or in particular areas of the setting. If so, this could indicate a hidden hazard, or that there needs to be a change in the amount of supervision or in the layout of an area.

Name	Date and time	How injury happened or existing injuries when child arrived	Type and bodily location of injury/accident/incident	Action taken and any subsequent action	Treated or witnessed by	Signature of parent or carer
Ben Day	6.6.06 5pm	Arrived at setting with injury	Bruised and cut knee		Playleader Joy Hind	Mrs Day
Ellie Smith	11.7.05 5.30pm	Tripped on playground when playing football	Grazed nose, hands and knees	Bathed wounds, removed dirt and comforted until calm	Playleader Joy Hind	Mr Smith

An accident book

Every setting will have records of where to contact parents in an emergency. Parents provide this information when their child first joins a setting. Emergency contact information should be checked regularly and updated if necessary by a designated member of staff, usually the supervisor. An example of the information required is shown below.

Child's name _____

Address _____

Telephone number _____

Emergency contact (1)

Name _____

Address _____

Telephone number _____

Emergency contact (2)

Name _____

Address _____

Telephone number _____

CONSOLIDATION

What would you tell the children to do in each of the following situations:

- if they heard a fire alarm while they were indoors
- if a stranger approached them while they were playing outdoors
- if they became separated from the rest of the group while on a trip?

Write down what you would say in each case and explain why these instructions are appropriate for your setting.

END UNIT KNOWLEDGE CHECK

1 Describe three different levels of supervising children

2 What is the difference between hazards and risks?

3 What procedures do you need to follow when administering medicines?

4 Describe five checks that might be carried out in the play setting to ensure children's health and safety.

5 In the event of an accident in the play setting how should adults arriving on the scene react?

6 Explain why regular practices of fire/evacuation procedures are important.

7 Give one example of potential difficulties that may occur during each of the following emergency procedures: fire, missing person.

8 List three things children may be allergic to and describe possible symptoms.

9 What information would you give to a parent whose child had been stung by a wasp?

10 What are the benefits of behavioural agreements?

Develop and promote positive relationships

The ability to develop positive relationships with children and their parents or carers is an important skill for playworkers to develop. Positive relationships create a good atmosphere, which means that children can feel relaxed and will enjoy coming to the setting. Good relationships are also the key to managing children's behaviour in a way that allows boundaries to be set in partnership with the children.

This unit is divided into four sections:

- PW8.1 Develop relationships with children
- PW8.2 Communicate with children
- PW8.3 Support children in developing relationships
- PW8.4 Communicate with adults.

Playwork values

The playwork values relating to this unit are shown in the table below.

Value	Details
1	The child must be at the centre of the process; the opportunities provided and the organisation which supports, co-ordinates and manages these should always start with the child's needs and offer sufficient flexibility to meet these.
2	Play should empower children, affirm and support their right to make choices, to discover their own solutions, to play and develop at their own pace and in their own way.
3	Whereas play may be enriched by the playworker's participation, adults should always be sensitive to children's needs and never try to control a child's play so long as it remains within safe and acceptable boundaries.
6	Every child is an individual and has the right to be respected as such. Each child should feel confident that individuality and diversity are valued by the adults who work and play with them.
7	A considerate and caring attitude to individual children and their families is essential to competent playwork and should be displayed at all times.
8	Prejudice against people with disabilities or who suffer social and economic disadvantage, racism and sexism has no place in the environment which seeks to enhance development through play. Adults involved in play should always promote equality of opportunity and access for all children, and seek to develop anti-discriminatory practices and positive attitudes to those who are disadvantaged.

Value	Details
10	Play is essentially a co-operative activity for children both individually and in groups. Playworkers should always encourage children to be sensitive to the needs of others; in providing play opportunities, they should always seek to work together with children, their parents, colleagues and other professionals and, where possible, make their own expertise available to the wider community. (The new standards will not be mapped completely to this value as playwork practice is not comfortable with the first sentence.)
11	Play opportunities should always be provided within the current legislative framework relevant to children's rights, health, safety and well-being.

Ofsted national standards

For related Scottish National Care Standards, please see Standards 1, 4, 6 and 8 on page 344.

Standard 3: Care, learning and play

The focus:

Children's care, learning and play are supported best where the registered person and staff are clear about the main purpose of the provision. The development of children's emotional, physical, social and intellectual capabilities is promoted when they take part in a wide range of activities. Staff meet children's needs through sensitive and appropriate interactions which promote children's self-esteem. They plan first-hand experiences which enable children to make choices when developing their knowledge, skills and understanding. Children's care, learning and play are supported well by staff who monitor children's progress and use this to provide for their individual needs.

Standard 3 describes the atmosphere and feeling a playworker will want to create in a play setting. It clearly states the importance of putting the children's and young people's needs first, so that everything that a playworker does helps and benefits the children.

Section 3 gives guidance on building positive relationships and developing children's self-esteem.

Standard 9: Equal opportunities

The focus:

Children need to feel valued and free from discrimination. Family members and staff should work together to share information.

Section 9.2 describes good practice with regard to anti-discriminatory practice.

Standard 10: Special needs

The focus:

Children with special needs have the right to be included and for their needs to be met.

Sections 10.4 and 10.5 give guidance on including all children and about consulting with parents.

Standard 11: Behaviour

The focus:

Children benefit most where adults adopt a consistent approach to the management of their behaviour.

Guidance is given in 11.2 and 11.3 about encouraging positive behaviour and about the adult's role.

Standard 12: Working in partnership with parents and carers

The focus:

The registered person and staff welcome parents into the setting and there is a two-way flow of information, knowledge and expertise. When thinking about information that needs to be given to parents and carers, consider how the information is made accessible.

What you must know and understand

For the whole unit

K1: The importance of good working relationships in the setting

K2: Relevant legal requirements covering the way you relate to and interact with children

K3: Relevant legal requirements covering confidentiality and the disclosure of information

K4: Relevant legal requirements covering the needs of disabled children

K5: The types of information that should be treated confidentially; who you can and cannot share this information with

K6: The meaning of anti-discriminatory practice and how to integrate this into your relationships with children and adults

K7: The basic stages of child development and how these affect the way:

- you behave with children
- you communicate with children
- children relate to and interact with others

For PW8.1

K8: Strategies you can adopt to help children feel valued and welcome in the setting

K9: What is meant by appropriate and inappropriate behaviour when interacting with children; the policies and procedures to follow and why these are important

K10: The importance of encouraging children to make choices for themselves and strategies to support this

K11: The importance of involving children in decision making and the strategies you can use to do this

K12: How to negotiate with children according to their age and stage of development

K13: Strategies that you can use to show children that you respect their individuality

K14: How to balance the needs of the individual with those of the group as a whole

For PW8.2

K15: The importance of clear communication with children

K16: Why it is important for children to ask questions, offer ideas and suggestions and how you can help them to do this

K17: Why it is important to listen to children

K18: How to respond to children in a way that shows that you value what they have to say

K19: The types of behaviour that show that you value children's ideas and feelings

K20: The importance of being sensitive to communication difficulties with children and how to adapt the way you communicate in different situations

For PW8.3

K21: How you can help children to understand the value and importance of positive relationships with others

K22: The importance of children valuing and respecting other people's individuality and how you can encourage and support this

K23: Why it is important for children to understand and respect other people's feelings and how you can encourage and support this

K24: Why it is important to be consistent and fair when dealing with positive and negative behaviour

K25: Strategies you can use to encourage and reinforce positive behaviour

K26: Strategies you can use to challenge and deal with negative behaviour which are consistent with your organisation's policies

K27: Why it is important for children to be able to deal with conflict themselves and what support they may need from you

K28: Why it is important to encourage and support positive relationships between children and adults in the setting and the strategies you can use to do this

For PW8.4

K29: Why positive relationships with adults are important

K30: Why it is important to show respect for adults' individuality and how to do so

K31: The importance of clear communication with adults

K32: The importance of being sensitive to communication difficulties with adults and strategies you can use to overcome these

K33: How and when it may be necessary to adapt the way you communicate to meet the needs of adults

K34: Typical situations that may cause conflict with adults and how to deal with these effectively

The importance of good working relationships in the setting

Your role as a playworker will involve you establishing and maintaining relationships with a variety of people.

Good working relationships will have benefits both for the children and young people in the setting and for the quality of the service you provide. If people feel welcome, are valued and can see the quality provision you provide, they will want to be associated with you and your reputation will be enhanced. Positive working relationships make for a happy setting, where people feel able to approach staff and voice their opinions, ideas and views.

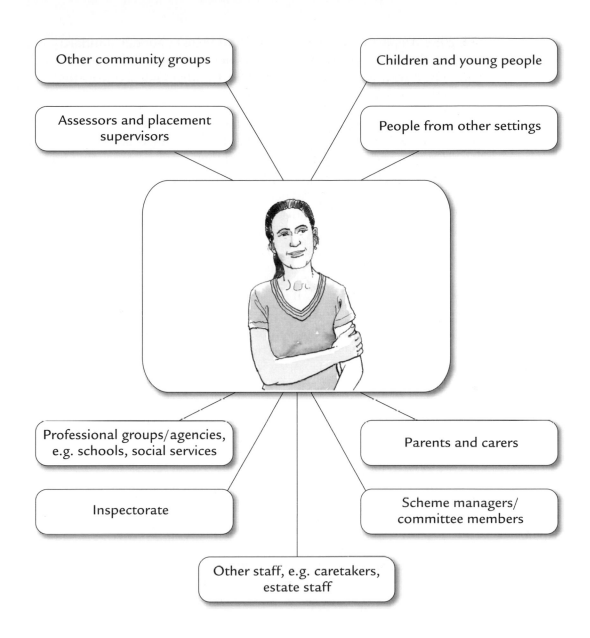

Other community groups

Children and young people

Assessors and placement supervisors

People from other settings

Professional groups/agencies, e.g. schools, social services

Parents and carers

Inspectorate

Scheme managers/ committee members

Other staff, e.g. caretakers, estate staff

You can achieve positive relationships with parents, for example, simply by talking to them when they bring and collect their children and providing them with information about their child's day. Once you have established a relationship it is important to remember to maintain it in order to keep it going.

Relevant legal requirements covering the way you relate to and interact with children

The Children Act (1989) was established to protect children and young people. The main aim of the Act was to provide a balance between the rights and responsibilities of the parents and the rights and well-being of the child. Within this Act are guidance points with regard to settings where children are cared for, and regular inspections are recommended to ensure that the correct standard of care is met.

The DfES (Department for Education and Skills) national standards are a baseline for quality, below which no provider should fall (see Standard 3: Care, learning and play on page 86). The Children Act requires that providers meet these standards.

A requirement is that each setting will have its own policies and procedures and these must be linked to the current legislation, i.e. the Children Act 2004 and the Every Child Matters programme. It is vital that you remember that policies are only effective if they are implemented correctly and are reviewed and updated regularly. For example, every play setting needs a policy on behaviour management, and everyone within the setting must agree with it and follow it. Where a policy is not followed, or where people within a setting do not agree on how to manage behaviour, children are often given very mixed messages; this makes it hard for them to know what is and is not acceptable.

In order for policies to work, it is therefore useful if settings regularly review procedures and agreed strategies, especially if there has been a change in staffing. New members of staff should be given copies of policies, and it is useful to spend time talking with them about the strategies that are used and the way in which incidents of unwanted behaviour are reported.

Confidentiality

The Data Protection Act (1989) and the Freedom of Information Act (2005), which operates alongside the Data Protection Act, provide clear guidelines on the legal responsibilities that everyone, including playworkers, has with regard to confidentiality and the disclosure of information that is kept on record. These regulations are confirmed and integrated within the Children Act (1989).

Remember that all personal information that you have should be stored securely and access should be limited to team members, who may require the information to work safely with the child, and outside agencies, especially for child protection issues and Common Framework Assessments.

Some information that you become aware of may be confidential due to its nature, for example, medical conditions, family issues, criminal activity, child protection issues, etc. In these cases you should only share the information with those whom it is absolutely necessary to tell and even then you may not go into detail. For example, if a parent has told you that she has a relationship problem, you would not share this unless you thought that there may be child protection concerns and the well-being of the child is at risk, and then it would only be shared with the relevant people (see Unit PW12, page 260).

ACTIVE KNOWLEDGE

Look at the list below and tick the boxes to show whom you would share this information with.

Type of information	Who to share the information with				
	Other children	The child's parents	Other playworkers	Other parents	Your manager
A child has had an accident and has bumped her head					
A playworker has phoned in to say he will not be coming to work due to a family death					
You have produced details about a proposed off-site visit to the local woods					
A child has had an accident and has wet his pants					
The setting has had a successful grant application for play equipment					
Two children have built a den and have requested that it stay intact for the session the next day					
A parent tells you that she was abused as a child					

Legal requirements covering the needs of disabled children

Guidelines for working with children with disabilities are included within the Children Act. Your setting will have a policy regarding meeting the specific needs of all children and this includes those with a disability. It will have been written to meet legal requirements and probably the Ofsted guidelines with regard to:

● the commitment of the setting and the staff team with regard to the support they can offer
● how the physical environment will meet individual needs
● how children with specific needs will be included in the setting
● confidentiality.

There will also be guidelines in the setting's diversity policy about how to meet individual needs and the importance of respecting individuals and of integration. Policies are only effective if all of your playwork team are aware of them and the policies are regularly reviewed and updated.

Many useful sources of information on the needs of disabled children can be found on the internet. Some of these are shown in the table below.

Topic	Website
Communication impairment	www.afasic.org.uk
Sight impairment	www.rnib.org.uk
Hearing impairment	www.rnid.org.uk www.hearingconcern.org.uk
Autism	www.nas.org.uk
Cleft lip and palate	www.clapa.com

CONSOLIDATION

At each team meeting include an agenda item on your setting's policies. Choose one for each meeting to discuss, review and if necessary update. This will be the ideal time to refresh your team's memory, to challenge any instances of poor practice and to highlight your good practice.

Element PW8.1 Develop relationships with children

To become an effective playworker you will need to develop relationships with the children and young people in your care. Initial interactions play a vital part in the developing of relationships, especially with children and young people.

What you need to demonstrate you can do

- Interact with children in a way that helps them feel welcome and valued in the setting
- Adapt your behaviour to the age, needs and abilities of individual children
- Negotiate with children about their needs and preferences and involve them in decision making as appropriate to their stage of development
- Apply inclusive and anti-discriminatory practices in your relationships with children
- Make sure your behaviour with children is appropriate
- Give attention to individual children in a way that is fair to them and the group as a whole
- Respect confidential information about children

Interact with children in a way that helps them feel welcome and valued in the setting

Like most adults, many children find it stressful to go into a new environment where they do not know many people. You can help by making all children who come into your setting feel comfortable and welcome. Remember that older children may present themselves as being relaxed and confident, yet in reality be unsure of themselves. The way in which you welcome children will be slightly different according to their age and needs.

Welcoming younger or less confident children

Younger children often seek and need adult attention and supervision. It can be a good idea to allocate one member of staff – a key worker – to take a particular interest in each child from the beginning. The key worker can talk to the child about the opportunities and play that is taking place and help them join in, guiding them if requested. Some younger children will find it hard to ask for the toilet or for drinks, so it can be helpful if they are told about these early on. In some settings, older children enjoy taking care of younger ones; this too can be a useful way of welcoming the younger child.

Welcoming older or more confident children

Older children still need reassurance and adult support, but this might be given in a more discreet way with adults taking the lead from the children. For example, you might ask a child, 'Do you want me to introduce you to Kira, who I think lives near you?' This approach allows children either to take up the offer of help or, if they are confident, to find their own way. Even with outwardly confident children it is still a good idea to keep an eye on them at first, in case they are finding it hard to join in with the others.

If any behavioural agreements have already been established, you could discuss these so that older children understand the framework of the setting. It is important not to have too many ground rules, but to balance the health and safety issues against the risk, challenge and learning that can occur from negotiation.

Greeting children

Even when children have settled into a new setting, it is still important that they are made to feel welcome. Take time to greet each child, and have a word or two with them. This will allow you to pick up on any signs that a child is not happy, for example, they may have had a bad day at school, may be feeling tired or may not have had time for breakfast.

Most settings have areas where children can sit and be quiet if they wish. If they don't feel like joining in with the other children straight away, these can also be places where you can chat to children. They may want to tell you what they have been doing or how they feel, or they may want to discuss their favourite music or computer game.

Planning activities to help children to get to know each other

In some settings, several children will start at once. It is a good idea to have some free play materials and equipment which will allow the children to get to know each other and be able to play with each other. Children will give out play cues to each other and these are usually received positively. They often do not need an adult to talk for them and organise them but will soon get to know each other.

✓ ACTIVE KNOWLEDGE

The next time you have more than one child starting at your setting try putting out a range of lengths of material, some props, pegs and some torches.

1 What do the children do?
2 How quickly do they interact and get to know each other?

Interacting with children and young people

If a playworker interacts with children and young people as individuals, showing and giving respect, then it will be returned. Children need to feel safe and secure. They need to know that the adults around them are interested in them and value what they say.

Children and young people need to be respected

Keys to good practice: Interacting with children and young people

✓ Always use language the children and young people will understand.
✓ Listen carefully and show them that you are listening.
✓ Use eye contact.
✓ Respond to any cues from them.
✓ Show an understanding of their views and opinions even if you do not fully agree with them.
✓ Empower them to have the confidence to share their views and opinions.
✓ Use humour appropriately.
✓ Negotiate and discuss issues.

Adapt your behaviour to the age, needs and abilities of individual children

The children and young people in your playwork setting may cover the whole age range. This will mean that you will need to adapt your interactions so they are appropriate to the children with whom you are working. For example, if you are working with a group of 4- or 5-year-olds, the things you say and do would be different from when you are working with 13- or 14-year-olds. It is important to get this right and not to patronise children or talk down to them.

Individual children's development will occur at different ages. By getting to know the children in your care you will be aware of this and will learn to interact accordingly.

Negotiate with children about their needs and preferences and involve them in decision making

For children to be comfortable with you and the environment you are providing, it will help if you encourage them to ask questions, offer ideas and make suggestions. The aim is to make them feel that they are active participants. Some adults find this difficult at first, especially if in their previous experiences adults were seen very much as all-powerful and the decision makers, while children were expected to be passive. As an adult, you need to keep sight of your overall responsibility to keep children safe and protected, but you can still create secure and respectful relationships so the children can really talk to you.

While encouraging children to feel that they can be active in their communication with you, you should be aware that some children may use this as an opportunity to test the boundaries of politeness. Try to see this as a learning process for children, though you will need to explain to children when their comments are not appropriate.

If children and young people are to reach their full potential, it is important that they acquire the skills of negotiation and it is never too soon to begin. Even very young children need to understand the power of negotiation and they need to practise these skills if they are to improve them. By supporting children and allowing them to make choices for themselves their self-confidence will increase.

Initially this may mean small achievable steps, for example, allowing them to choose their own sandwiches or drinks, or paint, etc. Gradually children will be able to make bigger decisions as they become more confident, for example, planning their own play. A setting that is too structured gives little opportunity for children to gain these skills, as do adults who are very directive in their interactions.

Think about it

Consider these situations:

1 Leah is 9 years old. You see her go over to Danielle (aged 7), snatch something out of her hand and run off. Danielle chases after her and when she catches her she tries to recover the item. As you get closer you see that it is a watch. You remember seeing the watch in the dressing-up box earlier.

2 Harry, who is 6 years old, desperately wants the hammer that Tyrone is using. He tries to snatch it from Tyrone but Tyrone will not let go. Harry tries again, this time trying to hit Tyrone. Again Tyrone will not let go but now shouts out telling Harry to go away. Harry tries a third time to get hold of the hammer and it is now being waved around as they struggle.

Decide what action you would take from the following:

- immediately shout out to stop the arguing
- support the children to try to sort it out themselves
- let the children fight it out as long as it does not become too out of hand
- take away the item and tell the children if they can't play nicely then they will not play with it at all
- sit down with the children and allow them to discuss the situation rather than fight
- ignore the situation and hope that a colleague deals with it.

You might find that you will use a different technique depending on the ages and stages of development of the children involved and the antecedent (what happened before), but whatever you decide you should always allow for negotiation and encourage the children, wherever possible, to sort out their differences for themselves. In some cases you may need to act as a facilitator or an advocate during this process, especially with younger children.

Apply inclusive and anti-discriminatory practices in your relationships with children

Anti-discriminatory practice is about taking positive action against discrimination. This can be done by challenging any discriminatory remarks or actions and being a good role model; this means being positive about diversity. As a playworker you will be in a position to influence and guide the children and young people to accept other people's differences and act appropriately towards others. To have a consistent and positive approach to diversity and to challenging discrimination will enhance the relationships that you establish with the children and young people.

The children and young people in your setting will come from a variety of social and cultural backgrounds and will have values and beliefs that are unique to their own lives. They will hold their own opinions and ideas about what they want and what is important to them. The team of playworkers should accept the differences and should lead by example. They should welcome the diversity that children and their families bring and show a respectful acceptance of major events in their lives and of society as a whole.

Anti-discriminatory practice requires that children are treated as individuals and equals. This does not mean that they will necessarily get exactly the same amount of attention or help. For example, a younger child might require more adult attention than an older child who has been attending the setting for a number of years, although all children have a right to some individual adult attention.

Be sure to speak to and greet all the children for whom you are responsible; do not spend so much time with one child, or group of children, that others find it unfair.

Avoid labels and assumptions

In some settings, children and young people quickly gain labels such as 'shy' or 'attention seeking'. Labels are potentially limiting for children, who often then live up to their reputation or label. As a playworker it is important to be careful when commenting on children to other members of the team, especially when the comment suggests a specific type of behaviour.

Similarly, playworkers should not make assumptions about children based on their lifestyles, gender or any other characteristic. Classifying children is another way of labelling them and prevents people seeing them as individuals.

Think about it

Look at the situations below and think about how you would challenge these comments:

1 Ben attends the play setting every night after school; he is poorly dressed but is excited about his birthday as his mum has promised him some new Adidas trainers. On his birthday he arrives with some new trainers that are of a chain store make. He is obviously disappointed but is hiding this from the others. You overhear Jamaal say, 'I thought you were having Adidas trainers, not those cheap ones.'

2 Charlotte returns after Christmas and as she comes through the door you hear Katie say, 'Charlotte has just come in. Let's go and hide so we don't have to play with her.'

3 Carla has a sight difficulty and has to wear glasses. She is with a group of girls who are imagining that they are at the cinema. They have set out the chairs in aisles and have a tray of ice creams and sweets. You overhear Holly say, 'You can't be the one who sells the ice creams cos you can't see.'

As well as challenging the comments, it is important to support the victim in a positive manner.

Make sure your behaviour with children is appropriate

For children to feel safe and secure, playworkers must ensure their physical and emotional safety. This means being aware of their feelings and insecurities, for example, considering whether a child is being bullied, or encouraging children within the setting to play together.

You need to make sure that children see you as a responsible person who will look after them if they have a problem. It is unwise and unprofessional for playworkers to tell their own problems to children.

You can help children to feel safe by supervising their play activities and keeping an eye on relationships within the setting. This can be done sensitively, yet in a way that allows children to see that there are people around who will take care of them.

A confident and effective playworker needs to understand what is meant by appropriate and inappropriate behaviour when interacting with children and young people. To ensure anti-discriminatory practice, each child should be treated as an individual according to his or her needs so he or she feels valued and respected. Flexibility in the way you react to and interact with children will mean you are a good role model for the children. This will help the children and young people to become well adjusted and open-minded.

ACTIVE KNOWLEDGE

Look at the chart below and tick the suitable box.

Behaviour	Appropriate	Inappropriate
Discussing personal issues in front of the children		
Interrupting conversations and butting into conversations between children		
Standing back and waiting to be invited to join in the conversation		
Offering choices and options		
Being authoritarian and strict		
Responding honestly to questions		
Using sarcasm and put-downs		
Using correct terminology		
Ignoring children and young people		
Having favourites		

CASE STUDY

You are outside and the children and young people have built a den near the trees. A group of girls and boys aged 9 and 10 are kitting it out to make it into a house. You are observing from a distance but can hear the conversations. Jemma sends Leah to get some plates and cups and Josh to get some cutlery. Leah runs off towards the play centre and Josh appears outside the den looking lost and confused. He stands still and gazes around.

1 What would you do at this stage? Would you just ignore Josh or would you go over to see if he understood what Jemma meant?
2 Give reasons for your decision.

Give attention to individual children in a way that is fair to them and the group as a whole

In a child-centred environment where the children and young people feel safe and secure, adults will need to respond to the cues that the children send out with regard to the type and amount of attention they would like. Effective playworkers will have established appropriate relationships with the children and young people. This will give them an insight into the children's needs and allow them to be sensitive to these needs. This may mean spending more time with one child than another or being available to provide unobtrusive supervision.

At times the staff ratios will allow key workers to spend time with individuals. It is important to capitalise on these opportunities to spend quality time with specific children. However, you should be aware of the importance of balancing the needs of the individual with those of the group as a whole.

Respect confidential information about children

The Data Protection Act and the Freedom of Information Act give guidance about confidentiality. (See page 305 for guidance on respecting confidentiality and who you should and should not share information with.)

CONSOLIDATION

Think about a really positive relationship that you have developed with one of the children or young people in your setting. What techniques did you use to develop the relationship? Now think about a child or young person with whom you have very little interaction. How could you develop your relationship with the child or young person further? Consider whether you can use some of the strategies you used to develop the positive relationship and also that you have read about in this section.

Element PW8.2 | Communicate with children

The most successful playworkers are those with good communication skills who are also able to develop an affinity with children. Without effective communication children will be disadvantaged and their development delayed. There are many different reasons for communicating and you will need to use different strategies, styles and methods depending on the individual child.

What you need to demonstrate you can do

- Communicate with children in a way that is appropriate to their age, needs and abilities
- Listen to children and respond to them in a way that shows you value what they say and feel
- Ask questions, clarify and confirm points
- Encourage children to ask questions, offer ideas and make suggestions
- Recognise when there are communication difficulties and adapt the way you communicate accordingly

Communicate with children in a way that is appropriate to their age, needs and abilities

Most people working with children find that although their style of communication varies slightly with the ages and needs of the children they are working with, the basic principles such as listening remain the same.

Forms of communication

When communicating with children several forms of communication may be used at once. It is important to use the methods that are appropriate to the situation and meet the child's individual needs. Some options are shown in the following diagram.

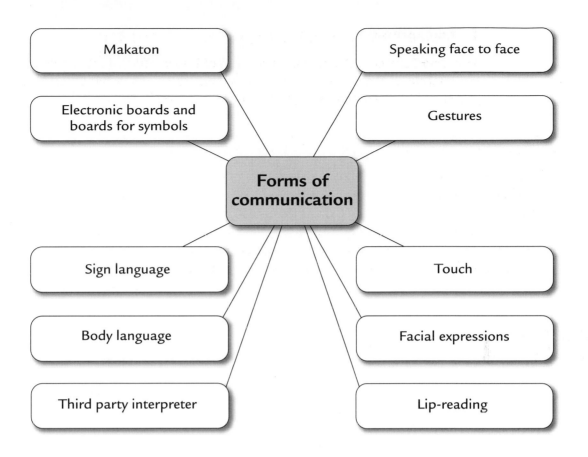

Makaton

Electronic boards and boards for symbols

Speaking face to face

Gestures

Forms of communication

Sign language

Body language

Third party interpreter

Touch

Facial expressions

Lip-reading

Basic communication skills

Most people find that they have basic communication skills, although they may not be able to identify these and understand how they work. There are many facets of good communication: the four elements outlined below are particularly important.

Listening

Many children feel that adults are not very good at listening to them. Younger children, for example, may need time to think through what they want to say, whereas older children often want to talk in detail.

For children to understand that you are interested in what they are saying, you need to use active listening skills. Do not interrupt children or burst in with suggestions, but allow them to talk to you at their own pace. Show in your face and your body language that you are interested.

Speaking to children

Children recognise and dislike adults who patronise them or order them around. It is therefore essential that you talk to children at an appropriate level, which shows them respect. Many children equally dislike adults who pretend to be one of them, so you need to try to adopt the role of being supportive but friendly.

Facial expression

Facial expressions are sometimes more important than words. People's faces can show interest, boredom or anger, as well as warmth. Your face will tend to show what you are feeling, and children will notice whether this matches what you are saying, so they will detect whether or not you are sincere in what you are saying.

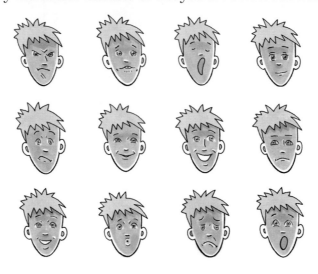

Tone of voice

Your tone of voice will also send out messages. It will tell children whether or not you are being sincere, whether or not you are really interested in what they are saying, and whether or not you really care for them and respect them.

Other methods

You may need to communicate using other methods, for example, Makaton. This is a type of sign language where actions mean words or phrases. Some examples are shown below.

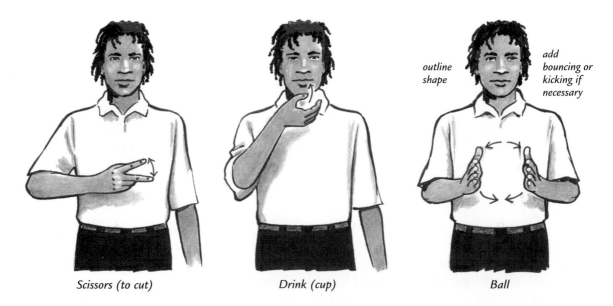

Scissors (to cut)   *Drink (cup)*   *Ball*

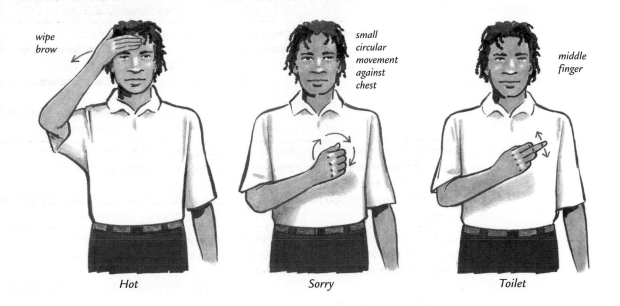

wipe brow

small circular movement against chest

middle finger

Hot

Sorry

Toilet

The basic stages of child development and how these affect the way you communicate with children

To effectively communicate with children, you will need to use a range of communication styles appropriate to the developmental age of the child or young person. Understanding how children of different ages and stages of development communicate and what they like to talk about is crucial for rewarding interaction. Being aware of typical chronological development at all ages will help you to assess the type of communication method to adopt. It is, however, important to draw on your own knowledge of a child's or young person's developmental level in order to be able to choose effective and appropriate methods of communicating with that particular child or young person.

The table overleaf shows typical language and communication development.

Age	Development	Effective communication techniques
Birth–12 months	Communicate using a range of noises and movements, for example, facial expressions, cries, grunts, gurgles, coos, body movements, etc.	Respond quickly (with smiles, etc.) Make the most of times when you are facing the baby (when feeding, changing, etc.) Provide meaning to the baby's communication efforts Pay attention to the baby's style of expressing emotions and preferred level of activity
12–36 months	Communicate with a combination of gestures and grunts, one word sentences, two word sentences, positive and negative emotional expressions and body movements	Respond quickly to communication efforts Expand on one- and two-word sentences Label emotions Follow their lead in play and let them create play Provide an explanation to go with requests
3–6 years	Can now talk in full sentences that are, surprisingly, grammatically correct Sequencing of stories comes more easily by 6 years Experiment with imaginative and pretend play Often talk to themselves when playing alone	Encourage discussion about past events Encourage discussion about feelings, both positive and negative Create opportunities for imaginative and pretend play When requesting and discussing issues use explanations to explain Allow children to talk to themselves uninterrupted – self talk helps them focus on what they are doing
6–12 years	Talk in full sentences and enjoy conversations and discussions Ask more questions and can relate and recall past experiences Can understand and talk about the perspectives of another person Are beginning to recognise the influence that their behaviour has on others Can handle more than one piece of information at a time Enjoy playing with and talking to peers	Use conversation to develop play and learning experiences Allow them to talk to each other uninterrupted Use discussion to solve problems and to negotiate behaviour Use rationale when making requests Encourage them to talk about feelings and the possible reasons for their emotions Use conversation to help manage conflict
12–18 years	Are interested in talking in depth about themselves and their relationships with others – they want to understand who they are becoming and what others think about them Like to talk about how different they are from their parents and carers and the rest of the world Often show more challenging behaviour and have conflicts (and conflicting views) with their parents and carers Are more skilled in getting their needs met and in the art of negotiation	Be actively sensitive and responsive to their feelings Be flexible and allow for negotiation – remember to see things from their point of view Maintain the relationship as this will be more helpful as they get older Recognise that they will be developing ideas that are often very different from yours, and unless they are in danger of harm, accept this as a stage of individual development Use conversation to keep up with their lives and stay interested in what they have to say

Communicating with children of different ages

Playworkers have to adapt their communication according to the ages of the children they are working with. For example, a younger child will enjoy an adult saying 'Well done' because they need reassurance, while an older child might find this patronising. It is hard to define any particular rules about how to communicate with different ages of children, but in general, communication with older children should recognise their independence and their need to talk at a more grown-up level.

Keys to good practice: Communicating with children

✓ Face the child or young person when you speak to them.
✓ Try to find something to talk about that the child likes.
✓ Be aware of body language.
✓ Smile, speak calmly and quietly.
✓ Use child friendly language.
✓ Observe and pick up on cues.
✓ Mirror their body position.
✓ Consider the child's stage of development.
✓ When talking to a small child, try to get down to their level.

ACTIVE KNOWLEDGE

Look at the examples below and decide which are appropriate to use with a child aged 6.

- Shouting across the room for the child to come and have a drink.
- Sitting on the floor chatting about the child's birthday.
- Asking how the child acquired the fracture of the femur.
- Standing very close and looking down at the child to ask if he or she wants to go outside.

Listen to children and respond to them in a way that shows you value what they say and feel

There are several levels at which people listen depending upon the reason for listening. For example, if you are being given directions you need to concentrate and take notice. On the other hand, if you are in the car with the radio on, it is often just background and incidental listening where you do not give your full attention as you are concentrating on something else.

The term active listening is used to describe the manner in which you listen attentively and respond to show you are interested and really value what is being said. This is the technique you need to adopt when talking to the children and young people in your setting. Try to remember that communication is a two-way process and that you can help to improve it.

Listening skills

To listen effectively involves three main processes.

- Hearing – this is the physical process that allows a person to distinguish sounds within the close environment.
- Listening – this process is an awareness of these sounds without a real evaluation of them.
- Understanding – this is the most important process and involves understanding what is being said.

When developing listening skills you need to be aware of how easily these processes can be interrupted by the environment (by distractions, etc.) and also from within ourselves (by talking too much, interrupting, etc.).

ACTIVE KNOWLEDGE

Complete the sentences below.

1 An active listener always …
2 An active listener gives …
3 An active listener will show …
4 An active listener looks …
5 An active listener does not …
6 An active listener will never …

You may find that you have included some of the points below.

Keys to good practice: Using active listening

Do:
✓ face the child and give eye contact
✓ look interested
✓ make encouraging sounds to show you are following the conversation
✓ give your full attention.
Don't:
✓ interrupt mid sentence or take over the conversation
✓ try to rush the conversation
✓ walk away while the child is still talking
✓ look bored.

Ask questions, clarify and confirm points, and encourage children to ask questions and offer ideas

Children and young people will gain a sense of security in you and the setting if they feel that they are listened to and valued. It will empower them and give them confidence to ask questions, voice their opinions, share their ideas and discuss their emotions if they feel they are in a safe and secure environment without fear of ridicule.

At times it may be appropriate for you to ask questions as this will help you to understand and clarify or confirm points. However, it is important to remember that it is their opinions and ideas you require and so you should not take over the idea or conversation.

Asking questions and giving opinions is a developmental stage in life, which may occur at different ages depending on the opportunities and experiences children have had. As a playworker you can play a vital role in helping children to develop these skills. The diagram below shows why it is important to encourage the development of these skills.

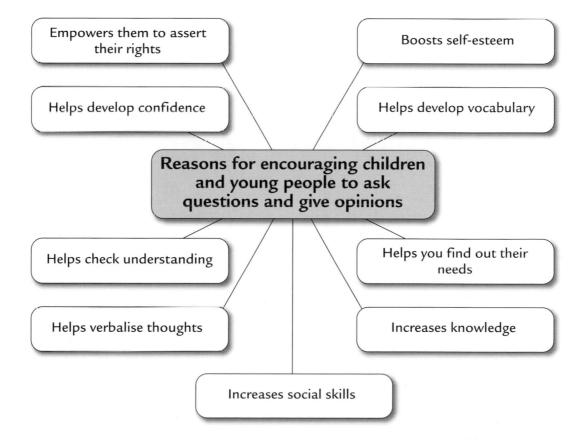

Empowers them to assert their rights

Boosts self-esteem

Helps develop confidence

Helps develop vocabulary

Reasons for encouraging children and young people to ask questions and give opinions

Helps check understanding

Helps you find out their needs

Helps verbalise thoughts

Increases knowledge

Increases social skills

Keys to good practice: Encouraging children and young people to ask questions and give opinions

✓ Use opportunities as they arise for talking and discussion.
✓ Adopt a non-judgemental attitude.
✓ Show unconditional acceptance of children and their families.
✓ Offer alternatives rather than advice.
✓ Set aside time for discussions and ideas.
✓ Follow up ideas and act on suggestions.
✓ Use routines and tasks as a tool for conversation.
✓ Be a good listener.
✓ Create a forum and encourage participation.
✓ Make requests rather than demands.
✓ Use a tone of voice, body language and facial expressions that encourage participation.
✓ Use open-ended questions.

The types of behaviour listed above show that you value children's ideas and feelings. If a suggestion is put forward and you decide not to act upon it, be sure to offer some rationale for this. To ignore a child or reject their opinions and suggestions will make a child feel undervalued and this could affect their self-confidence and self-esteem.

PORTFOLIO EVIDENCE

Think of a way that the children and young people can put forward suggestions on a specific topic, an area of the setting or something they would like to do. This could be in the form of a suggestion box, a questionnaire or a discussion. With your team, plan how this could be organised.

Record this and present it to your assessor as portfolio evidence for this unit.

Recognise when there are communication difficulties and adapt the way you communicate accordingly

It is not always easy for children to understand adults; sometimes it seems to children that adults just do not get the point or that they are not listening. Often adults may tell them something, then five minutes later feel they need to repeat it. This can seem frustrating, and, just like adults, children sometimes feel frustrated because they feel that adults do not understand them. They may lack the skills needed to express themselves, they may not know the words or they may not be easily understood.

As a playworker you need to be aware of the importance of being sensitive to communication difficulties with children and of how to adapt the way you communicate in different situations. Always remember that communication is a two-way process and that you will often need to overcome obstacles or barriers to enable communication to flow.

Barriers to communication

Barriers to communication may be physical or psychological.

Physical barriers

Barrier	Explanation
Hearing	If a child's hearing is impaired the child may need different types of help to enable him or her to hear. For example, the child may need a playworker to sign for him or her, someone who knows Makaton, or a picture board (electronic or cardboard). Alternatively, the child may just need his or her hearing aid checking out as the batteries may be low, or it may not be switched on or adjusted properly. A child with hearing difficulties may lip-read so ensure that your mouth can be seen and you speak clearly.
Speech difficulties	A child's speech may be impaired for a range of reasons, for example, a medical condition, emotional difficulties or just a lack of good language opportunities.
Language	English may not be the child's first language and so the child may need a playworker who speaks his or her first language. If this is not possible, a phrase book or board could enable the child to be understood and the team as a whole to learn some phrases and words so that they can communicate. Sometimes children who speak English as their second language may need explanations for phrases and words that have a regional meaning.
Dialect	Even if a child does speak English he or she may come from a different area of the country and possess a regional accent. Take time to listen and try to speak clearly. Remember that you also may have an accent or may use local phrases that are not understood in other regions.
Body language	The signals you give can affect the confidence and attitude of a child when communicating with you. Some body language gives the impression that you are not listening and the child will be quick to interpret this and lose interest. Body language may be used differently in some cultures so an awareness of this will enhance communication.
Physical distance	If you stand too far away from a child you may need to shout and this can be quite frightening for the child. On the other hand you may be too close to the child and actually be invading his or her personal space, which may make the child feel uncomfortable.
Background noise	Excessive background noise can make talking and listening difficult. This is a renowned problem for those with hearing aids as they pick up every sound. A quieter room or place will aid communication.
Family members	The presence of family members can inhibit communication. Children may feel embarrassed about talking in front of their parents or carers, or they may feel restricted in what they say due to loyalties to the family members.
Misinterpretation	Humour can be a good thing. However, it is important to remember to use it appropriately. It is easy for children and young people to misinterpret what you say and become offended or upset, especially if they do not understand humour. It is particularly important with children who have autistic tendencies as sometimes they take comments literally and this can be very confusing for them. For example, if you said it was raining cats and dogs, some children would be looking out for them coming from the sky.

Psychological barriers

Psychological barriers can also affect communication.

Barrier	Explanation
Emotional difficulties	Children and young people may have emotional problems and difficulties which can easily become barriers to effective communication. As a playworker it is vital that you are patient and give encouragement to boost self-esteem and confidence. Some children simply refuse to communicate, and are sometimes known as 'elective mute'. This may stem from emotional difficulties. If a child always refuses to communicate, and not just because he or she is upset or angry, it would be appropriate to put the common assessment framework (CAF) into action.
Safeguarding issues	Some children and young people may have child protection orders and/or may have been abused. This may cause communication problems and it is important to spend time gaining the trust of the child. This process cannot be rushed, and you will need to be patient and understanding.
Behavioural difficulties	A child or young person may have behavioural difficulties; these could be related to medical conditions (for example, Attention Deficit Hyperactivity Disorder, or ADHD) or to other aspects of their care and upbringing. As a playworker you must understand the emotional difficulties that the child or young person is experiencing and look beyond his or her behaviour. You should unconditionally accept the child and build a trusting relationship. This in turn will enhance communication.
Social difficulties	As with behavioural difficulties, a child or young person with social difficulties will have very little understanding of socially acceptable behaviour and language. As a playworker you will be in a position to enhance their communication skills and encourage their social skills by interacting with them.

Overcoming communication barriers

Finding solutions to communication barriers means overcoming obstacles and this may mean learning as you go along. To develop your listening skills you will need to take time to really listen and to understand. Try to use encouraging words rather than negative ones, and remember not to use discouraging tones. Be honest but gentle, be patient, and remember you should never give up.

CASE STUDY

You have just returned after the Christmas break. You are with a group of six children who are in the process of making a theatre so they can put on a performance. You notice that Bailey, aged 9, is not really interacting as she usually does. She is quiet and standing very close to Summer, who seems to be organising the group. When Summer talks, Bailey moves even closer and Summer loudly tells her to get away from her 'face'. Bailey moves away slightly but when Summer says something else, again Bailey is very close. Summer is getting cross with Bailey and asks her to put up the curtains. Bailey ignores her. Summer then shouts to her, 'What's the matter? Are you deaf?' There is a sudden silence within the group. The children all turn to you to see if you have heard and await a reaction.

1 What would you do?

ement PW8.3 Support children in developing relationships

Young children learn from observing and then copying. This means that the people they spend the most time with become the educators with regard to establishing and maintaining relationships. As children get older they will gain experience of developing relationships for themselves.

Very young children go through a stage of social development in play where they are egocentric; they only seem concerned with themselves and what is happening to and for them. In the next stage of social development they begin to interact with others and finally are able to join in and play.

If a child's development has been disrupted or delayed (for example, if they have had emotional disturbances or some form of medical condition), the child will have missed or not reached these developmental stages. This will affect the child's ability to play and build relationships.

As a playworker you can help build children's social skills and confidence so they are able to integrate and take a full and active part in all the opportunities in the play setting. All settings should provide for inclusive experiences by planning the setting to meet individual needs as well as the group's needs.

It is important that children understand that they need to be able to interact and build relationships with others. Confident and effective playworkers will be able to help children and young people build skills, strategies and techniques for developing and maintaining lasting relationships. Good positive role models are a vital link in this process.

What you need to demonstrate you can do

- Support children in developing agreements about ways of behaving in the setting and how to put these into practice
- Support children in understanding other people's feelings
- Support children who have been upset by others
- Encourage and support children to sort out conflict for themselves
- Encourage and support adults to have positive relationships with children

Support children in developing agreements about ways of behaving in the setting

If your setting is to be a child-centred environment where children and young people have ownership of and respect for the environment and what happens within it, they need to be given the autonomy to develop agreements about the kinds of behaviour that they want to see in the setting. The best behaviour policies are those that are simple and contain very few guidelines and boundaries.

It is important that children learn to take responsibility and that they are not always governed or controlled by what adults see as correct behaviour. You should remember that your setting is not a school or military establishment, but a place where children and young people can 'chill out' after a day spent conforming in school or where they can spend their school holidays and free time. The atmosphere in the setting should be relaxed and friendly, where adults respect and value the children and where the children are not shouted at all the time and expected to perform just to please adults.

At the same time you will need to ensure that children are aware of the need to meet health and safety regulations and those of the inspecting authority if you wish to keep your registration. No one wants an unsafe environment but parents and carers should realise that children will have opportunities to take risks. The skills they develop to assess these risks will contribute to their development of independence, social skills and, of course, health and safety.

Behavioural agreements should be developed with the children and young people in a manner that reflects a positive attitude to behaviour. If the children have ownership of these agreements, they are more likely to keep to them and challenge others who do not adhere to them.

Encouraging children's positive behaviour

It is always a good strategy when working with children to encourage positive behaviour, and to have a policy that encourages wanted behaviour rather than focusing too much on unwanted behaviour.

What is positive behaviour?

Positive behaviour is behaviour that you wish to encourage in children in order that they can socialise effectively. This includes being able to share and co-operate with others as well as being able to take on responsibility.

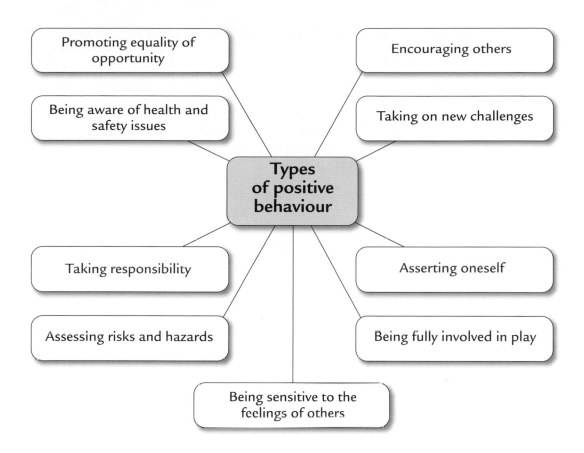

Promoting equality of opportunity

Being aware of health and safety issues

Encouraging others

Taking on new challenges

Types of positive behaviour

Taking responsibility

Assessing risks and hazards

Asserting oneself

Being fully involved in play

Being sensitive to the feelings of others

Praising children's positive behaviour

It is always worth acknowledging children's positive behaviour: this is a great encouragement for them, especially if praise is given at the time. It is also a good idea to explain to children what effect their behaviour is having. For example, you might say, 'It's good that you were ready to move up like that to allow Alicia to join in – that will have made her feel welcome.' This helps children to learn why positive behaviour is so important.

The way in which you give praise will tend to vary according to the children you are working with. Older children, who have reached a stage when they may feel embarrassed, sometimes prefer discreet praise which is given when no one is listening. Rather than saying, 'Well done', you could say, 'You really handled that well.' With younger children the approach might be different: they may prefer a wider recognition, and 'Well done' said in front of others will often be welcomed.

Reinforcing positive behaviour by example

Studies on the way children learn show that learning through watching other people is extremely powerful. This is sometimes called social learning, or learning by modelling. This means that adults who work with children must act as good examples. Another term used is role models.

Children imitate many people around them, including those whom they see on television or in videos, but it has been shown that they especially model themselves on adults whom they admire in some way. If you have won the respect of a child, you may be able to influence their behaviour positively.

It is a good idea to explain this concept to the older children too, so that they can feel that they are contributing to the positive atmosphere and behaviour in the setting.

Fostering positive behaviour

Another way in which you can help children show positive behaviour is by ensuring that the time they spend in settings is enjoyable. Children who are feeling bored or who feel they are in 'babyish' settings are more likely to show unwanted behaviour. Look carefully at the types of opportunities available to the children who attend the setting and make sure that they are fun, challenging and appropriate.

This is not always an easy task: some settings are working with a very wide age range, and the play needs of younger and older children will often be different. When working with wide age ranges, some settings create spaces where older children can play together, with periods for the whole group to come together, whereas other settings work in a more integrated way. It is also a good idea to look at activities and consider how they can be made simpler or more challenging as necessary.

Providing opportunities for children to show positive behaviour

In order to foster positive behaviour, you need to create an environment in which children have opportunities to learn and to use the relevant skills. This will often mean making sure that children can take on responsibility; true co-operation and sharing come from within rather than being imposed.

Co-operation is an aspect of positive behaviour that should be encouraged

Using behavioural agreements effectively

Behavioural agreements will give children a clear understanding of the boundaries in the setting. Most goals and boundaries are very simple. They should be designed to make sure that children respect one another and do not put themselves or others in danger.

In some settings behavioural agreements are decided on by the staff alone, while in others children are given the opportunity to contribute. There are many advantages of involving children in the process of drawing up behavioural agreements, one being that this enables them to take on responsibility.

How to draw up behavioural agreements

There are several ways of drawing up behavioural agreements with children. In some settings, staff ask all the children to come together for a general discussion about what they think the behavioural agreements should include; in other settings, members of staff work first with smaller groups, and then all the ideas are pooled together. The choice of approach will probably depend on the number of children and the group dynamics within the setting. The advantage of splitting into smaller groups is that the younger or less confident children may feel more able to contribute their ideas – the aim, after all, is to create a situation where all children's views are heard.

The next step is to look at the behavioural agreements that have been suggested and consider the reasons behind them. Most groups of children are very interested in fairness, and are able to establish some good behavioural agreements. If you feel that there are important issues that have not been covered, you can always ask the children how these should be addressed.

It is important that behavioural agreements are written in a positive manner. For example, if the children think that there should be no name calling, this could be written along the lines of 'Speak to others as you would like them to speak to you.' Never use the word 'don't' or 'no' to start a clause. Check that all the adults in the setting are aware of the clauses in the behavioural agreement.

Once the behavioural agreements have been drawn up, most settings find some way of recording and displaying them. Sometimes the children themselves take responsibility for this. In other settings, staff members might write them up and then display them. Settings that encourage children to draw up behavioural agreements find that children tend to enjoy this process, and it is easier later to deal with situations in which a child has not kept within the agreed limits.

Behavioural agreements for particular activities

You may also need behavioural agreements for particular play opportunities, especially where there is a safety element, for example, when going out on trips or playing certain games. A good approach is to gather together the children who are involved and ask them to think about the potential difficulties and what the rules need to be. You are then helping the children to think through situations instead of imposing rules on them.

In some situations this may not be possible, and you might need to say to the children, 'Look, just before you start, can I remind you that you will need to think about making sure the ball does not stray into the road. It's probably a good idea if you play away from the fence.'

ACTIVE KNOWLEDGE

At your next team meeting discuss ways to reduce the number of clauses in your behavioural agreements. Reflect on when they were last reviewed and how you could now update the agreements.

Ensuring that adults are aware of the behavioural agreements

It is essential that all adults in the setting come to some agreement about behavioural agreements, otherwise tensions can be created. If you are responsible for a setting's policy on behaviour, consider reviewing agreements regularly and ensure that everyone knows this will happen from time to time. If you feel that a clause set by an adult is not appropriate, talk this through with colleagues first, rather than with children; this prevents staff from feeling undermined.

Playworkers will have their own views and opinions on what they feel should be included in a behavioural agreement. These will often relate to their own values and beliefs as well as their previous experiences of working with children and young people. It is important not to try to force your opinions on other team members or on the children and to be aware that other people will have different values to yours. Open-minded discussions are important, remembering that the child should be at the centre of the discussion and not the playworker.

Challenging behaviour

Encouraging positive behaviour is always better than reacting to unwanted behaviour, but there will nevertheless be times when you will have to respond to unwanted behaviour.

There will be many occasions when you have observed and dealt with challenging behaviour. One factor to keep in mind when addressing challenging behaviour is to ask yourself whether the child or young person is actually causing harm to himself or herself or others, or is seriously damaging property. If the answer is no then think again before you say anything. Be sure that you have a firm and rational explanation as to why you are challenging the behaviour rather than just because 'it's not nice'. As you develop a respecting and understanding relationship with the children, you will be encouraging them to become more confident and they will hopefully then feel that they can challenge what you say if they are not happy with the content.

The concepts by which many playworkers were brought up were often very different from those of today's society. To be open to change in attitude and behaviour shows that you are a forward-looking and thinking playworker. If you remember this when challenging behaviour within the play setting you will be enabling the children and young people to take responsibility and learn how to address their behaviour for themselves.

CASE STUDY

It is a lovely day in the summer holidays and at lunchtime you are all sitting outside eating your packed lunches. You glance across and see that Joel is eating his yogurt with his index finger.

1 Do you:

- shout across to him to stop as it's 'disgusting'
- think it looks a fun thing to do
- offer the use of a spoon
- send him away to eat in private so that no one needs to watch
- watch intently to gain some skills yourself
- make a sarcastic remark about the way he is eating
- suggest you all try it?

Promptly identifying unwanted behaviour

You need to identify unwanted behaviour as soon as it happens. By stepping in quickly and in a positive way, problems can often be solved easily. This means that your setting must provide good supervision of children's play activities, and you should watch carefully to see whether children's body language indicates a potential problem. In some cases, simply strolling past the children's activity, or a direct look across at a child, might be sufficient to help children remember the behavioural agreements of the setting. In other cases, you might have to move quickly to avoid children hurting themselves or each other.

Strategies for dealing with unwanted behaviour

There are various strategies for dealing with unwanted behaviour. Many playworkers find that some work better than others with particular children. The choice of strategy may also vary according to the age of the child with whom you are working. Getting to know the child is almost as important as the strategy itself.

Whatever strategy you adopt when dealing with unwanted behaviour, always remember that children have a right to respect and dignity. Your methods should not humiliate children or be aggressive, either in voice or in action. (Adults who employ methods that humiliate children tend to be less effective in dealing with unwanted behaviour, as children feel alienated.)

Keys to good practice: Dealing with unwanted behaviour

Do:
✓ remain calm
✓ make sure that the child and others are safe
✓ consider taking the child aside
✓ listen to the child
✓ explain to the child why his or her actions are inappropriate
✓ involve the child in deciding how to prevent the unwanted behaviour from recurring
✓ consider whether there is an underlying reason for the child's behaviour.
Don't:
✓ jump to conclusions
✓ shout
✓ be aggressive
✓ humiliate the child
✓ ignore what the child is saying
✓ isolate the child (e.g. 'You have to wait outside')
✓ use physical restraint or punishment.

The following are useful strategies for dealing with unwanted behaviour.

● Talk to the child away from other children: privacy prevents children from feeling embarrassed and from losing confidence. It is effective with all ages of children, but is particularly important with older children. The aim is to have a word with the child quietly, without the other children in the setting necessarily knowing that you are dealing with behaviour.
● Explain why the behaviour is inappropriate: children do not always know why their behaviour is unwanted, especially when they have simply become overexcited during a play activity. It is always helpful to explain briefly why they need to stop their behaviour. This should be done in a non-confrontational way. For instance, 'Look, I know that you're having a lot of fun, but the bad news is that you might get hurt if that stick gets near your eyes.'
● Offer alternative activities: in some cases, you can distract children by offering them alternative activities. This is particularly useful if the reason for the

unwanted behaviour is partly that children feel unchallenged or that the children are not co-operating with each other. Alternative activities should be offered in a way that does not feel like a punishment.

- Help children to consider the consequences of their behaviour: it can be helpful if children are encouraged to think through the consequences of continuing their unwanted behaviour. Again, this should be done in a non-confrontational way, and is useful as a strategy with older children. (Younger children are not always able to empathise with others or to consider the results of their actions in the same way.)

The importance of being consistent and fair when dealing with positive and negative behaviour

Whatever strategies you decide to adopt when addressing challenging behaviour, you should share your practice with your team. As a team, you can discuss the effectiveness (or not!) of your strategies and this will help team members to be consistent in their approach.

Children, and especially young people, will have a strong sense of fairness and will challenge inconsistency. They will soon become aware of the strengths within the team and if the team do not support each other by adopting a consistent approach, the harmony of the team may be disrupted leading to insecurity among the children and young people. Maintaining a consistent approach does not necessarily mean treating everyone the same, but treating children and young people according to their individual needs in a consistent manner. If questioned by the children and young people a discussion on diversity will often suffice.

The same tactics should be adopted when addressing positive behaviour. Sometimes positive behaviour is not dealt with consistently, for example, if playworkers expect more from some children than others they may forget to acknowledge all children's positive behaviour.

Support children in understanding other people's feelings

It is important for children to understand and respect other people's feelings. If playworkers show children care, consideration and respect, they will encourage children and young people to do the same.

By providing a range of experiences where children can safely act out and show their feelings, using a range of media, materials and equipment, the children and young people will become aware of their feelings and how to respond and react in an appropriate manner. They will also develop an understanding of feelings in general, including those of others.

Some children and young people within your setting may have exceptionally good social skills. These children will be able to develop and maintain relationships in which they understand and can empathise and sympathise with others. They will also act as role models to the other children.

Support children who have been upset by others

Whenever challenging behaviour takes place you need to be aware that not only do you have the incident to deal with, but you also have the aftermath. This could be the victim in cases of discriminatory practice, the casualty in an overzealous argument or even the children and young people who have witnessed the incident and have become frightened or upset by it or the people involved. To sympathise with and support children and young people in an appropriate manner is important. This may mean talking through the situation and reassuring them, it may mean explaining and apologising for the behaviour of others or it may just mean acknowledging that they were upset and that it was fine for them to show that they were upset.

Encourage and support children to sort out conflict for themselves

If the children and young people in your care are to become well balanced caring adults who interact with individuality, but integrate within society, then you must help equip them with the tools to foster and develop personal attributes and strategies. One of these vital skills is that of negotiation and the ability to sort out conflict for themselves. As with most skills, unless you have the opportunity to practise you cannot become proficient. You would not expect a child to be able to ice skate without practise, likewise with sorting out conflict, without the opportunities to practise they will not develop the skills. Unless the conflict is getting totally out of hand and there is a possibility of someone getting hurt, then allow the children to try to sort it out. It may mean that you are around to observe and if necessary facilitate or support, often just your presence will give them the confidence to negotiate rather than become angry and aggressive (see page 65).

Encourage and support adults to have positive relationships with children

It is important to encourage and support positive relationships between children and adults in the setting. You can do this by showing children care, consideration and respect. In order to build positive relationships with children, it is essential that you respect them and show this in the way that you work with them. This means listening to them, taking on board their ideas and feelings, and making sure that you do not patronise them or make them feel uncomfortable by your tone of voice. Adults who do not show children care and consideration are at best tolerated by children and at worst avoided. If they feel that they are not liked or wanted, some children may even refuse to come to the setting.

The presence of good role models makes for a friendly and secure setting.

Keys to good practice: Supporting a colleague who finds it difficult to build relationships with children

✓ Include an 'issues' topic on the agenda of your weekly team meetings and use this to look at effective communication skills.
✓ Support and encourage the colleague by highlighting his or her positive aspects (without being patronising) to help build confidence.
✓ Provide information to the whole team on courses on communication and relationship building.
✓ Discuss ways of building relationships in appraisal/supervision sessions.

CONSOLIDATION

Think of two (or more) children who do not usually interact well together. At your next team meeting discuss the opportunities you could provide to help them to interact.

ement PW8.4 Communicate with adults

There are times when adults will visit the play setting, including parents and carers as well as adults from other agencies and settings. The manner in which you interact with these people will be watched in many cases by the children in your care and this is one of the most important reasons why you should communicate effectively with them.

What you need to demonstrate you can do
- Communicate with adults politely and courteously and in a way that is appropriate to them
- Show respect for adults' individuality, needs and preferences
- Respond to adults' requests for information accurately within the agreed boundaries of confidentiality
- Actively listen to adults, asking questions and clarifying and confirming key points
- Recognise when there are communication difficulties and adapt the way you communicate accordingly
- Handle any disagreements with adults in a way that will maintain positive relationships

Communicate with adults politely and courteously

Most good relationships depend not only on respect but also on good communication. Good communication can help prevent potential misunderstandings, as well as helping parents and carers to feel that they can talk to you openly about their children and give you feedback about what you are doing.

There are many ways of communicating with and passing information on to parents and carers. Even if they can rarely visit the setting, you may still be able to maintain some contact.

The following list shows some of the methods of communication that are commonly used:

- face-to-face contact
- notes home
- telephone calls
- open sessions
- home book or diary
- newsletter
- noticeboards
- photos and videos.

Dear Mrs. Martin,

Just a quick note to let you know that Mark has settled down really well. This week he has especially enjoyed playing with the mini-golf set we have here.

Hope to see you in the near future.

Please do not hesitate to get in contact.

Best wishes

Sarah Godwin

Manager, Clowning Around out-of-school club

A note to a parent

22nd August

Ling has had a good day today, despite seeming a little drowsy at times. Could this be a side effect of the medication? She enjoyed our treasure hunt in the garden this morning and also the painting activity this afternoon. We have put one of the paintings in her bag. Please could you send in some spare clothes tomorrow, because we are going to have the water out if it is a hot day.

Jenny

23rd August

We have not had a very good night! You might find that Ling is very tired today as she had a fit last night. I am going to take her to the doctor tomorrow to check whether this new medication is working.

Ling showed us her painting and we have put it up in the kitchen.

I have put two changes of clothes for Ling in her bag as well as some photographs of our new kittens. She loves the kittens – one is called Max and the other is called Theo.

A home book

PORTFOLIO EVIDENCE

Recall a time when you felt that you communicated politely and courteously with a parent or carer. Write this up on an evidence sheet and evaluate your practice by commenting on:

● why you felt it went well
● how you would have altered what you said or did if it had been another parent or carer
● what you learnt from the incident.

Another way of communicating politely with parents and carers is to welcome them when they come into the setting (see Unit PW14, page 298).

Why positive relationships with adults are important

Positive relationships with adults bring benefits to both the children and the setting. One way of developing positive relationships is to make adults, including parents and carers, feel welcome when they come into the setting.

Show respect for adults' individuality, needs and preferences

One of the key factors in building good relationships with parents and carers and making them feel welcome is valuing and respecting them. This means showing a non-judgemental attitude. Whatever the situation, always remain polite and courteous to all parents. For example, find out how they would like to be addressed, rather than assuming that you should call them by their first names.

Respecting parents and carers also means that you must accept that each parent and carer will have personal views and a personal lifestyle, as well as individual ways of relating to their children. This is often easier to say than to do, but it is essential in showing good anti-discriminatory practice. Valuing and respecting parents and carers does not only mean saying and doing the 'right' things. It also means thinking positively about them, remembering that your tone of voice and your body language send out messages which might make people feel unwelcome.

Respond to adults' requests for information

There is a range of information that parents and carers might need once their children attend a play setting. An important part of the playworker's role is to ensure that when parents and carers request information they are given it accurately and promptly, unless this is likely to break confidentiality. If you are unable to provide information, you might refer the parent or carer to your line manager, or give suggestions as to where they might find it.

ACTIVE KNOWLEDGE

Look at the following types of information that parents and carers might need:

- information about the costs of sessions
- reassurance that their child has settled in
- information about the types of activities and resources on offer to children
- details about opening and closing times
- information about finding lost property
- more information about how an accident occurred
- information about how a parent or carer can help in the setting.

1 Why might parents and carers need each of these pieces of information?
2 In what ways might this type of information be passed on?
3 Why is it important that parents and carers are given accurate information promptly?

CASE STUDY

Daisy returns to the setting after the Christmas break. Her mother tells you that they have been experiencing difficulties as she will not respond to anything that they ask her to do. Her mother seems very concerned that Daisy is being 'naughty' and ignoring everyone on purpose. She asks you who she was playing with before Christmas and if they are rude.

1 What would you say to Daisy's mother at this stage?
2 What information would you give her about the other children?

You manage to calm Daisy's mother and agree to keep an eye on Daisy during the day. You also agree to set aside some time to talk to her mother in more detail when she collects Daisy. During the day you see that Daisy is ignoring the other children and does not respond when you ask her if she would like to be involved in a creative opportunity that she usually loves. You begin to realise that she may not be able to hear what is being said so you monitor and record instances to show to her mother. Daisy comes and sits with you in the quiet area and tells you that her ear has just started to hurt. You are about to respond when her mother comes through the door.

3 What would you do now?

Actively listen to adults

If you are holding a conversation with a parent or carer it is important that you observe basic communication skills (see page 101). This will show that you are interested in what they are saying. By maintaining eye contact and giving signs that you are listening, for example, by nodding to show that you agree or by facial expressions, you will emphasise the value of what is being said. If you are unsure about exactly what a parent or carer is saying, you should ask questions to clarify their ideas and then confirm the key points.

Parents will have different views and opinions on all types of subjects, especially on aspects of the play and care that you provide. Some may have very strong views, whereas others may be less opinionated. However strong their views, it is important to acknowledge that everyone has a right to their own opinions. It is good practice to address issues in a non-confrontational way, always giving an explanation for what you are saying and trying to back this up with reasons linked to legislation, theory or procedures relating to practice. This will give the message that you are taking them seriously.

If you ask for people's views it is important to act upon the replies that you receive. Otherwise, people will feel devalued and will be reluctant to contribute in the future.

CASE STUDY

You are planning for the summer holidays and one worker suggests an overnight stay at an activity centre. You agree to ask the parents for their views on this suggestion.

1 How would you take the situation forward to ensure that all have the opportunity to contribute their views?
2 How would you make sure you understand exactly what each parent is saying?
3 What would you do if the views were really varied?

Recognise when there are communication difficulties

There will be times when you come across parents and carers who have communication difficulties. It is important that you are able to recognise these and are able to provide them with all the relevant information in a sensitive manner and in a form which they are able to understand. The Ofsted Standard 12 requires you to consider how the information you provide is made accessible (see page 87).

Different languages

It is useful to have your literature reproduced in a variety of languages to suit the needs of the parents in your community. However, you will need to ensure that you are aware of the spoken language within the home and not assume that those families automatically speak the main language of their country.

Interpreters

In some cases you or your staff may be able to speak other languages. This is always an asset to the setting as this will help parents and carers feel more at ease and informed. If you do not have staff who can interpret, you may be able to find a member of the child's family who could act as an interpreter for you. If this is not possible, you could 'hire' the services of an interpreter.

It would be useful to investigate these possibilities before it becomes an issue. There may be a network already set up within your area or within the community that you are able to use.

Audio and video tapes, etc.

These are excellent means of communication and can be provided easily and with little cost. They will enable parents and carers with literacy, sensory and memory difficulties to access all the information about the setting. You will need to ensure that they are presented in a clear and precise manner that can be understood by the audience.

Braille

For parents and carers with sight difficulties literature can be made available in Braille. If you experience difficulties regarding the translation, your local RNIB institute will be able to advise you. Alternatively, you could try their website: www.rnib.org.uk.

Signing

You or your staff may have the expertise to be able to understand sign language. If not, and you need to be able to communicate with parents who use sign language, you can get advice and help from someone who is able to use sign language. You may find that Makaton (a basic form of sign language) is understood (see Active Knowledge on page 103). This is an easier format than British Sign Language.

Other ways of producing literature

As well as having literature reproduced in a variety of languages, it would also be useful to have some copies in large print, in different typefaces and on different coloured paper. This will help those with sight difficulties and may also help those with word association problems (for example, dyslexia). You could also use easily understood words or illustrations to help those with literacy difficulties.

Keys to good practice: Being sensitive to communication difficulties

✓ Investigate the local facilities that could help you to provide for those with communication difficulties.
✓ Encourage staff development to aid communication methods (for example, sign language) in the setting.
✓ As a setting, learn and use Makaton signs.
✓ Learn basic welcome words from other languages.
✓ Provide a poster showing the word 'welcome' in other languages and in Braille.
✓ Remember always to be sensitive in your approach.

CASE STUDY

You are organising a visit to the coast. The letter that you are sending home gives all the information about what the children need for the visit. When Lila's mother comes to collect her, she receives the letter and is told to return it by the end of the week. You are aware that she has difficulties with literacy.

1 What could you do to ensure that all the information is understood?
2 How would you do this in a sensitive manner?

Handle any disagreements with adults in a way that will maintain positive relationships

Most play settings that maintain good relationships with their parents and carers rarely have disagreements with them. However, there may be times when misunderstandings occur. These misunderstandings could be between a variety of people and they may impact on the children and young people in your setting. This may then lead to a disagreement or area of emotional disturbance, which then becomes a conflict.

A misunderstanding could simply be a confused message, for example, a child could have told his or her parents that you are no longer providing drinks of juice whereas you may have said that you were only providing sugar-free drinks. These simple misunderstandings can easily escalate and it is then that they can become a serious issue. When a misunderstanding or a disagreement occurs it is important to ask yourself whether it is something you can clear up and deal with yourself or whether you need to ask for help or advice, or need to pass it on to someone else.

Disagreements can produce bad feeling. If left unresolved, the parent or carer may withdraw the child. In many cases, disagreements can be avoided by having clear policies and procedures and making sure that parents are aware of these when the child starts in the setting. Disagreements can also be avoided by involving parents and carers when planning, and by not making assumptions about their needs and wishes.

In some cases, disagreements with parents and carers may be unavoidable. It is important to manage them when they arise, to handle them carefully and tactfully, and to remain polite and courteous.

Conflict may also arise from situations where you are required to pass on information to other agencies when you suspect that the welfare of the child or young person is at risk. You have a responsibility under the Children Act, as well as the policies and procedures of the setting, to safeguard the welfare of the children and young people. In areas such as child protection it is important that you follow your policies and procedures at all times.

Think about it

Look at the issues listed below and think about which ones you would keep confidential and which ones you would pass on:

- a medical condition, for example, bed wetting
- a disclosure of abuse
- a parent's work telephone number
- a suspicion that a child is being severely punished at home
- a child's family situation
- information about criminal activity that would put the child at risk
- details regarding a parent's employment status.

Keys to good practice: Managing disagreements

Do:
✓ remain calm and friendly
✓ find a private area to discuss issues with parents and carers
✓ try to find out any relevant information beforehand
✓ apologise if the setting has been in any way partly to blame for the disagreement
✓ listen to what is being said and investigate further if necessary
✓ try to work out a compromise solution
✓ thank parents and carers for coming in to talk with you
✓ consider arranging a way of keeping in contact or following up on the discussion
✓ record details of what has been said or agreed
✓ consider referring the disagreement to your line manager for guidance.
Don't:
✓ become angry and defensive
✓ make any promises that you cannot keep
✓ refuse to listen to what parents and carers are saying
✓ pass on any comments about situations unless you have investigated first
✓ breach confidentiality.

CASE STUDY

Read the following scenarios.

- Miss Harvey has telephoned you to ask why her son Jamie was not included in the visit to the pantomime that you are proposing for the Christmas holidays. Before you can answer she says that she thinks that it is very unfair that all the other children have had letters about the trip and that her son has not. She goes on to say that she is considering taking the matter further as she feels that he is being discriminated against.
- John, Ellie's father, asks to have a word with you in private. He says that he has heard that you have a new computer with games and that all the children are given a time on it except his daughter. He says that you should have more computers or have a better system so that everyone has a turn, like the play facility that Ellie went to before they moved house.
- You have organised a dance session at the local studio which costs £2. Jackie has two children at the setting. Your playwork assistant is at the door checking and taking payments. She asks Jackie for the money for her children. Jackie storms over to you and complains that she is very embarrassed by this as she has completed the form for them to attend and has already paid the money.

1 Work out how you would handle each of these cases. You could role-play them with a partner or write down what you would do.
2 Why is it important to try to understand parents' and carers' points of view?

PORTFOLIO EVIDENCE

Think of all the different adults that you interact with in and around the setting. Choose one person whom you have spoken to recently and write down how you communicated and how you adapted your style to meet the needs and requirements of that person. This can be used as portfolio evidence.

CONSOLIDATION

Think about all the different adults that you have contact with during each session and the way you interact with each one. Could you have improved your interactions in any way? You could refer to the chart (page 195 in Unit PW10) where it is suggested that you comment on different aspects of your work. List your strengths and areas for development in working with others and discuss this with a colleague to see if they agree.

Value	Details
10	Play is essentially a co-operative activity for children both individually and in groups. Playworkers should always encourage children to be sensitive to the needs of others; in providing play opportunities, they should always seek to work together with children, their parents, colleagues and other professionals and, where possible, make their own expertise available to the wider community.
11	Play opportunities should always be provided within the current legislative framework relevant to children's rights, health, safety and well-being.
12	Every child has a right to an environment for play, and such environments must be made accessible to children.

Ofsted national standards

Standard 3: Care, learning and play

The focus:

Children's care, learning and play are supported best where the registered person and staff are clear about the main purpose of the provision. The development of children's emotional, physical, social and intellectual capabilities is promoted effectively when they take part in a wide range of activities. The playwork team meet children's needs through sensitive and appropriate interactions which promote children's self-esteem. They plan first-hand experiences which enable children to make choices when developing their knowledge, skills and understanding. Children's care, learning and play are supported well by staff who monitor children's progress regularly and use this information to provide for their individual needs. (Scottish National Care Standard 5; see page 344.)

What you must know and understand

For the whole unit:

K1: Relevant playwork assumptions and values that apply to this unit

K2: The short and long term benefits of play

K3: The playworker's role in supporting play

K4: Indicators/objectives you can use to evaluate play provision

K5: Behavioural modes associated with play

K6: The range of play types that are commonly accepted

K7: How to provide for the range of play types

K8: The mood descriptors associated with play and how to recognise these

K9: The main stages of child development and how these affect children's play needs and behaviours

K10: The particular needs of disabled children and how these need to be met when planning for and supporting play, including helping them to manage risk

For PW9.1

K11: Why it is important to identify children's and young people's play needs and preferences

K12: The types of information you can use to identify play needs and preferences and how to access these

K13: The barriers to access, including disability but taking account of others, that some children and young people may experience and how to address these

K14: Why it is important to consult with children and young people on play needs and preferences

K15: Effective methods of consulting with children and young people

K16: The range of different types of play spaces that can meet children's and young people's needs and preferences

For PW9.2

K17: How to plan play spaces that meet children's and young people's play needs

K18: Why it is important to create spaces that children and young people can adapt to their own needs

K19: How to obtain and/or create resources needed for a range of play spaces

K20: How to involve children and young people in the creation of play spaces

K21: The importance of access for all children and how to ensure this happens

K22: The health and safety requirements that are relevant to play spaces and how to ensure you take account of these

For PW9.3

K23: Why it is important for children and young people to choose and explore play spaces for themselves

K24: The types of support you may need to provide and how to decide when it is appropriate to provide support

K25: Why it is important to leave the content and intent of play to children and young people

K26: Why it is important to allow play to continue uninterrupted

K27: Why it is important to allow children to develop in their own ways and not to show them 'better' ways of doing things when they are playing unless they ask

K28: The main stages of the play cycle

K29: How to define a play frame

K30. How to identify play cues

K31: How to identify when and how to respond to a play cue

For PW9.4

K32: Why risk is important in play and how to encourage and support acceptable risk taking

K33: Levels of risk acceptable according to organisational policies and procedures

K34: The range of hazards that may occur during children's play and how to recognise these

K35: The basic stages of child development and the implications these have for levels of risk

K36: How to assess risk according to age and stage of development

K37: The importance of balancing risk with the benefits of challenge and stimulation

Short and long term benefits of play

There are many benefits of play. Every time children engage in play activities they discover something new and learn through first-hand experience. Play is an end in itself and should be encouraged for its own sake. It is through play that children will develop to their full potential socially, physically, intellectually, creatively, emotionally and culturally. Play has a vital role in helping children achieve the five key outcomes of the Every Child Matters agenda.

that the play is not interesting enough. A style of working which supports rather than directs the child, is what adults should aim for.

Behavioural modes associated with play

There are many definitions of play. It may be:

- personally directed – children choose how they do it
- intrinsically motivated – children choose why they do it
- spontaneous – freely chosen
- goalless – children do it for no external goal or reward
- where the content and intent is under the control of the children and young people.

When you consider these definitions you need to reflect on your role as a playworker and why you focus on providing a programme of activities that are adult-led and often have a tangible end product. There is a real danger that the occupational standards may lead playworkers into providing activities rather than supporting play which is created and driven by the children themselves. It would be detrimental to the child if playworkers constantly 'do' rather than 'understand and reflect'. Playworkers should strive to provide, maintain and protect an environment where children can play according to where their imagination takes them.

The mood descriptors associated with play and how to recognise them

When children and young people play they will probably be showing certain feelings within the play activity. This is referred to as a mood descriptor. As a playworker it is important to be able to recognise and help children and young people to be aware of these qualities in themselves and in others.

Descriptor	How to recognise this
Happy	Probably the easiest descriptor to recognise – the children are involved in play, often smiling and co-operating with each other
Independent	The child is self-sufficient and free, happily working alone or leading a play opportunity; the child will explore and develop play opportunities
Confident	Children are self-assured and positive in their actions often taking the lead; they are uninhibited and creative when playing
Altruistic	Children are unselfish and self-sacrificing when playing with other children, allowing others to take control or have the most desirable piece of play equipment
Trusting	Children have faith in others and are happy to be led by other children, following their direction without question
Balanced	Children are stable and even-handed, taking turns and being aware of the needs of other children during play
Active or immersed	Children are engrossed and absorbed in play, making no demands on staff or other children
At ease	Children will get on with whatever they are doing with minimal intervention; the play is simple and straightforward, and generally undemanding

Stages of child development and how they affect children's play needs and behaviours

Children's stages of development may affect their play needs and behaviours. Bear this in mind when planning new play opportunities and also when judging how much supervision or support a group of children might need.

Although there is a strong link between age and stage of development, you need to get to know children as individuals as their experience can affect their development. In some areas of development children may have developed some skills but not others. For example, a child may be good at using social conventions such as showing table manners yet find it hard to share with others during a play activity.

The table below shows some of the areas of development and children's play needs and behaviours.

Areas of development	Children's play needs and behaviours	Ways in which the playworker can encourage children
Language and communication	Being able to communicate is extremely important when socialising. By 5, most children are beginning to use language fluently, but it is not until around 8 years that children have mastered a language. Children who have a language or communication impairment or who do not speak the language of the setting fluently may find it hard to get others to understand them. This can lead to isolation and frustration.	Praise the child when he/she tries to communicate. Provide play opportunities that do not rely heavily on language and communication.
Cognitive/ intellectual	Children's intellectual/cognitive stage of development affects the way in which they play. Younger children tend to enjoy more hands-on activities and role play. Older children tend to enjoy games and activities that rely on their abilities to follow rules, use their memory or think in the abstract, e.g. noughts and crosses, crosswords, board games. Children's intellectual and cognitive development tends to follow a certain pattern which relates to their age and experience, with most children being able to follow and understand rules by the age of 6 or 7.	Younger children and children with learning difficulties may need adult support when playing games which require following complex rules. Make sure that some games and activities are provided which do not rely heavily on intellectual skills.
Emotional development	Children's emotional development and social development are often inter-related. Skills such as being able to take turns and share gradually develop, along with empathy – children learn to be thoughtful and to think about how others might be feeling. Children who lack confidence or have poor self-esteem can find it harder to make relationships with children of their own age. Some children tend to be aggressive, while others might be attention-seeking.	Make sure that children are given praise and feel valued. Plan some play opportunities for pairs and very small groups.

Collect and analyse information on play needs and preferences

You will need to collect evidence for this section of the unit from a wide range of sources and then analyse and comment on the evidence. This will include consulting with the children and young people on their play needs and preferences.

What you need to demonstrate you can do

- Collect information on children's and young people's play using a range of methods
- Investigate and take account of the needs of children and young people who experience barriers to access
- Analyse information to identify play needs
- Consult with children and young people and take account of their ideas on play needs and preferences
- Research and identify a range of play spaces and resources that will meet the play needs of children and young people

Collect information on children's and young people's play

From your work you must show that you have collected information from the following sources:

- researching playwork theory and practice
- observing children and young people at play
- interacting with children and young people.

An excellent method for providing evidence for this section would be to review your play setting and decide how it can be enriched to improve the outcomes for children. You could then implement the changes and evaluate the impact. You should also observe and interact with children and young people in your setting to involve them fully in this project. This could be evidenced using photographs or video – but do remember to get written consent from parents before you do this.

Although some observation of this element by your assessor is possible, you will need to demonstrate to your assessor that you have read and researched a variety of books, papers, journals and websites. You could write reflective accounts and include written observations of the play cycle, play types, children's use of space and resources, who they play with, and how and when they play. Such observations can be of children in your workplace, in local parks or public spaces. You should consider including children playing in all types of settings, as well as conversations, consultations and interactions with children.

The conclusions you reach and the actions taken as a result may be evidenced by minutes of meetings, action plans, photographs and witness statements.

Investigate the needs of children and young people who experience barriers to access

There may be many barriers to a child accessing play opportunities. These may be as simple as a parent not wishing the child to get his or her clothes dirty or the child wearing inappropriate footwear such as flip-flops or fashion shoes. It might be that a child has English as a second (or even third) language. It is important that playworkers take account of these barriers and investigate ways of helping the children and young people overcome them.

There is no single solution to meeting the needs of children with disabilities as this is a broad-ranging term which can cover a child who has breathing difficulties and uses an inhaler through to a child who is a wheelchair user and beyond. The important thing is to consult with the relevant people. Speak to the child, the child's parent or carer, the school and anyone else who is involved with the child. They will be able to advise you on the abilities and skills of the child and also the possible risks and limitations that you may need to be aware of. The whole staff team will need to be equipped with this information to allow them to support the child in the most appropriate way. It may also be helpful to give other children some information so that they can avoid inadvertently harming or excluding a child from a play activity.

Further information about the needs of children and young people who experience barriers to access can be found in Unit PW6 (see page 32).

CASE STUDY

Petra, who is 10 years old, is a wheelchair user who has recently started attending the local playscheme. She is becoming increasingly frustrated because the other children insist on pushing her in the wheelchair when she prefers to push herself. She feels the other children are treating her like a baby in a pushchair. The playworker in charge has a quiet word with Petra and asks her if she would be happy for a group discussion about this so that everyone is aware of what is acceptable and what is not. Petra agrees that this would be a good idea.

1 How could the playworker introduce the discussion?
2 What do you think the reaction of the other children might be?
3 How might this situation have been avoided?

Analyse information to identify play needs

In Unit PW6 there are ideas, suggestions and information that will help you to gather and analyse information about play needs (see page 17).

Using the information you have collected on children's and young people's play, think about what the play needs might be of the children in your setting.

Consult with children and young people on play needs and preferences

It is important that children take ownership of their play. For this to happen they need to be involved in the planning and their ideas, wishes and preferences should be paramount. There may be times when for one reason or another their wishes cannot be met, but if this is the case you need to discuss this with them and explain the rationale. There are many effective ways of consulting with children and young people. Information on the range of methods can be found in Unit PW6.1 (see page 15).

Research a range of play spaces and resources that will meet the play needs of children and young people

Play spaces are not just about the physical spaces that children can play in but they also include the equipment and materials provided for activities. A stimulating environment for children is important but we also need to address in a variety of ways how children feel within different play spaces and activities. For example, some children who are involved in an activity in a wooded area might be stimulated and excited by the environment while others might feel frightened by the darkness and trees and be anxious about being stung by nettles.

Objectives you can use to evaluate play provision

There are many indicators or objectives that can be used to evaluate play provision, but the seven play objectives described in *Best Play* are designed to form the basis for any quality assurance evaluation.

Objective	Definition
1	The play provision extends the choice and control that children have over their play, the freedom they enjoy and the satisfaction they gain from it.
2	The provision recognises the child's need to test boundaries and responds positively to that need.
3	The provision manages the balance between the need to offer risk and the need to keep children safe from harm.
4	The provision maximises the range of play opportunities.
5	The provision fosters independence and self-esteem.
6	The provision fosters children's respect for others and offers opportunities for social interaction.
7	The provision fosters the child's well-being, healthy growth and development, knowledge and understanding, creativity and capacity to learn.

From *Best Play*, National Playing Fields Association, March 2000

It is possible to evaluate how well a setting is delivering by looking at objectives 1–4 as they are relatively short term and can be observed while children are playing. objectives 5–7 are potentially more difficult as they require evaluation over a period of time to identify long term benefits. You will also need to be aware of the fact that children are subject to influences outside the play provision which will affect their growth, welfare and development. Whether playworkers can evaluate using these criteria will depend on their skills of observing and interpreting what they see.

Reflective practice is an important tool when evaluating play provision and is the basis of the evaluation process. For more information on reflective practice, see Unit PW10 (pages 170–190).

Most local authorities will have created or adopted quality assurance schemes which can be adapted to suit the play setting. These may be local schemes or ones developed for national organisations. Your local Children's Services Department will be able to give you support with this process and will advise you on the most appropriate scheme for your setting. A survey completed by parents and children is another valuable evaluation tool as it is important to seek their views.

CONSOLIDATION

Think about the information that you have collected and analysed on play needs and preferences.

1 Have you researched all aspects of different play needs?
2 Have you checked these against the preferences of the children and young people in your setting?
3 For your playwork award you could use these topics in a professional discussion with your assessor.

ment PW9.2 Plan and prepare play spaces

Planning and preparing effective play spaces should be an exciting and challenging task for a motivated playworker. It is vital that you use the information and data on play needs and preferences that you have collected and analysed to enhance your planning and preparation of play spaces.

What you need to demonstrate you can do
- Plan play spaces that meet the needs of children and young people and can be adapted by them to meet new needs
- Make sure the play spaces provide for a range of different play types
- Obtain the resources needed for these play spaces
- Work within the available budget or find other creative ways of obtaining or making resources
- Create the planned play spaces involving children and young people wherever possible

- Make sure that the range of play spaces will be accessible for all children and young people who could take part
- Make sure the play spaces take account of health and safety requirements

Plan play spaces that meet the needs of children and young people

The term 'play space' covers not only what you see, but also what you can feel. The layout, the furniture and the equipment of a setting are important, but so too is the atmosphere created by the staff. Children are very sensitive to their environment and quickly distinguish between play spaces that they like and those in which they feel uncomfortable.

Providing a good play environment is like doing a jigsaw: several pieces must be put together for it to be complete.

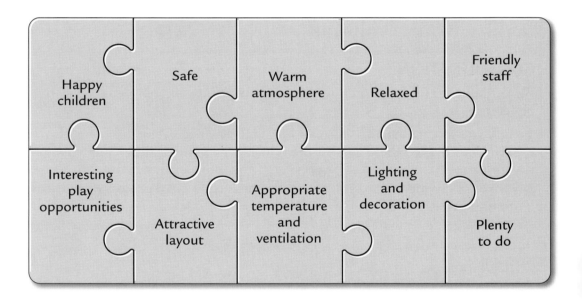

Characteristics of a good play space

ACTIVE KNOWLEDGE

1 What do you think are the strengths of your own play setting?
2 Are there any drawbacks to your setting?
3 Copy the jigsaw puzzle above and ask the children in your setting to look at it. Can they think of anything else that is important?

An effective play space is one which:

- pays attention to and supports the variety of feelings and moods children may bring with them or have during play
- has particular spaces, areas or resources that at different times encourage the experience or expression of a range of emotions
- seeks to develop, via diverse means, an overall feeling and atmosphere of welcomeness, acceptance, freedom and playfulness
- fully considers, supports and evokes children's feelings and moods during play and therefore uses space, lighting, colour, sounds, images, materials, etc. accordingly.

The diagram below shows the different types of play space.

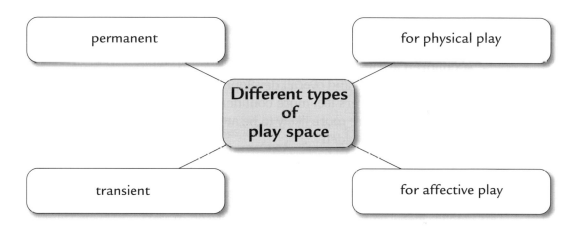

A transient play space is one which is not permanent. It could be a space that changes and/or gets adapted by moving a wide range of resources, props, materials and structures. The space could be changed by playworkers or by children breaking up the wider physical space into smaller spaces for different kinds of play. For example, an outside den could become a house, be brought inside for the night and then be used the next day as a picnic area for a snack.

Playworkers or children may at different times:

- create dens and hidey-holes
- use fabrics, props and loose parts to create imaginative places like a beach, a hospital or a forest
- shift furniture back or around to accommodate particular games, for example, making the quiet area smaller and more cosy by moving the chairs, beanbags and screen while a game of indoor rounders takes place.

A transient play space could be a couple of cubic feet behind a piece of furniture or a whole room or field; it could be spontaneously created or planned in advance.

ACTIVE KNOWLEDGE

✓

1 Draw a diagram of the layout of the play space in your setting on one day and describe the play opportunities within that space. Explain the benefits and disadvantages (if any) of this layout.

Making the play space friendly, attractive and stimulating

As well as making sure that the physical environment is safe and interesting, it is also important that the general atmosphere in the play space is welcoming. Children are particularly sensitive to atmosphere, and this will often determine whether or not children want to return.

Creating a good atmosphere

Creating a good atmosphere is a little like cooking a cake – it needs a mix of several ingredients. One of the main ingredients is the staff themselves. Staff who are warm, friendly and genuinely interested in working with children will help to create a good atmosphere, although it is important that they also work together as a team.

Another essential ingredient is the way in which the play space is maintained. A messy and grubby environment indicates that staff take no pride in their workplace, while an attractive environment sends out a very positive message.

A third essential ingredient is the children themselves! If children are happy and enjoying being in the environment, they will create a lovely atmosphere. This will happen only if they enjoy the play opportunities and feel that they are being valued.

Keys to good practice: Creating a good atmosphere

✓ Make sure that children, parents and carers are warmly greeted when they enter the setting.
✓ Consider creating a reception area with plants, posters and photographs.
✓ Make sure that equipment that is not being used is properly stored away.
✓ Prioritise finding storage solutions that will allow children to access resources easily.
✓ Make sure that the setting is properly cleaned.
✓ Ask children for ideas on how they would like their play spaces to look.
✓ Put up display boards and encourage the children to create colourful displays.
✓ Work with the children to produce programmes of play opportunities, activities and outings.
✓ Encourage parents and carers to be involved in the setting, for example, helping with play opportunities.
✓ Look for ways to strengthen teamwork, such as a communications board, nights out and staff meetings.

ACTIVE KNOWLEDGE

1 Does your setting create a good atmosphere? If so, how does it do this? If not, what would help?
2 Are there any areas you can identify as needing to be developed?
3 Explain how this might be done.

Obtain the resources needed for these play spaces

Most play settings have limited resources and limited budgets, so staff have to make the best use they can of the resources they have available. This sometimes means thinking about individual pieces of equipment and considering other ways in which they might be played with or used. A slide, for example, could become a good den if a sheet were draped over it, and a basketball net might be used for devising a new team game.

Children love to make dens out of available materials

Visiting other play settings

Visiting another play setting may spark off new ideas – another setting might have different games, for example.

Making an audit of equipment

An audit of equipment from time to time helps everyone in the setting to remind themselves exactly what resources are available. Items sometimes get forgotten in cupboards.

Work within the available budget or find other creative ways of obtaining or making resources

A wide range of materials and equipment are available in catalogues and stores and can be bought to enhance play. However, there is no need to buy expensive toys and equipment as children and young people have great imaginations and will use any interesting materials you provide for all kinds of play activities. That is not to say that you need not buy any materials or equipment, but you could use resource centres and contacts, for example, local firms, parents, carers, local industries, etc. to supplement the resources and help save on the budget.

Reporting and acting where there are resource problems

Where there is a clear shortage of resources, take action. A poorly resourced setting will find it hard to provide stimulating opportunities for children. In some settings a clear case will need to be made for new equipment, for example, if a management committee needs to be persuaded. If this is the case in your setting, consider using the equipment audit to show that there is an identifiable problem. Be very clear about what you are requesting. Instead of simply complaining about equipment, offer ideas about what you need and how much it would cost. Before going ahead and either buying in equipment or fund-raising, check out any policies with your line manager. There may be a policy about accepting second-hand toys, for example.

Combining resources

Sometimes resources can be combined to make a new play opportunity, for example, toy cars can be combined with the sand area to make a safari race track, or rollerblades and balls can be combined to produce a new game of dodgeball on skates!

Sorting and repairing equipment

Sort out equipment that is no longer safe or that is broken. Before throwing away any resources, check with the manufacturer whether spare parts are available. These are quite often free or very inexpensive.

Create the planned play spaces involving children and young people wherever possible

One of the keys to a successful play setting is continual reflection upon what is happening. It is very easy to get into a comfortable 'rut' and for routines and activities to be carried on because they have become 'tradition'. This is dangerous: new children may come into a setting and find that their needs are not met, and staff may become less motivated and challenged. It is often harder for permanent settings to realise that they need a change of routine or layout unless regular reviews are carried out. Yet the benefits of developing the play environment are enormous. Such reviews can help the team:

- motivate staff and volunteers
- make sure that equipment and resources are up to date

- make sure that the play space meets all children's needs
- provide variety and stimulation
- prevent children from feeling bored
- keep up to date with health and safety regulations.

Encouraging children to 'own' the play environment

While it is important that staff take pride in the play space, it is also important that children feel that it is theirs. Making sure that children have a stake in the play space contributes to their development, as it encourages them to work co-operatively, considering not just their own needs but also those of other children. Having access to a setting that they feel is 'theirs' is also very important for children who are feeling insecure in other areas of their lives, for example, if they are not enjoying school or if their home life is unsettled. The benefits are summarised in the diagram below.

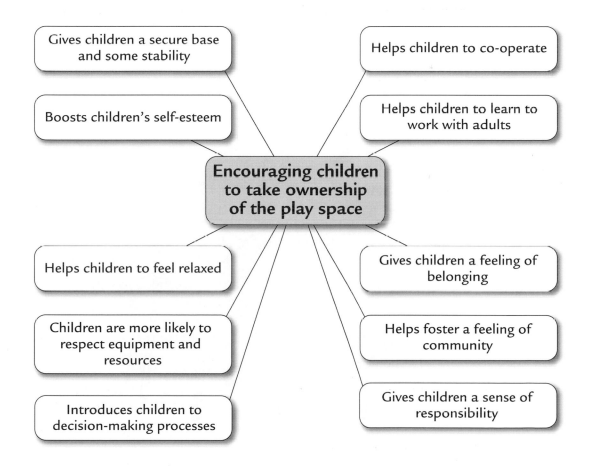

Gives children a secure base and some stability

Boosts children's self-esteem

Helps children to co-operate

Helps children to learn to work with adults

Encouraging children to take ownership of the play space

Helps children to feel relaxed

Children are more likely to respect equipment and resources

Introduces children to decision-making processes

Gives children a feeling of belonging

Helps foster a feeling of community

Gives children a sense of responsibility

Sharing responsibility

If children are to feel that the play space is their own, they must be given opportunities to take responsibility for it. They must be involved in decisions, encouraged to make suggestions, and allowed to improvise and adapt equipment, providing that safety is maintained.

Helping children take responsibility for their environment does not mean that playworkers take a back seat and leave everything to the children, however! This would not work, particularly in settings with very young children. What it does mean is that playworkers need to find ways of working alongside children, listening to them and giving them opportunities to contribute. This is quite a skill: children may need to be guided as to how to make fair decisions, how to listen to each other and how to consider what is practicable.

Children can be encouraged to share responsibility

There are many ways of encouraging children to contribute, and most settings use several. Common strategies include:

- holding meetings with all the children
- encouraging groups of children to hold their own meetings to discuss specific issues
- giving children choices wherever possible – for example, using preference sheets
- having a 'suggestions' box
- carrying out surveys and evaluations
- having a 'comments' noticeboard for the children.

For children to feel that their suggestions are valued, it is important that you act upon them whenever you can. If this is not possible you should explain why, for example, there may be financial or health and safety restraints.

ACTIVE KNOWLEDGE

Think of a recent occasion when you encouraged children to make suggestions about their play space.

1 Explain the circumstances and how you did this.
2 Were you able to act upon their suggestions?
3 If not, write about how you explained this to the children.

Make sure that the range of play spaces will be accessible for all children and young people

There are many ways of making sure that the play space remains interesting and challenging and accessible for all children.

- Staff might go on training courses, which will give them new ideas and help them keep up to date with current good practice.
- Many staff find it very helpful to visit other settings. Local networks can be formed to facilitate this type of exchange.
- Looking at brochures and visiting exhibitions may make staff aware of new products and equipment. Introducing some of these can help to develop a play setting.
- Children and young people can often contribute useful suggestions, provided that they are given the opportunities and encouragement to do so (see also page 15).
- By bringing in visitors, holding open days and actively encouraging parents and carers to be part of the setting, you can develop the setting further. Involvement and interaction like this helps everyone to feel motivated and energised.
- Approach specialist agencies for advice and support about access issues for children with limited mobility or other access issues.

Make sure the play spaces take account of health and safety requirements

No play space will ever be risk-free. You need to strike a balance between the needs of the children to play and their right to be safe.

When thinking about the activities that you provide and that the children choose, you should consider the risks and decide how these can be minimised. Children will inevitably be taking some risks in order to be able to explore and play freely, for example, climbing up a tree has an element of risk as the child might fall.

A playworker needs to be able to assess the risks and provide a safe environment without being over-protective. This allows the children to learn to take 'safe risks' and to gain confidence and independence.

One way in which you can minimise unacceptable risks is by carrying out regular checks on the environment and the equipment. This should also include looking at the cleanliness of areas such as the toilets and the kitchen. Some settings devise checklists in order to help staff remember what areas in particular they should be concentrating on.

More information on health and safety requirements can be found in Unit PW7.

ment PW9.3 | Support self-directed play

One of the main qualities required of an effective playworker is that of being able to support the children and young people in an appropriate manner. This means allowing for and encouraging self-directed play, knowing how and when to respond to play cues and holding play frames when necessary.

What you need to demonstrate you can do

- Encourage children and young people to choose and explore the range of play spaces for themselves, providing support when necessary
- Leave the content and intent of play to the children and young people
- Enable play to occur uninterrupted
- Enable children and young people to explore their own values
- Ensure children and young people can develop in their own ways
- Hold children's and young people's play frames when necessary
- Observe play and respond to play cues according to the stage in the play cycle

Encourage children and young people to choose the range of play spaces for themselves

Playworkers must encourage children and young people to explore the range of play spaces for themselves. Play allows children to try out new things and to go that one step further without fear of ridicule or failure. This is the idea behind play being used to 'extend' children. Playworkers have an important role to play in helping children to extend themselves as children can lack confidence in certain areas of their development. For example, a child might want to climb a little higher or try cycling without stabilisers, but is slightly afraid or unsure.

The key to helping children to overcome their own barriers is to allow them the space and time to edge further towards their goals at their own speed. It is essential not to 'push' children, as this can curb their confidence – and in any case, children should want to learn to do things from choice rather than to please adults. Pushing children into situations where they fear failure can also lower their self-esteem: they may become disappointed with themselves because they cannot do as much as they want.

You can help children by praising what they can already do, and be ready to help them when they want to 'have a go'. In practical terms, this might mean standing underneath a climbing frame ready to catch them, or giving a steadying hand when a young person is learning to rollerblade. Take your lead from the children, asking them what type of support they would like: they are then more likely to meet their own goals.

There may be times when children will need particular help, for example, during a treasure hunt a younger child might need help in reading the clues. Supporting children needs to be done sensitively, so as not to undermine a child's confidence or 'credibility' in front of other children. This is particularly important when helping older children.

When giving support to an individual child, be sure that other children do not feel neglected and that they too are given the adult support they need. Children can easily feel resentful, and parents and carers might think that playworkers have 'favourites'. Treat every child as an individual, and make sure that you listen to and interact with each one on a one-to-one basis at some time during each session – even if this is simply a greeting – and find out whether they are enjoying the session.

In order to balance the needs of individual children with those of the group, you may have to 'juggle' between children. One way in which you can give children high levels of individual support is by maintaining good staff ratios. Bear this in mind when planning and consider the supervision requirements of the range of activities you propose.

Leave the content and intent of play to the children and young people

Play is essentially an adult-free experience where children can decide what they want to do and when they want to do it. Children have generally learned their skills and limitations through a process of trial and error, and through play they also learn to improve skills and performance. The nature of the play experience is a matter for the children involved and in general they are the best people to decide what they want to do and why. Play should not be seen as an entertainment or diversion but as an integral part of a child's developmental process.

Self-reliance and independence are important skills for children to develop. Children who are confident enough to have a go at activities are more likely to enjoy them and persevere with them. Self-reliance and independence also allow children to be more creative in their play, because they are not afraid of doing things 'wrong'.

The following diagram shows the benefits to children of acquiring these qualities.

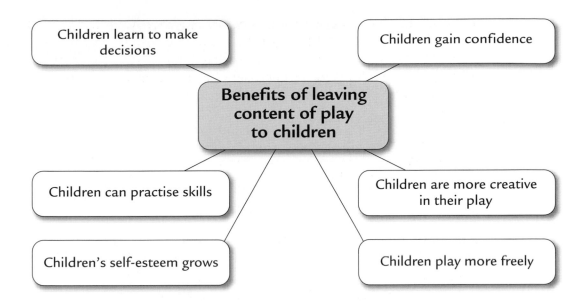

Children learn to make decisions

Children gain confidence

Benefits of leaving content of play to children

Children can practise skills

Children are more creative in their play

Children's self-esteem grows

Children play more freely

Whenever possible, encourage children to be independent and self-reliant. This does not mean refusing to give them assistance, but making sure that you do not 'take over' an activity, and looking for ways to encourage them to take on responsibility. An example of this would be if a young child wanted some help cutting some fabric: the playworker might look for a sharper pair of scissors so that the child could do the cutting himself, or ask the child to hold the fabric in place while it was being cut. You can also help children to be independent by making sure that they have access to equipment and resources.

Enable play to occur uninterrupted

When children are happily playing and enjoying their play, it is not a good idea to join in. Children gain more from being able to play freely with each other.

In some cases, children will ask a passing adult whether she or he wants to join them. In such a situation you need to make a judgement: will they still continue their game without you? Unless they seem really keen for you to join in, decline their offer pleasantly.

When children have made it clear that they wish to play alone

In some situations you will see from children's body language and play that they wish to be away from adults. They may huddle and create a den, or their play may stop as adults come near. Once you have satisfied yourself that their play is safe, you should leave them to play on their own. If play seems particularly secretive, however, you should maintain a close but discreet eye in case the children are doing something dangerous.

When children's safety may be compromised

If equipment is not designed to take adults or if you might put the children in danger, you should not join in. Even if children wish you to join in, you should not be tempted on to equipment that is not designed for adults, such as swings and climbing frames.

Remember too that your body weight and size might create a dangerous situation, for example, if during play you toppled onto a child.

When an adult's presence will inhibit children

Sometimes children may invite you to join in, but you might see that your presence would stop them from gaining the most from their play. For example, they might wish you to join in a performance they are putting on. By not taking part, however, you will be able to give the children greater ownership of, and so more satisfaction from, the activity, which they will then have done by themselves.

Sometimes children will invite you to join in but remember they are in charge

Children gain a lot of skills from being able to play independently of adults, so once children seem settled into their play, consider looking for ways of leaving them to it. Do this without disrupting the play or making the children feel that the play is not interesting enough. In some situations, especially with younger children or where you have been involved in the play activity, spend time withdrawing from the activity gradually. You might ask another child if she would like to play on your side during a board game, or in a role play situation, and then begin to say less and less. This tends to work better than abruptly leaving the play activity. In other situations, if you can see that children no longer need you and have become very involved themselves, you might acknowledge how well they are doing and ask if they still need you.

If you originally joined in the play because of a conflict or tension, it is a good idea once you have left the play to remain nearby in case the difficulty reappears. Where you have helped younger children in their play, you might need to keep popping back discreetly in case they need further support.

✓ ACTIVE KNOWLEDGE

Recall a time when you joined in and then left children to play on their own.

1 Explain how you left their play without disrupting it.
2 How can children benefit from being able to play without the involvement of adults?

Enable children and young people to explore their own values

Play is a process of 'trial and error' and children will frequently behave in ways that we, as adults, may regard as inappropriate, oppressive or risky; however, in these situations, they are always evolving.

Children play within their personal code of behaviour as well as those of their own culture and society. At times, play tests these codes, and this can give concerns about play and how adults manage it.

Play is important to the child, providing an arena for behaviour that is not overwhelmingly dominated by adult views and values. It is an important part of the experience, which may look like mistakes or bad behaviour from other points of view, from which children learn the appropriate behaviours for their own adulthood. Some boundaries are required, but these need to be skilfully drawn and applied if the benefits of play for the child are not to be eroded.

From *Best Play*, National Playing Fields Association, March 2000

Zoe and Tyronne are both 6 years old. They have made a house out of some lengths of material and used boxes and other equipment for furniture. They have dressed up and are sitting watching television (an old cardboard box). Tyronne pulls out a small building brick from his pocket and pretends that it is his mobile phone. He 'talks' to his mate and you overhear part of the conversation.

'Hi man, what time tonight? ... Okay ... At 12ish brother ... Where? ... At the end of the street? Okay, I'll bring the dosh.'
Zoe takes on the role and says, 'Where are you going?'
Tyronne also keeps in role and says, 'Never you mind, it's men's business. You stay here and make the dinner for when I get back.'
Zoe slips out of role and says, 'Is that what your mum does?'
Tyronne replies, 'Of course!'

1 Would you do or say anything at this stage, later or not at all? Explain your answer.
2 Before you have a chance to say or do anything (if you were thinking of that line of action) you hear Zoe say, 'Well my mum wouldn't make dinner at that time of night.' Do you now think that you should have said something?

Ensure children and young people can develop in their own ways

A playworker's core function is to be a facilitator who creates a stimulating environment for play and provides opportunities for a wide range of play experiences. Play is performed for no external goals or rewards, therefore children should not be persuaded to take part in a particular activity.

Each child will have slightly different needs and interests, so each child will respond in different ways to play opportunities. Some children might wish to repeat certain types of play for long periods of time; others might be more restless and enjoy changing activities frequently. The play opportunities that you plan and provide must therefore be flexible enough for children to develop their own interests. For example, a child who loves dinosaurs might happily play with them in the sand pit, whereas a football enthusiast might enjoy creating a league table to record matches.

Children benefit greatly from being able to develop play in their own way, as shown in the following diagram. Look for opportunities to encourage them.

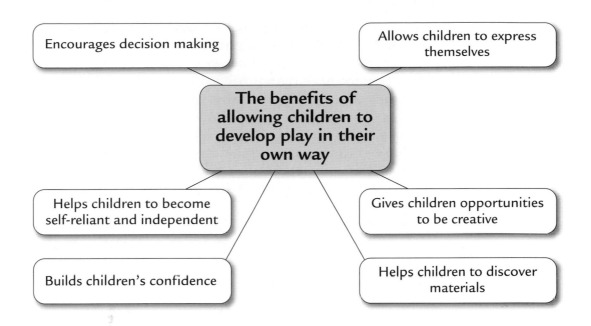

Encourages decision making

Allows children to express themselves

The benefits of allowing children to develop play in their own way

Helps children to become self-reliant and independent

Gives children opportunities to be creative

Builds children's confidence

Helps children to discover materials

Hold children's and young people's play frames when necessary

A play frame is a material or non-material boundary that keeps the play intact. Playworkers may need to support children and young people in maintaining a play frame so it continues as long as the children want it to. This enables children to play uninterrupted for as long as they wish to. This can be quite a challenge as children may affect the frame by including others, moving objects or starting to play in a different way.

Observe play and respond to play cues according to the stage in the play cycle

In the following example of a play cycle, the playworker responded to the play cues by not interfering but respecting the boy's preference to play on his own.

A boy (10) rolled a tyre into the fence. He watched it settle, then with a flurry of activity, began to lug all the tyres out one by one and started placing them carefully next to each other. It was clearly hard work. A worker came over and stood nearby, but not too close, and watched and waited. He ignored her and seeing that he was utterly absorbed she moved away. He carried on placing these tyres for over half an hour without stopping. Other kids moved deliberately around the outside of the tyres but none of them interrupted. Finally, he stood back and looked. He then rearranged one or two tyres and stood back again. Then he dusted himself off and went inside and was later completely unconcerned when some other child moved a couple of tyres elsewhere.

Source: Ali Wood, *Building Blocks* – a consultancy specialising in Playwork training, assessment, verification, writing and research

If you wish to research the theory of play further, you could read the paper produced by Gordon Sturrock and Perry Else on Psycholudics which you will find at www.ludemos.co.uk. This provides more information on play cycles and how they impact on the play process.

CONSOLIDATION

Recall times when you have:

- responded to a play cue and then withdrawn to enable play to continue
- held a play frame to enhance play.

1 Evaluate what you did and why.
2 Write these examples up as a reflective account and produce them as evidence for your portfolio.

Element PW9.4 | # Help children and young people to manage risk during play

Traditionally the health and safety definition of a hazard has been 'a physical situation that could be harmful or a source of potential danger'. When assessing risk in play settings, playworkers may therefore have only considered physical hazards such as broken play equipment, spills, etc. However, there are now four types of hazard in the standards to consider:

- physical
- emotional
- behavioural
- environmental.

Many playworkers will already instinctively recognise these other kinds of hazard, but all adults need to be aware of them when assessing risks – emotional and behavioural hazards are often more likely to result in unnecessary accidents.

Information on physical risk and some environmental risks can be found in Unit PW7.

What you need to demonstrate you can do

- Allow children and young people to experience and explore risk during play
- Identify hazards when they occur
- Assess the risks that these hazards pose in a way that is sensitive to the nature of the children and young people involved
- Raise children's and young people's awareness of hazards and encourage them to manage risks for themselves
- Balance the risks involved with the benefits of challenge and stimulation
- Only intervene if the level of risk becomes unacceptable

Allow children and young people to experience and explore risk during play

It is important that children and young people are allowed and at times encouraged to experience and explore risks during play. Children need to learn how to manage risks, for example, when they are climbing, they need to be aware of how to minimise the risk of falling. Being able to manage risks gives children confidence and develops their independence. Children seek out opportunities for risk-taking and the play provision must respond by providing an exciting and stimulating environment that balances risk appropriately against safety.

One way in which you can help children to manage risks safely is by talking to them about the potential risks in the environment and encouraging them to think of strategies to manage the risks. For example, you might ask children what the risks are when they are cooking, and how they could minimise these. Playworkers need to be quite skilful in deciding to what extent a child is mature enough to minimise a risk, as the overall responsibility for the safety of children still rests with the playworker. Playworkers therefore need to spend time getting to know the children they are working with, and observing them in the play setting.

Think about it

Think about a time when you allowed children to experience risk in a safe way.

1 What risks were the children experiencing?
2 How did they manage the risks?

Identify hazards when they occur

Within every play setting there will be times and instances where hazards will occur. In Unit PW7, which relates to health and safety, there is information about physical and environmental hazards. This section will help you to address the issues that arise from other types of hazard.

Environmental hazards

Most environmental hazards are well known and may be considered as physical hazards. More specifically they include things such as:

- extreme or freak weather conditions (as well as being potential hazards these also affect children's behaviour)
- the presence of animals
- light, for example, strong sunlight, darkness, dusk or fading light, etc.

Emotional hazards

Children will bring their moods and feelings from their day at school to a play setting and this often affects the way they behave and interact with others. They will also experience all kinds of feelings when playing – sometimes by choice and sometimes unexpectedly. Playworkers need to be aware of how children are feeling in case they need to intervene to distract or support children in expressing their feelings through play.

Behavioural hazards

More often than not, whatever children are feeling will influence the way they behave and certain behaviours are potentially hazardous. Again, playworkers need to be sensitive and ensure that they do not intervene unnecessarily. Children do not always behave well when they play (this is one way in which they learn and test out social skills) and playworkers are not there to ensure that they do. However, playworkers do need to be aware of behaviours that could create unacceptable risk.

There are many resources available that you will find useful, for example from Kidscape (www.kidscape.org.uk) or Incentive Plus (www.incentiveplus.co.uk).

Mood/feeling	Behaviour
Boredom	Bullying
Excitement	Attention seeking
Fear	Egging on
Anger	Showing off
Frustration	Hyperactivity
Tiredness	Experimenting
Insecurity	Immersion
Over-confidence	Exclusion
Intensity	Competitiveness
Anxiety	Dominating
Stress	Intruding on others' space or game

Potential emotional and behavioural hazards which may be experienced by groups or individuals

Assess the risks that these hazards pose in a way that is sensitive to the nature of the children and young people involved

It is tempting to intervene immediately when children and young people demonstrate behaviour that is considered negative or unwanted, but the skilled playworker will constantly observe and assess the risks – often without the children being aware of this. As mentioned earlier, play should give children the opportunity to experiment and explore situations and experiences without intervention wherever possible.

CASE STUDY

Matt and Shuna are arranging for a group of children to go rollerblading. The group includes children of different ages and they realise that the activity will be safe for the older children but not for the younger ones.

1 How could Matt and Shuna handle this situation?
2 What will they need to think about when assessing the risks of this activity?

Playworkers need to be aware of the following:

● children with disabilities or with learning difficulties who both want and need full inclusion in the play space and the opportunities it offers – playworkers need to understand their ability levels in order to support them and prevent unnecessary risks
● children with 'behavioural problems' – playworkers need to understand and recognise the causes and triggers of their difficulties so that the hazards these may cause are minimised

What you must know and understand

K1: Why reflection on practice and evaluation of personal effectiveness is important

K2: How learning through reflection can increase professional knowledge and skills

K3: How reflection can enhance practice and use personal experience to increase confidence and self-esteem

K4: Techniques of reflective analysis

K5: Reflection as a tool for contrasting what we say we do and what we actually do

K6: How to use reflection to challenge existing practice

K7: The difficulties that may occur as a result of examining beliefs, values and feelings

K8: How to assess further areas for development in your skills and knowledge through reflection, feedback and using resources such as the internet, libraries, journals

K9: How to develop a personal development plan with objectives that are specific, measurable, achievable, realistic and with timescales

K10: The availability and range of training and development opportunities in the local area and how to access these

K11: The importance of integrating new information and/or learning in order to meet current best practice, quality schemes or regulatory requirements

Element PW10.1 | Reflect on your practice

As a professional in a play setting it is important that you continually evaluate the effectiveness of your own personal performance and practice.

What you need to demonstrate you can do

- Monitor processes, practices and outcomes from your own work
- Evaluate your own performance using best practice benchmarks
- Reflect on your interactions with others
- Share your reflections with others and use their feedback
- Use reflection to solve problems and improve practice

Monitor processes, practices and outcomes from your own work

An essential task in becoming a creative, reflective and critical thinking playworker is to monitor processes, practices and outcomes from your own work. This will include asking yourself questions such as the following.

In my interactions with children:

- Do I wait for a play cue from a child or young person?
- Do I aid or hinder play?
- Do I enable play to occur uninterrupted by me?
- Do I jump into situations too quickly?
- Do I leave the content and intent of play to the children and young people?

When I observe the children and young people do I ask myself:

- What type of play is taking place?
- What is actually happening?
- Are there any play cues being given out?
- If so, what are these?

When I consider the actual environment do I ask myself:

- What is stimulating?
- What has/hasn't changed in the last week and why?
- Are my colleagues observant?
- Are the materials provided suitable for stimulating play?

Evaluating your own work

Taking time to consider your own performance and to evaluate your own work is always worthwhile. Doing this allows you to consider how you might handle things differently in the future as well as why things are working well.

To help you evaluate effectively, it is worth thinking first about what you actually need to do in your job role. Job roles vary enormously from one playworker to another, and most people have several strands to their jobs.

Tasks that playworkers might do include the following:

- liaising with social services and other agencies
- supervising other playworkers and volunteers
- working as part of a team
- working to provide play for children and young people
- liaising with parents and carers
- checking and providing equipment and materials
- record keeping
- encouraging health and safety while still allowing for challenge and risk
- ordering and obtaining resources
- marketing.

ACTIVE KNOWLEDGE

● Write down the tasks that you carry out in your organisation. (You might like to use the list on the previous page to help you.)
● Why are these important to the smooth running of the organisation?

Useful strengths for working with others

As a playworker you will have many strengths. Below are a selection that you may already have, or you may wish to develop.

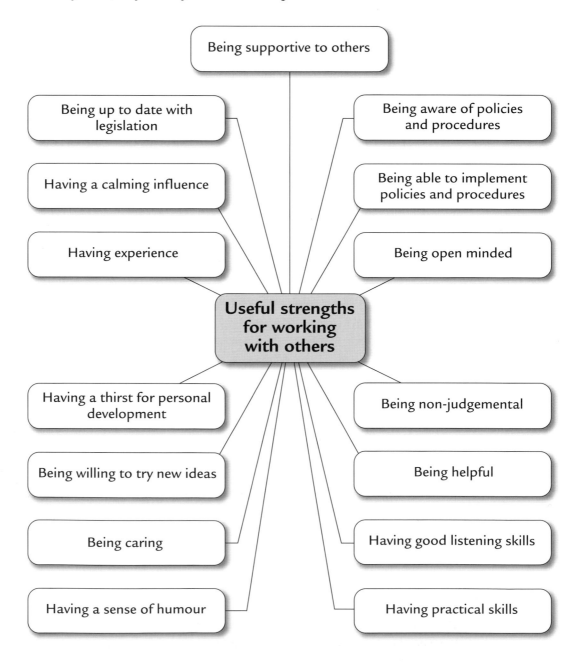

Being supportive to others

Being up to date with legislation

Being aware of policies and procedures

Being able to implement policies and procedures

Having a calming influence

Having experience

Being open minded

Useful strengths for working with others

Having a thirst for personal development

Being non-judgemental

Being willing to try new ideas

Being helpful

Being caring

Having good listening skills

Having a sense of humour

Having practical skills

Evaluate your own performance and reflect on your interactions with others

Personal observations

One way to evaluate your practice is through your own observations. You might notice that children and young people seem to enjoy talking to you, or that you are able to empower them to manage disagreements for themselves. These are strengths. In the same way, if you think about all areas of your work, you might be able to identify some areas of development in practice. For example, you might run out of glue because it was not reordered, or you may notice that you find it harder to relate to particular children. To be able to analyse strengths and weaknesses in this way, you need to look carefully at the reactions of others to your work. You also need to think about the reasons for your strengths and areas for development.

CASE STUDY

Ajaz has been working as a playworker for three years. He is keen to gain his S/NVQ Level 3 in order to start applying for supervisory positions. He tries to reflect on his strengths and areas for development. He realises that he is particularly good with the older children, who often seem to play for longer periods when he is working with them. He thinks that this is because he has a relaxed approach with them, and is good at acknowledging their ideas and helping them develop play. When he considers his weaknesses, he identifies that his organisational skills could be improved – he noticed that a colleague was irritated the other day because he had forgotten to bring in some art materials.

1 If you were Ajaz what would you do?
2 If you supervised Ajaz what would you suggest to help him?

In order to evaluate your own performance, you need to become a reflective practitioner.

The reflective practitioner

A reflective practitioner is a person who monitors and evaluates his or her practice using a variety of evaluation methods and sources, for example:

ACTIVE KNOWLEDGE

List the things you value in life then look at the picture below and see how they compare.

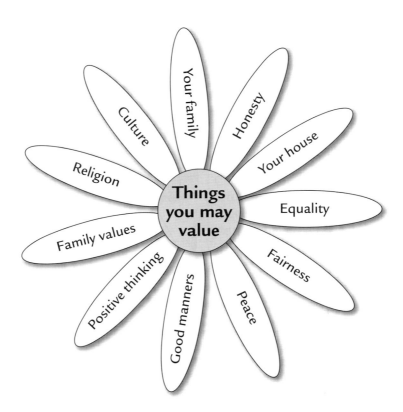

You may find that some of the things you value are materialistic and some are personal, spiritual or religious. Your values, beliefs and feelings may change over a period of time according to your circumstances. For example, ten years ago the things you valued may have been very different from what they are now.

ACTIVE KNOWLEDGE

Think back to your life ten years ago and list the things that were important to you then. Now compare this with the list of things you value now. How many are actually the same?

When your values are challenged

Sometimes you will experience personal inner conflict when someone challenges the feelings or values that are integrated into your practice. You may have to examine your values and actions and realise that you are being perhaps judgemental or even discriminatory. For example, you may have a parent who owes you money, or who has not sent in a packed lunch for a child and tells you that he or she cannot afford it. You then see that the parent has a packet of cigarettes. It may cross your mind that the parent can afford to smoke but not provide a lunch or pay for the child. However, you may not be aware of the underlying circumstances that may have an effect on the parent and the parent's life. A playworker's approach should always remain non-judgemental.

Inner turmoil will show that you are in fact questioning yourself and your practice, and this in turn will show that you are open-minded and prepared to change.

The diagram below shows how you can use these challenges and reflections to your advantage and to bring about change within yourself. It is called a reflective learning cycle. Think of this as a wheel that is continually turning.

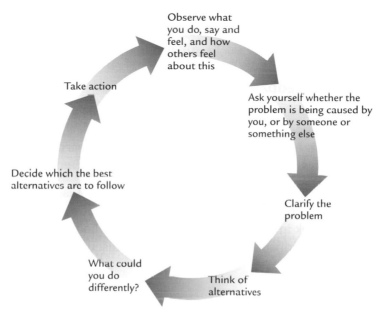

Observe what you do, say and feel, and how others feel about this

Ask yourself whether the problem is being caused by you, or by someone or something else

Clarify the problem

Think of alternatives

What could you do differently?

Decide which the best alternatives are to follow

Take action

The reflective learning cycle

 **ACTIVE KNOWLEDGE**

Use the reflective learning cycle to help you make a change in your own practice.

 Keys to good practice: Being aware of the values and beliefs of others

✓ Do not judge others against your own values.
✓ Try to understand that all families are unique and have their own values and beliefs.
✓ Be aware that there may be cultural differences.
✓ Be aware of the different festivals and religious days that families celebrate.
✓ Try not to press your own beliefs on others.
✓ Do not criticise others – you may not be aware of the pressures they are under.

Using interviews

Another way of collecting feedback is by interviewing people, or talking to them. You can do this with a list of prepared questions, which you then ask, noting down the replies. Interview questions can be 'open'. These allow people to talk generally about particular topics, for example, 'What do you think about taking the children out on visits?'

Interviews have the advantage that people will often say more face to face than they will write down. You can also add supplementary questions if you need clarification. Interviews are also useful in situations in which people might have difficulty filling in forms.

Feedback from children and young people

Children are always a good and reliable source when you require feedback. They should be encouraged to express their wishes, views and opinions on a regular basis. If you show that you value their opinions by acting upon their suggestions, they will feel more willing to be open and share their views with you. If, on the other hand, you ask their opinions and then disregard or 'rubbish' them, they will be less inclined to participate in the future. So an open mind and a non-judgemental attitude are required.

Older children might enjoy designing their own evaluation and feedback sheets before filling them in, whereas younger children might prefer just to talk about what they enjoy doing or the equipment that they would like.

✓ ACTIVE KNOWLEDGE

List the types of topic you could use to encourage children and young people to share their views. Your list should include some of the areas below:

- décor and use of space
- materials you provide
- snacks you provide
- equipment you buy
- staff attitudes
- visits you could arrange
- specialist activities and instructors you could arrange
- routines.

The list could be endless. Always remember that the children are your reason for being there. Asking for their views will make them feel that the provision is child centred and belongs to them.

There is a variety of methods that you could use when requesting the views and opinions of children and young people. You could use informal approaches, for example, as-and-when discussions or chats in a non-threatening atmosphere. Alternatively you could use more formal approaches, such as a suggestion box where ideas and opinions can be posted anonymously, evaluation sheets, questionnaires, true or false statements, multiple choice questions, etc.

Always choose an evaluation method which:

- the children or young people can understand
- is interesting for them
- relates to specific topics you wish to address
- you can analyse easily.

Below is a practical example.

Stansville Play Centre

Activity: <u>Environmental play in the woods</u>   Date: _____

Age: _____

I thought that:

The place chosen was:	☺	😐	☹
The food was:	☺	😐	☹
The free time to play was:	☺	😐	☹
The equipment provided was:	☺	😐	☹
The time we stayed there was:	☺	😐	☹

Things I would have liked to do _____

_____

_____

Things I did not like _____

_____

_____

Thank you for completing this form. Please put it in the box near the door.

A questionnaire for children

ACTIVE KNOWLEDGE

Think of an opportunity or activity that you have provided recently. Ask the children or young people to help devise an evaluation form.

Feedback from parents and carers

Because they benefit from the service you provide, parents and carers will have important views on the type of provision they require for their children. Remember that if you do not meet their expectations, it is likely that they will withdraw their children from your setting. The implications of this could be unfortunate for your scheme, whether the parents pay for the service or not. There are many ways that you can ask for feedback from parents and carers. As with the feedback from children, the methods you choose need to be relevant and the data collected needs to be measurable and useful.

Feedback method	Example	Follow-up
Suggestion box/book	Provide a box and bring this to the attention of parents and carers, leaving it where it can be clearly seen. Provide pens and paper.	Take suggestions seriously and give them the consideration they require.
Questionnaire	Prepare a questionnaire that is easy to complete. Ensure every parent and carer receives one. Explain why you are asking them to complete the questionnaire.	Check all questionnaires are returned. Evaluate and provide a response for the parents and carers.
Parents/carers meeting	Promote the meeting, or include it in another activity such as a coffee evening or fund-raising event. Make sure that notes are taken.	Act on suggestions and provide some form of feedback to parents.
Discussions	These can be informal and can take place whenever the opportunity arises. Remember to provide opportunities for discussion with all parents, not just those you get on particularly well with.	Follow up all feedback received. Keep a record of what was said, maybe in a special book.

Feedback methods

When you receive feedback you should always remember to be objective and have an open mind. Do not take it personally, but look to see how it can improve practice. If you act on their feedback, people will feel a sense of belonging and that their input is valued.

Feedback from other adults

There is probably a range of other adults who visit the setting. This could include:

- committee members
- volunteers
- students
- social workers
- other playworkers
- play development workers
- inspectors (Ofsted/fire brigade)
- visiting speakers
- specialist activity workers
- S/NVQ assessors
- your team
- support workers
- Sure Start workers.

The list could be endless. These people could, like the parents and children, play a valuable part in providing feedback. They could help you to identify areas of good practice and highlight areas for development.

✓ **ACTIVE KNOWLEDGE**

List the other adults who visit your setting. Prepare a book to collect their comments like the one below:

We are continuously evaluating our setting and would appreciate any help you could give us on highlighting good practice and areas we could improve. Thank you!

Date   Comments   Name/Agency

Next time you have visitors, ask them to comment in your book.

Getting feedback from colleagues

Your colleagues can be a good source of helpful feedback. You can share your self-evaluation with them and ask for their comments, or just chat informally about how things are going. You may also have the opportunity to have a formal appraisal, where your line manager or a senior colleague meets formally with you to discuss your work and development needs. For more information on appraisal, see page 194.

Acting on feedback

Recording information

In order to make good use of feedback, it is essential that the information you gain is recorded correctly. This might be in note form, but may need to be in more detail if an important issue has been raised. For example, if a parent has made a strong criticism, write down exactly what was said and in what context, and pass this on to your line manager or other members of the team.

Handling others' criticism constructively

As a result of receiving feedback from others, you might find that some criticisms or comments are linked to work for which you are responsible. A colleague might comment that a rota system does not seem to work, or that she or he is often not informed of changes that are taking place.

It is never easy to take criticism, especially if you have put 100 per cent effort into your work, but in order to improve your professional practice it is always necessary to listen to what others are saying. Try not to become defensive; instead, see this as a learning process. You might be learning about the way other people perceive situations, or you might be learning about the disadvantages of a certain way of working. One way of coping with criticism is to consider what you can learn from it. The diagram below shows some questions that you could consider asking yourself.

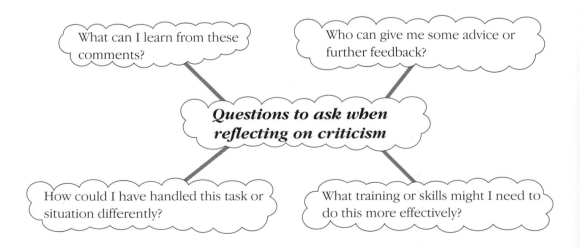

What can I learn from these comments?

Who can give me some advice or further feedback?

Questions to ask when reflecting on criticism

How could I have handled this task or situation differently?

What training or skills might I need to do this more effectively?

Acting on suggestions for improving service

You must be prepared to act on suggestions and try out new ideas if you are asking for feedback. However, you may find that some suggestions are not viable for a variety of reasons, for example, there may not be adequate staffing levels and expertise. If you have not acted upon particular suggestions, you should provide feedback to explain why not.

When considering changes or new ideas you will always need to ensure that they offer challenge and an element of risk. At the same time they will need to meet health and safety regulations and the policies and procedures for your setting, as well as legal requirements. See page 188 for more advice on assessing the impact of potential changes.

Keys to good practice: Trying out new ideas

✓ Make sure any new idea is monitored for effectiveness before it becomes permanent practice.
✓ Inform everyone of the changes and make sure they are open-minded about the idea.
✓ Provide time to listen to feedback.
✓ Remain open-minded yourself.
✓ Do not be afraid to stop the new activity if, after a given time, it is not working.

ACTIVE KNOWLEDGE

Ask each team member to submit an idea for improving a routine, to take effect next month. Discuss these at a team meeting and choose relevant ideas to be implemented.

Use reflection to solve problems and improve practice

Comparing what was achieved with what was planned

Most organisations review and monitor their plans. This allows them to see how effective the plans were, and informs future planning. Reviewing can take place on an informal basis, or it might take place more formally, for example, during staff meetings. In some cases an organisation's funds might be dependent on formal evaluations which monitor the quality of the provision.

There are many ways in which an organisation might monitor and review its plans. Some organisations keep a day-to-day log book in which they evaluate each session's activities, whereas others simply ask staff members to review plans at the end of the week.

St Nicholas Community Playscheme log book	
Date	
Monday 21st July	*Today, we went to the park as the children fancied a picnic outdoors. This was quite a success, although a letter needs to go out to remind parents about sending in sunscreen. Afternoon session went particularly well – a new version of stuck in the mud was invented by one group.* *Jasmina Hurd – Leader*
Tuesday 22nd July	*A wet day meant that the children were unable to go out doors for much of the day. Some tensions in the group at first over the computers until a solution was found. Several children are working on a dance routine and a talent show is being organised for Thursday!* *Jasmina Hurd – Leader*
Wednesday 23rd July	*The children are getting really excited by the talent show and now most of the group is keen to take part in some way. Posters are being designed, competition rules are being drawn up and Michaela's mum has promised to send in a video camera.* *Martin Hargreaves — Deputy*

A playscheme's log

Evaluating events, activities and routines

It is also useful to evaluate your performance on specific tasks. For example, after organising an outing, you could think about how smoothly it went and what lessons you can learn for the future.

It is easy to dwell on the areas of development of any event or activity, but it is also important to consider the positive aspects of events that have been planned. If you can identify the ingredients for success, you will be better able to repeat this in the future. It is not always easy to identify the reasons for success, but often some key features can be recognised in each case. Typically these key features will include the following:

- good forward planning
- strong time management skills
- enthusiasm of staff
- sufficient resources
- active involvement of children in planning
- appropriate timing of the activity
- enough time allowed for the activity.

What lessons can you learn from a successful outing?

✓ ACTIVE KNOWLEDGE

Make a quick evaluation of the types of play opportunities that you provide in your setting by completing a table like the one below.

Types of play	Always	Often	Occasionally	Never
Communications play				
Creative play				
Deep play				
Dramatic play				
Exploratory play				
Fantasy play				
Imaginative play				
Locomotor play				
Mastery play				
Object play				
Role play				
Rough and tumble				
Social play				
Socio-dramatic play				
Symbolic play				

Using reflection to help you make changes

Sometimes it is helpful to think reflectively about how things work on a day-to-day basis in your setting. You can use reflection and feedback both to identify potential problems and improvements and to help you put changes into action.

CASE STUDY

Jo, the deputy manager at an after-school club, feels that homework is a potential issue that might need to be discussed. Several parents have made comments about the difficulty they have in finding time to supervise homework at home, and one parent has withdrawn her child because the club offers no facilities for children to do their homework. Jo asks the manager if they could stay behind one night to talk about the issue of homework. She has the exit questionnaire that was filled in by one parent recently, and she has also noted down the comments of several other parents. Jo realises that many playworkers feel uncomfortable about bringing homework into the club, because they want to create a play environment for the children and are working hard to make the club feel different from school. During the discussion with the manager, Jo puts forward different points of view regarding homework, and especially that the ethos of the club is play. They agree that more information is probably needed before they can make a final decision. They agree on the following action plan.

Action points	By whom?	By when?
Find out the views of children in the club	Jo	End of March
Send out a questionnaire to parents	Jo	End of March
Raise the issue of homework with team during a team meeting	Manager	15 March

1 Why was it important for Jo to ask for some specific time to talk this through with her manager?
2 Why is it a good idea to collect further information before making any decisions?
3 Why is it useful to record information on an action plan?

Assessing the impact of potential changes

When assessing the impact of potential changes, you need to think about the following things carefully.

- Team support and morale – it's important to discuss and explain changes carefully in order to make sure the team are happy with the change and are prepared to give it a try. If the team are unhappy with the proposed change, it's worth finding out why and seeing if a solution can be found.
- Staffing requirements – do the proposed changes mean that staff might need to change their hours and/or duties? If so, this will need careful discussion and thought.

- Children's/young people's needs – these are paramount. All changes should be thought through to check that they benefit the children. It is good practice to ask them about proposed changes, if these are likely to affect them.
- Parents' needs – parents and carers are important partners. Any changes that might affect them (such as changes to opening hours or fees) should be carefully assessed.
- The budget – the cost of the proposed change will need to be carefully worked out. Balancing priorities with the needs of the budget can be tricky. For example, buying a new fridge as a result of a health and safety audit may not seem as attractive as buying some new equipment for the children, but it may have to take priority if the setting is to keep its registration!
- Health and safety – this must be taken very seriously. If a setting is found to be breaching codes of practice, registration and insurance can be withheld. Risk assessments will be required. Suggested changes must be evaluated with health and safety in mind. For example, changing the layout of a room might make it more difficult to evacuate the building in an emergency.
- Other organisations – you may need to consider how changes would affect other organisations with which you work. For example, you might be renting your premises from a school, or be based in a workplace or leisure centre.

Techniques of reflective analysis

To analyse something means to examine it in detail. Here are some techniques you could use to analyse areas of your work.

Technique	How to use it	Example
Questioning what, why and how	Choose something that you have done recently and ask yourself: **What** did you do, **why** did you do it and **how** well did it go?	Think about what happens when the children arrive at your setting.
Seeking an alternative	Ask yourself: Could you have done something different or better?	Think about when you provided a snack and the children commented on the snack.
Keeping an open mind	Invite constructive criticism, ideas or opinions and then acknowledge these and act upon them.	Think about when a colleague suggested something that you have never tried before. Think about how you replied and how you reacted.
Viewing things from a different perspective	Look at something from a child's or parent's point of view.	Think about some materials you provided. Were they really interesting to the child? What did the parent/carer think?
Thinking about consequences	Think about the effects of the materials you provide for other people. Think about them from the point of view of health and safety and other requirements.	Think about some materials you provided when the children were really enjoying themselves but were making a mess which you knew would be tricky to clear up.

Technique	How to use it	Example
Testing ideas through comparing and contrasting	Try different ways of doing things, compare how they went, and contrast them with other options.	Think about home time. How do you manage when there are children leaving at different times? How can you still offer opportunities that are not disrupted when children leave?
Asking 'what if ...?'	Think about situations where you took a risk and a dangerous situation could have occurred.	Think about when there was a fire drill and an aspect of safety was not followed correctly.
Synthesising ideas	Bring together ideas from different sources, e.g. trying out something a colleague suggested, something seen on television or something heard about in training.	Think about how you could make an existing activity even better by trying out an idea someone has suggested, e.g. having a camp fire to cook marshmallows.
Seeking, identifying and resolving problems	Think about a problem before or as it arises, and look for a solution.	Think about what you did last time one of your workers phoned in sick.

Techniques of reflective analysis

Keys to good practice: Using reflection

✓ Use reflection as a tool for contrasting what you say you did and what you actually did. Think carefully about things and ask for feedback from others, then take this on board.

✓ Use reflection to challenge existing practice, get feedback and analyse the situation. Then use the data as a tool to challenge and change the practice in a professional manner.

Advantages of reflective practice

The table below shows the advantages of continually improving your practice in the play setting.

Benefits for you	Benefits for the children	Benefits for the organisation
Increases your knowledge and skills Identifies strengths and areas for development Confirms your good practice Boosts self-esteem and confidence Identifies areas for development	Ideas about opportunities are updated Current initiatives and legislation are implemented Variety of different opportunities are available Children can observe a good role model Contented atmosphere is maintained Children's welfare is addressed	Current trends and developments are implemented A high standard is maintained A good example is set to other team members Reputation of the setting is upheld/increased Inspection requirements are met

Advantages of continually improving your practice

ACTIVE KNOWLEDGE

1 Think of a time when a child or young person reminded you that you had said that you would do something, and then you did it your way and not the way they wanted you to.

2 Use the next team meeting to look at a certain routine and ask for suggestions on how you could change it to bring it more in line with meeting the children's needs.

CONSOLIDATION

Think about a recent session or task during which you were responsible for providing the materials.

1 Explain what you did and why you did it.

2 Evaluate your own performance:

- Did the session go as well as you had planned?
- Were there any ways in which you could have improved your performance or the children's enjoyment?
- What were your strengths?
- What have you learnt from carrying out the session or task?

ment PW10.2 | # Take part in continuing professional development

This part of the unit requires you to think about your personal and professional development and to recognise the need to continually update your personal skills and understanding.

What you need to demonstrate you can do

- Identify areas in your knowledge, understanding and skills where you could develop further
- Develop and negotiate a plan to develop your knowledge, understanding and skills
- Seek out and access opportunities for continuing professional development
- Use continuing professional development to improve your practice

Identify areas in your knowledge, understanding and skills where you could develop further

Identifying areas for development

A positive way of looking at weaknesses is to refer to them as areas for development. This will enable you to see areas of weakness not as a personal insult but as an area of your practice that can be developed.

Areas for development can be identified in many ways, and many of these have been suggested in the previous section, PW10.1.

Steps in identifying areas for development

1 Use personal reflection and feedback to work out your strengths and areas for development (see page 173).

2 Consider which areas you might want to develop. For instance, you may have realised that you have a talent for working with older children, while also identifying that you never seem to have enough time to keep the paperwork up to date. These might be two areas that you could consider for development, especially if you wish eventually to take on some managerial responsibility where keeping on top of the paperwork will be essential.

3 Discuss the areas you have identified with your manager and colleagues. When working in a team it is important to keep your colleagues informed of changes you want to make. You should also get your line manager's approval and help, especially if the changes are part of moving towards a longer-term career goal. You may well want to discuss the areas you have identified for development in a formal appraisal meeting (see page 194).

4 Think about what you need to do in order to develop these areas. You and your manager might decide that you need some specific training, for example, on the theories of play or to gain a qualification. Or you may feel that you could get the experience you need by swapping roles with a colleague, doing some research or visiting another setting to observe how things are done there.

CASE STUDY

Anife works in a nursery which also runs a playscheme. The nursery will shortly be opening an after-school club. Anife is pleased about this as he has already started his S/NVQ in Playwork and is working in the holidays on playschemes. Below is a table that he has used to help him identify his areas for development.

Short term	First aid training Finish S/NVQ Level 3 in Playwork Basic computer course
Medium term	S/NVQ Level 4 in Playwork Gain Assessor's Award A1 Apply for positions as deputy manager Bookkeeping classes
Long term	Manage an after-school club and playscheme

1 What else might Anife add to the development plan?
2 If he worked in your setting, whom could Anife present the development plan to?

Develop and negotiate a plan to develop your knowledge, understanding and skills

Once you have identified some areas of your work that you would like to develop, you can work on a formal development plan. You will need to involve your line manager in this, possibly in the context of an appraisal (see page 194).

Personal development plans

As a professional person you should continually assess your performance, highlighting your strengths and areas for development. Once you have identified these you should record them in a personal development plan, in a manner that is easy to understand and that allows the plan to be monitored. This could be done formally at appraisal with your line manager or as a personal exercise, although it is good to have some input from a trusted and honest colleague.

Keys to good practice: Composing your personal development plan objectives

✓ Ensure the objectives are **specific**, giving clear details of the development activity.
✓ Ensure they are **measurable** and include specific recognisable outcomes.
✓ Ensure they are **achievable**, which may mean breaking down goals into smaller objectives.
✓ Ensure they are **realistic**, so your actions and targets can be met within the time set.

ACTIVE KNOWLEDGE

Look at the proforma for a personal development plan below. You could:

● use it to set up your own personal development plan
● compare it to your own existing plan to see if there are ideas you can use to improve your plan.

Personal development plan			
Name:		Date:	
Area for development	Action	Timescale	Review date
Health and safety training	Check out courses available and book on to convenient one	To start as soon as possible	At next appraisal or within six weeks
Cultures different from your own	Research into local play forum courses and workshops on celebrating festivals Research into cultural materials and equipment	To start immediately	At next staff meeting
Knowledge of play theories	Research the theories of play	To start as soon as possible	At next appraisal

Appraisal

An appraisal is a formal meeting in which you are able to discuss and address issues surrounding your performance. Your partner in the appraisal meeting should be someone you feel confident with and can trust to be honest and sincere. It is important that your partner can offer an unbiased opinion and help you in your reflection on practice. Due to the structure and size of staff teams in play settings, appraisal will often take place with a line manager or senior colleague.

An appraisal meeting should always be a pre-planned arrangement in which you are both given the opportunity to suggest topics for discussion. Appraisal meetings should:

● have guidelines with regard to the confidentiality of information
● have set time limits
● be held on a regular basis.

Notes should be taken and agreed by both parties before being stored securely to protect confidentiality. Appraisal notes should not be available to other staff members.

Why bother with appraisal?

Appraisal is useful as it:

● aids personal development
● builds on and gives support in your role
● gives the opportunity to think through and discuss new ideas
● can help sort out personal grievances
● highlights training needs
● enables people to feel valued
● helps people to focus on future responsibilities
● helps people to reflect on aspects of good practice
● provides a chance to address areas that need improving.

Well run appraisals can bring benefits both for you and for your setting. To be honest and open in appraisal is important because it will help you to progress, develop and make improvements in your role. Without frankness and honesty the appraisal would become worthless and you would be unable to create a culture of trust and respect. Badly run appraisals can actually hinder the relationships within the setting.

PORTFOLIO EVIDENCE

When preparing for an appraisal or any other meeting to discuss your work, try using a chart similar to the one below but including topics relevant to your specific role. Complete the chart yourself before the appraisal, ensuring that you comment on every score that you give yourself. Then either take it with you to the appraisal for discussion and comments, or give a copy to the person who is carrying out the appraisal. Ask this person to score and add comments and then compare the results in your appraisal session.

Topic	Very good	Good	Fair	Requires improvement	Comments
Interactions with parents and carers		✓			I always try to talk to parents and build relationships with them.
Communication with colleagues					
Communication with children and young people					
Support for colleagues					
Punctuality					
Preparation for sessions					
Including all types of play opportunities					
Awareness of risks and hazards					
Managing a team					

You could include the chart as portfolio evidence for your S/NVQ.

ACTIVE KNOWLEDGE

Look back at the chart about methods of personal and professional development and identify the ones that you have used. Choose another method and add this to your development plan at your next review.

Use continuing professional development to improve your practice

Continuous learning

To become effective in your role as a playworker it is vital that you develop your knowledge and your practice. Learning needs to be a continuous process which can involve formal and informal learning, linked to both your job role and your personal development. The circle of continuous improvement is shown in the diagram below.

Circle of continuous improvement

The diagram below will also show you how this works.

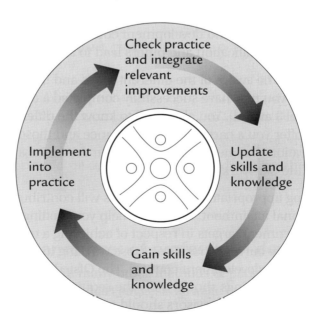

Continuous learning is important for a variety of reasons. Continuous learning:

- helps you evaluate your practice
- means that you are constantly updating your skills
- can keep you on track to realise your ambitions
- can make you more enthusiastic
- introduces you to new ideas and practices
- can increase your motivation
- improves your career possibilities.

Reviewing your personal development plan

It is essential to keep on reviewing your personal development plan and checking progress towards goals. It is equally important to change your goals if they start to seem irrelevant or less important.

Your personal development plan should be an active document that is kept up to date. This means reviewing it regularly, either as a personal task or in a meeting or appraisal with your manager.

It is also important to keep on listening to feedback and to ask people who have provided feedback to tell you how they think you are doing.

Integrating new information

For your personal development to be of value, you should use the results to enhance your work. You can make sure you put your new knowledge into practice by:

- dissemination – passing on your learning and skills to others in your team
- implementation – making changes in the organisation as a result of your learning.

There is a range of initiatives which can be undertaken by your setting to recognise and acknowledge that you provide a quality provision. This includes:

- gaining a quality assurance award
- providing feedback from an inspection
- providing a brochure explaining what you provide and why
- producing a monthly newsletter
- holding an evening where parents and carers are invited in
- using a news board to give information to parents and carers.

Your local Children's Services Department, the local council, local playwork centres or play forums and your allocated play development worker will be able to help and advise you about this process. (See also Unit A320, 'Allocate and monitor the progress and quality of work in your area of responsibility' which is available on the Heinemann website.)

Standard 4: Physical environment

The focus:

The environment should be warm and welcoming to children, staff and parents. It should be safe and secure, with space organised to meet requirements and used appropriately to promote children's development. (Scottish National Care Standard 1; see page 344.)

Standard 9: Equal opportunities

The focus:

Children need to feel valued and free from discrimination. Where staff are committed to equality they recognise that children's attitudes towards others are established in these early years. They understand relevant legislation and plan to help children learn about equality and justice through their play. The provision is carefully organised and monitored to ensure that all children have access to the full range of activities. Family members and staff should work together to share information. (Scottish National Care Standard 2; see page 344.)

What you must know and understand

For PW11.1

K1: Why effective, inclusive teamwork is important and how it contributes to the quality of the provision

K2: Why it is important to carry out agreed responsibilities and duties and what may happen if you do not do this

K3: The importance of sorting out duties and responsibilities that you are unsure about

K4: Why you should only vary responsibilities and duties with the agreement of colleagues

K5: Situations in which you should ask for additional support and why

K6: The importance of making suggestions as to how the team's work could be improved

K7: Why it is important to keep the appropriate colleagues up to date and informed of progress

K8: How to participate in team meetings

K9: Why it is important for the team to anticipate the needs of users

For PW11.2

K10: Why it is important to give colleagues constructive criticism

K11: Why it is important for colleagues to receive recognition for their contributions

K12: How to give constructive criticism in a way that reinforces the person's self-confidence

K13: The types of situations in which colleagues may need support and how to respond to these

K14: Why it is important to share information and how to do this effectively

K15: Why diversity is important in your area of work

K16: Why discrimination and prejudice should be challenged and how to do so effectively and constructively

For PW11.3

K17: The types of conflict which tend to happen in teams and how to deal with these

K18: Why it is important not to disrupt the work of the team when conflict occurs

K19: Types of conflict which you can deal with yourself and conflict which must be referred to others

K20: Why it is important to compromise when possible and how to identify situations where compromises should not be made

K21: How to support colleagues involved in conflict

K22: How to make accurate reports of conflict which has happened and why

K23: Organisational procedures for dealing with conflict

The purpose of a team

The dictionary definition of a team is 'a group of people working together to achieve the same aims and objectives'. If you keep this definition in mind, you will have a good basis for working as a harmonious team.

Think about it

At your next team meeting think about the aim for your team. You need to take into account all that is important to you as playworkers as well as the nature of the provision at your setting.

Reasons why people work as a team

People work as a team for a variety of reasons, some of which are shown in the table below.

Reason	Rationale of working together
To make the most of individual skills and expertise	If team members recognise that everyone has different skills, they will be able to use these skills to the best advantage in different situations.
To keep up morale	Team members can support each other if they work together.
To help motivation	Team members can enthuse each other by a positive attitude.
To complete tasks	Team members can achieve things in an efficient manner if the team works together.
To encourage team members to feel at ease	Team members can discuss and share ideas and opinions if they feel supported within the team.
To support others	Helping each other and working together enhances the work of the team.
For security	By working together team members can ensure that they follow relevant policies, procedures, guidelines and legislation.
To develop originality and resourcefulness	Team members can share ideas and skills to enhance the provision.
To establish a consistent approach	A consistent approach helps establish security for the children and young people as well as the staff.
To share information	Sharing relevant information at an appropriate time and in an appropriate manner contributes to effective team working.

Reasons for working as a team

- Errors and accidents are avoided.
- Job security and career prospects are enhanced.
- Job satisfaction and motivation increase.

You should agree your duties and responsibilities with colleagues either at a team meeting or at a briefing before a session.

The smooth running of the setting

Teamwork is not just about the quality of relationships in a work setting; it is also about everyone working together and fulfilling their job responsibilities. A good team can be compared to a machine, with every part vital if the machine is to work well. If one part is not working properly, the machine's effectiveness is reduced. In the same way, if one member of the team is not working well, the smooth running of the setting might be affected.

Minimising conflict and resentment

If all the adults in a setting carry out their work responsibilities and duties competently, there is less likely to be conflict between team members. Once one member of a team is not completing his or her work tasks, or is doing them badly, resentment can quickly build up as other team members have to work harder.

Avoiding errors and accidents

In some areas of work, the consequences of staff not fulfilling their work responsibilities and duties properly or completely are potentially dangerous. Examples include not supervising children carefully and not following hygiene procedures. Errors might also be made when someone is not doing their work properly, for example, a child might be given food to which he or she is allergic because someone did not record the allergy on a form.

Enhancing job security and career prospects

If you are able to carry out your responsibilities and duties well and are seen as being reliable, you will significantly improve your job security and career prospects. Staff who do not fulfil their job responsibilities, on the other hand, may even find that disciplinary action is taken against them. Employers have a legal right to expect that their employees will carry out the work they have been employed to do.

Increasing job satisfaction and motivation

Most people find that they are happier when they feel that they are working well and effectively. Staff who are not working hard at their jobs tend to have lower satisfaction levels and are therefore less motivated. Motivated staff are likely to produce a better atmosphere and to work more effectively with children.

Understanding your responsibilities

In order to be able to fulfil your work responsibilities, you need to be clear about exactly what you have to do and the standard to which you must carry out this work. One way in which you can find out about your work responsibilities is to ask for and read your job description. This should give you some guidance; if this is not enough, you might ask for more details from your line manager.

ACTIVE KNOWLEDGE

Using a chart similar to the one below list your main duties and responsibilities, and say why they are important.

Responsibilities and duties	Why these are important
Completing the register when children arrive and depart	To ensure that each child/young person is accounted for in the case of an emergency

Promptly sort out any duties and responsibilities which you are unsure about

If you are unsure about your job role, your job description can be helpful in giving you an overview of your role in a setting. However, there may be times when you need more specific information. For example, you may know that you are responsible for picking up some children from their schools and accompanying them to the club, but you also need to know for which particular children and for which schools you are responsible. This type of specific information is important if you are to be able to carry out your responsibilities competently. Knowing exactly what is expected of you can also help you and the setting in other ways, as you will not waste time getting something wrong, or 'treading on someone else's toes'.

By understanding your duties in advance, you may also feel that you can be more prepared and better organised. For example, if you know that on certain days you are responsible for preparing drinks and snacks, you might start the session by checking that there are enough clean beakers.

Good communication and understanding of who is responsible for what are important in maintaining children's safety. Missing children or accidents due to poor supervision are sometimes the result of inadequate communication, with one person thinking that someone else is responsible.

Clarifying your responsibilities and work duties is therefore important. Although your line manager is responsible for making sure you understand what you need to do, you must also take the initiative and check that you understand. If you are new to a setting but have worked in another establishment, do not assume that the same policies and procedures will be used – each setting has its own way of working.

Report your progress and any difficulties to colleagues and participate in team meetings

It is good practice to keep colleagues up to date about aspects of your work, for example, if you have had difficulties managing a task or have had some success with a child with particular needs. This helps everyone in the setting to stay informed, which is essential, especially between team meetings. When everyone in the setting shares information about their work and progress, staff are able to support each other and managers are able to identify recurring difficulties which might indicate that staff training is needed.

Awareness of others' work also helps when a staff member is absent, as others then know what needs to be done. It could be, for example, that before going off sick a playworker had promised to carry out a particular activity with a group of children.

In some cases, a setting might be adopting a new policy or strategy. Regular feedback among colleagues could allow them to consider its advantages and areas of development.

The importance of regular team meetings

Team meetings are essential if staff are to pull together and share information. Snatching odd words here and there is rarely enough to be able to discuss issues or to make proper plans. Team meetings allow everyone in the setting to listen to the same information and to comment on it at the same time.

Many settings have to hold team meetings after hours or before sessions start. It can be tempting to hold very short and very irregular meetings. Although this approach may seem to save time, in the long run it tends not to be effective as people's ideas and feelings do not get aired. It can also mean that staff become very ineffective and disorganised. Motivated and effective organisations and teams tend to be those that have regular team meetings.

Regular team meetings are essential

Participating effectively in team meetings

For team meetings to be useful, everyone must attend and do so with some enthusiasm. Be ready to contribute as well as to listen to others' ideas.

Keys to good practice: Participating in team meetings

Do:
✓ read anything that has been given to you beforehand
✓ listen carefully to what is being said
✓ keep your comments to the point
✓ keep your ideas positive
✓ put forward your suggestions concisely
✓ acknowledge other people's suggestions
✓ respect others' points of view
✓ be ready to compromise and go along with the majority view.

Don't:
✓ be late
✓ switch off
✓ talk while someone else is speaking
✓ say nothing at the time and then gossip and complain to others afterwards
✓ nit-pick and comment just for the sake of it
✓ be critical of others or make personal remarks
✓ fidget and watch the clock.

PORTFOLIO EVIDENCE

Think of a recent occasion when you participated at a team meeting. Explain how you contributed to this meeting and why it is important that all team members are willing to put their views forward. You could write this up on an evidence sheet and present it as portfolio evidence for this element.

CONSOLIDATION

Think of all the ways in which you contribute to the work of your team and also how the other team members contribute. Make a note of one positive contribution that each team member makes and raise these at your next team meeting to reinforce good practice.

As well as being a good team member, you also need to have the skills and knowledge to be able to support your colleagues. These are essential when you are involved in or responsible for managing the setting.

This section looks at some of the skills and knowledge that are needed to monitor others' work and provide guidance and feedback.

What you need to demonstrate you can do

- Provide comment and constructive criticism to your colleagues in a manner which identifies good practice and reinforces their self-confidence
- Offer helpful support to your colleagues when they need it
- Share information with your colleagues which helps them to improve their work
- Show that you value diversity and will challenge discrimination and prejudice in your work with and support for colleagues

Provide comment and constructive criticism to your colleagues

Commenting on work and providing feedback to others

An important part of teamwork is to provide the team with feedback and comments. If given sensitively, feedback can give people reassurance and recognition for their work, as well as help them to feel that they can ask for help and guidance. Positive feedback should always be sincere. It is a good idea to comment first on what has impressed you about the person's work or development.

Positive feedback can benefit everyone in the setting. It helps to:

- motivate individual members of staff
- give people further confidence
- encourage people to take on more responsibilities
- make people feel valued
- create a friendly atmosphere
- maintain communication
- boost overall morale in the setting
- improve staff retention.

The importance of constructive criticism

Alongside positive feedback, you will also need sometimes to pass on concerns or to query aspects of practice. This is not always an easy thing to do, especially if you have a close working relationship with someone, or if the person is 'senior' to you or older than you. This part of your role, however, is just as essential as providing positive feedback; if you do not address issues as they arise, more serious problems might result and your abilities to supervise would be questioned. The following diagram outlines why constructive criticism is so important.

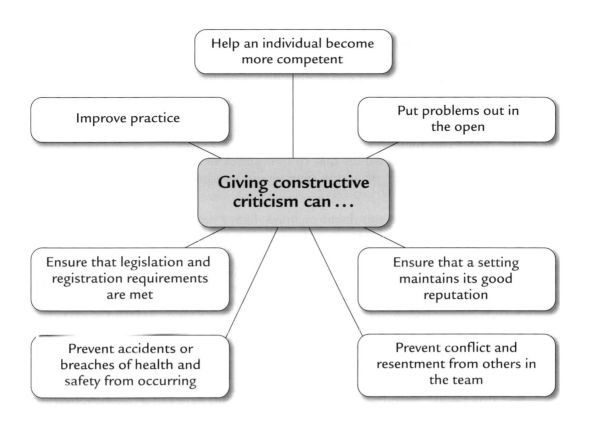

Giving constructive criticism can...

- Help an individual become more competent
- Improve practice
- Put problems out in the open
- Ensure that legislation and registration requirements are met
- Ensure that a setting maintains its good reputation
- Prevent accidents or breaches of health and safety from occurring
- Prevent conflict and resentment from others in the team

Giving constructive criticism

Feedback and constructive criticism must be passed on effectively and sensitively. If mishandled it will leave people feeling negative and demotivated. When you have some criticisms to make, try to ensure that these are discussed in private and at an appropriate time. Begin by making the person feel at ease, and comment on areas of their work that are good or improving. Then talk about the difficulties or concerns that you have. Most people find that an open approach is usually effective as the team member or volunteer does not feel that anything underhand is going on.

When bringing up concerns or difficulties, start by exploring whether the person concerned is aware of any problems, or has suggestions to resolve the difficulty. This allows you to get additional information that may include factors of which you are not aware. For example, an item of equipment may be broken, or the person may be spending time on another task.

Once you have explored the difficulty, explain or agree on how the matter is to be moved forwards. This can often be done verbally, but in some situations you may judge it necessary to record what has been agreed, such as further staff training. It is usually a good idea to agree also on a time when the matter discussed can be reviewed. Try to end the discussion on a positive note, as the person may otherwise concentrate only on the negative aspects of what has been said.

Advice and guidance

In some cases, people will need advice and guidance to help them manage their job role. Check before offering advice and guidance, otherwise the person you give it to may not follow it but instead may resent the fact that you have given it. For example, 'I think that there's a quicker way of doing that. Would you like me to show you?'

Training

You might realise that a person would benefit from some training in order to work more effectively. As with providing advice and guidance, discuss this with the person before organising the training. When people feel that they have been 'sent', they are less likely to benefit from training.

Share information with your colleagues which helps them to improve their work

There will be times when you will need to share information with colleagues so that they can do their work more effectively. For example, you might need to pass on some background information about a child which will help a playworker to understand the child's behaviour. There are many types of information that might be helpful, and it is your role to identify it and pass it on promptly.

Whenever you share information with someone, make it clear to them whether or not the information is confidential, so that it is not repeated to others by accident.

Types of information that you might need to share include:

- information about a child's circumstances or state of health (this is likely to be confidential)
- circulars or updates about current practice
- information about where to access further resources or equipment
- information about training courses on offer.

PORTFOLIO EVIDENCE

Think about some information that you have recently shared with a team member.

1 Why was it important that this information was passed on to them?
2 Explain why holding back information can sometimes damage relationships in teams.

Record this on an evidence sheet and submit it to your assessor.

Show that you value diversity and will challenge discrimination and prejudice

The staff team should all work together on specific aspects relating to the children and young people in their care. For example, they should have a consistent approach to behaviour agreements, challenging inappropriate comments, and acknowledging and meeting dietary needs. They should receive regular training and development opportunities to enhance their knowledge and understanding of important issues surrounding diversity. You may be able to access diversity courses from your local play forum or Children's Services, or you could join with another setting to invite in a speaker. As a team you should have a positive and consistent approach to actively promoting and implementing equality of opportunity and anti-discriminatory practice.

The Ofsted Standard 9 relates to this (see page 204).

✓ **ACTIVE KNOWLEDGE**

Look at the Ofsted guidance in Standard 9 (Scottish National Care Standard 8; see page 344) and discuss it at your next team meeting. Use the meeting to reflect on the work of your team and identify areas of good practice and areas for development. Remember to record this and review it regularly.

Valuing diversity

Diversity is essential in the workplace. In the same way that you should be valuing and encouraging social and cultural diversity, you should also understand that people will work in different ways and will bring to a setting their own ideas and values. You need to accept that other playworkers will work and relate to children in their own way, and that this in itself is a huge bonus in a play setting. It allows children to see that teamwork means working alongside people who have different styles. It also means that the team is more likely to be able to meet the varying needs of those with whom they work, as different children and parents will be able to identify with the styles of different team members.

Challenging discrimination and prejudice

As well as valuing diversity, you should also be aware of the need actively to challenge discrimination and prejudice. Make sure that colleagues are aware of your setting's equal opportunities and diversity policies and that these are being followed. If colleagues confide any difficulties they are having, let them know that you are supportive of them. Be ready to challenge or question practice if you feel that it encourages discrimination or prejudice. Never ignore it, even if challenging a person's behaviour leads to disciplinary action against a member of staff or talking to parents about their attitudes.

✓ **ACTIVE KNOWLEDGE**

Research task:

1 What is your work setting's policy on equal opportunities?
2 Do you have a complaints procedure?
3 How is everyone in the setting made aware of the procedures and policies?

- the child's or young person's needs are met
- the child's or young person's wishes are taken into consideration.

The parents and carers have rights, but they also have responsibilities. These are explained in the Children Act. One responsibility is to keep their children safe and secure from personal harm.

In all child protection investigations the Act states that:

- the child must be consulted about any decisions that are made
- wherever possible, the child or young person should be within their family (unless it would put the child in danger)
- parental responsibility must be taken into consideration
- the assessment framework guidelines about time limits for the different stages of an investigation must be followed.

The Common Assessment Framework

Each local authority will have a Local Safeguarding Children Board (LSCB). If a case of abuse against a child is being investigated, the committee will be made up of relevant people in the child's life. These may include the family doctor (GP), the social worker, the teacher or head teacher, the child protection officer from the police, etc. This committee must follow set guidelines laid down in the Common Assessment Framework. See Unit PW6, page 6, for further information on the Common Assessment Framework.

The Children Act 2004 updated the procedures for safeguarding children by encompassing the government paper 'Every Child Matters'. This focuses on the five outcomes for children:

- be healthy
- stay safe
- enjoy and achieve
- make a contribution
- achieve economic well-being.

All organisations involved in providing services to children – and this includes playwork – will team up in new ways to share information. LSCBs are designed to help ensure that key agencies work together effectively. Members of the LSCBs include local authorities, health bodies, the police and other agencies. The Common Assessment Framework now supersedes the assessment framework.

Policies and procedures

Each setting will have policies and procedures that playworkers must follow if they suspect abuse is occurring. These will be in line with the national standards set by the DfES.

The policies of your setting will have a section on child protection. A setting's policy on child protection will usually start with a statement and then include several areas, for example, those shown in the following list.

- Excluding known abusers – this section will state the conditions and requirements for all workers (paid and voluntary). It will include the requirement that all workers will be checked with the Criminal Records Bureau, known as a CRB check.
- Responding to a child arriving with injuries – this will explain the setting's procedure that will need to be followed.
- Responding appropriately to suspicion of abuse – this will explain how the setting will respond and whom will be informed.
- Keeping records – this explains in detail the records that will need to be completed and kept.
- Liaising with other bodies – this section gives details of the other agencies and bodies that will become involved, for example, social services and the NSPCC.
- Supporting the family – this explains how the staff and setting will support and work with the family.

ACTIVE KNOWLEDGE

Look at your policies to check:

- who the designated member of staff is
- what you should do if you suspect abuse
- what your specific responsibility is.

The role of the playworker

As a playworker you will have a unique relationship with the children and young people in your care. It will be closer to the relationship of an adult friend than the authoritarian relationship that they form with adults in school. It is important to develop this by getting to know the children and young people, actively listening to them, showing that you value what they say and showing that you care about them. With some children, where communication barriers exist, you can show this by your actions as well as your interactions. It is important that you use words that these children can understand and that you show patience in interpreting what they are trying to communicate to you.

The unique position that you are in will enable you to observe unobtrusively children's and young people's physical and emotional condition, for example, when they are carrying out routine tasks and activities. This will give you the opportunity to discuss, investigate and monitor conditions in a sensitive manner. It is important that you are aware of the policies and procedures of your setting and that you implement them correctly should you suspect abuse.

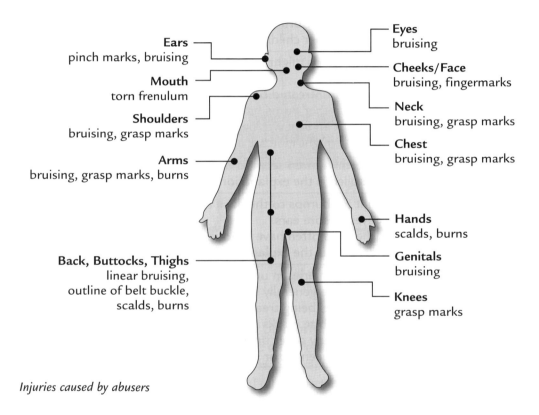

Injuries caused by abusers

Bullying

Bullying used to be thought of as inevitable in schools, but this attitude is now changing as people are beginning to understand the damage that bullying can cause. Bullying is any act of deliberate hostility that causes the victim distress. This includes verbal abuse and emotional intimidation such as 'sending someone to Coventry', as well as physical acts of violence.

According to Kidscape, a leading charity in preventing abuse and bullying, persistent bullying can cause the following.

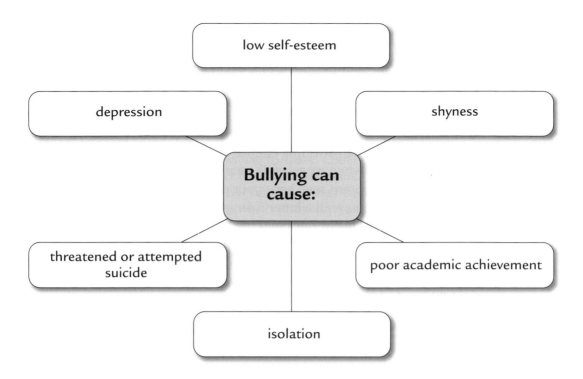

As well as looking out for signs of abuse, therefore, you should also be looking out for signs of bullying, especially if you are looking after children who come straight from school.

Watch for:

- children who do not take the shortest and most convenient route to the setting
- children who do not want to use the school bus
- children who come in looking frightened and dishevelled
- withdrawn behaviour
- unexplained bruises or scratches
- unexplained changes in behaviour
- children who say that they are not enjoying school.

Bullying can do untold emotional damage to children. It is essential that bullying is not allowed to occur in play settings. Be aware of children who might dominate others and who put others down by calling them names or by not listening to their ideas. When drawing up 'ground rules' with children, you may like to ask them to consider bullying as an issue.

Neglect

Identifying neglect

You may suspect that children are being neglected when adults fail to meet the needs of children and young people in their care. Neglect can include not ensuring the health, safety and well-being of the child or young person and not protecting him or her. However, these signs are sometimes due to poor parenting skills.

Indication	What to look for
Physical signs	In younger children there will be few physical signs; but older children may harm themselves and may take or smoke harmful substances. Look out for self-destructive behaviour: for example, self-mutilation by tattooing themselves, denying themselves food or taking harmful substances. These attention-seeking devices are ways of crying out for help. In severe cases, older children might even try to take their own lives.
Emotional signs	Children who are emotionally abused have very low self-esteem and confidence. They may be attention-seeking and look for popularity in inappropriate ways. Look out for children who seem very lonely or who act as the 'clown' to gain popularity. Consider whether children are particularly in need of attention or are clingy. Look out for children who are very worried and anxious, and who fear making mistakes. Consider whether children are very sensitive to criticism, or seem to have developed a 'don't care' attitude.
Behavioural signs	Children with low self-esteem might be extremely attention-seeking and 'needy', wanting a lot of adult time and support. Look out for children who burst into tears for no particular reason, or who seem very tense and anxious.

What to look out for

Remember that not all these indicators mean a child has been abused. Those who suffer emotional abuse are more likely to suffer other forms of abuse too. Bullying can also be classed as emotional abuse, depending upon the form it takes.

CASE STUDY

You set out an activity where the children are making passports. You ask the children to paint a picture of themselves. You notice Jade, aged 10, has painted herself looking solemn and very unattractive. She tells you that she looks like this at home and that her father has told her she is fat and ugly like her mum.

1 How would you respond to this?
2 Would you report it, or record and monitor it?

Sexual abuse

A range of indicators may lead you to suspect sexual abuse. Some you may observe and others you may just become aware of. Examples are listed in the following table.

Possible physical indicators	Possible behavioural indicators
Itchiness or discomfort in the genital or anal area Sexually transmitted diseases Blood stains on underwear Bruises or scratches on genital or anal area, or buttocks Bite marks on thighs and buttocks Abnormal swelling Frequent visits to the toilet In girls: ● pregnancy ● vaginal discharge In boys: ● pain when urinating ● penile discharge ● penile swelling	Excessive preoccupation with sex – always referring to sexual issues Eating or sleeping problems Excessive masturbation Sexual knowledge above the child's developmental level Not wanting to be with certain people Oversexualised behaviour that is not appropriate to the age or development level of the child Knowledge and use of sexually explicit language that is beyond the age and stage of development of the child Low self-esteem or lack of self-confidence Withdrawn and unnaturally quiet behaviour Anxiety and taking great care what they say to you

In matters of possible abuse it is important not to jump to conclusions. For example, just because a child is visiting the toilet more often than usual it does not automatically mean a child has been abused. The child may just have drunk a lot or have an infection.

CASE STUDY

You are sitting outside eating a picnic near some trees with Joel, aged 7. Joel tells you that he plays dens with some big boys in the woods near his house and they give him money and sweets every time he goes with them.

1 What might spring to mind?
2 What questions might you ask him?
3 If you are still concerned by his reply, whom would you tell?

✓ ACTIVE KNOWLEDGE

Try writing an imaginary report on the above case study. This will help you to understand how difficult it is to word a report and to keep it factual.

Summary

During your time as a playworker you may need to assess children and young people who you suspect are being abused. The abuse may be physical and more obvious or it may be sexual or emotional. These two types of abuse are sometimes harder to detect. The abuse may also involve neglect or bullying.

Whatever the form the suspected abuse takes it is important to be aware of the correct procedures. Your first concerns will be for the child or young person, especially if he or she is in need of medical attention or in personal danger. In these circumstances you must act quickly. However, you may just have suspicions and then you will need to discuss your concerns. You may need to observe and monitor the indicators until you have the required evidence to report the issue.

Think about it

Think about the situations below and decide which type of abuse you may suspect.

1 The weather has been very hot for a few days and a girl aged 7 years comes to the play centre wearing a backless top. Her shoulders and arms are very red and the skin is peeling. She tells you that she had to stay outside in the back yard for the whole of the day before as her mother had a friend round.
2 Josh is playing on the rope swing when his tee-shirt rides up and you notice a range of different coloured bruises on his lower back.
3 Bhavna, who is 12 years old, comes in for a drink. As she sits down she winces and lowers herself slowly on to a chair. She says that she bruised her private parts when she fell over at a family wedding at the weekend.

Consider any signs and indicators of possible abuse in the light of other information about the child

Other types of information to be considered

When a holistic view is taken of the child or young person other contributing factors will be looked at in line with the Common Assessment Framework. For example, the child might have sustained an accidental injury or several injuries through play, or other aspects of their circumstances and life may need to be taken into account.

These factors, which may make a child or young person more vulnerable to abuse, are called predisposing factors. They are often caused by difficulties and stresses in an adult's life or the adult's previous experiences. These may affect the adult's attitude to the child or young person, making the adult less tolerant of him or her. For example, the carer could:

- be living in crowded conditions, perhaps sharing accommodation or living in a flat that is too small for the family
- lack parenting skills – perhaps the carer did not have a positive role model in his or her own parents and so is unaware of a parent's responsibilities
- be financially insecure, surviving on very little money and unable to provide adequately for the children
- be on medication or drugs, which may be due to a medical condition or drug dependency
- be socially isolated with no family or friends living nearby to talk to and help the carer
- be used to physical punishment as a method of control and be repeating this with his or her own family

- lack love and attention so may be very unhappy and feel deserted and sad
- be immature and resent the responsibility of a child
- have been abused himself or herself when younger and have unmet needs of his or her own
- be experiencing relationship difficulties and be emotionally drained
- resent the child as the child could be less pleasing than the carer had hoped, for example, due to the child's gender (the carer might have desperately wanted a girl and had a boy, or the other way round) or to the child having a medical condition or disability.

Considering explanations and attitudes

It is always important to consider the explanation given both by the carer and by the child or young person to see whether these are consistent with the injury or indicator. Any inconsistencies will need further investigating.

In some cases the attitude of the carer can give cause for concern, especially if the carer blames the child or someone else for the injury or indicator, or if the carer admits to being responsible but does not show concern, remorse or guilt. If the carer denies anything is wrong or justifies the injury by saying that the child deserved it this would also give cause to suspect some form of abuse.

Think about it

Read through the following scenarios and ask yourself the following questions.

- Is it abuse?
- Could there be another explanation?
- Should you investigate further or report it?

1 You are listening to two children aged 10 and 12 who are having a conversation close by. You hear one child say, 'My daddy baths me late every Saturday night after my mum has gone to work. When he dries me he hurts me because he tickles me but I laugh so that he stops.' The other child says, 'I always bath and dry myself.'
2 You overhear a conversation between two single mums about working in the evenings at the local bingo hall. One says, 'I always get a taxi home.' The other says, 'Oh, I don't pay for a taxi. I get the babysitter to collect me when the kids are in bed.'
3 You notice a long thin mark right across Tom's back when his shirt rides up as he bends down to tie his trainer lace. You enquire if it hurts and how he did it. Tom looks uncomfortable and eventually says he fell against the door.

The impact of abuse on children and young people

Abuse can cause trauma and distress to the victims. This can affect all aspects of the child's or young person's development (physical, intellectual, linguistic, emotional and social). Some effects will be obvious and easily recognisable; others will be hidden and will often lie dormant until they come to the surface at some stage in the person's life, not necessarily during childhood. The most significant damage will almost certainly be to the self-image and self-worth of the child. To be abused is a degrading experience and will affect the potential of any child or young person.

Children who have been abused may show one or more of the following types of behaviour.

Type of behaviour	Example of behaviour
Withdrawn	May become isolated within a group May not communicate with peers
Aggressive and forceful	May be abusive and violent towards others May always want to take charge in situations and tell others what to do
Negative and unco-operative, unable to enjoy things	May be pessimistic and refuse to do things May be sad and unhappy with things and with life
Showing symptoms of stress, and physical and emotional problems	May have eating disorders, wet the bed, have temper tantrums and respond inappropriately to situations
Having low self-image and self-esteem	May think they cannot do things, that their thoughts and opinions are not worth mentioning
Unable to concentrate	May flit from one thing to another
Pseudo-macho	May talk with a knowledge above their years on certain adult topics and give an air of independence above the typical development level

These are just a few examples, and not all children and young people displaying these behaviours will have been abused. Often they respond in extremes and flit from one type of behaviour to the opposite extreme.

The relationship that playworkers should build with the children and young people in their care should be one in which the children and young people feel valued and listened to. The children and young people should feel at ease to exchange ideas, opinions and information, but also feel they can express their emotions (positive and negative) and thoughts freely to people who are understanding, caring and non-judgemental.

It is vital that the children and young people feel comfortable and safe in the play setting. Playworkers can aid this process by:

- working closely with parents and carers
- providing a welcoming, friendly atmosphere
- having a range of workers who are friendly, approachable and caring
- providing a range of play experiences where children and young people are able to express, show and deal with their emotions.
- promoting personal safety for children in discussion and activities
- encouraging and praising children to help them gain self-confidence and self-esteem.

Take action which is appropriate to the significance of the signs and indicators

> **Keys to good practice: Taking action if you suspect abuse**
>
> ✓ Take the child or young person somewhere more private to talk to him or her (be careful not to put yourself at risk).
> ✓ Monitor and record your suspicions and actions.
> ✓ Use the correct reporting forms and a body map to record the position of the injury if you suspect physical abuse.
> ✓ Follow the correct procedures of your setting.
> ✓ Inform your designated member of staff or, if that is you, report on your concerns.

Follow agreed procedures for confidentiality at all times

Your policies and procedures will have a section on confidentiality. It is important that you are aware of these and follow them as they will have been written with the Children Act and the Data Protection Act in mind (see Unit PW6, pages 5 and 8).

You should not discuss any details, suspicions or known facts with anyone not connected with the case, and this may include the rest of your team. They may be aware that there is a child protection referral or enquiry but the details must not be shared. Failure to follow procedures could jeopardise the safety of the child or young person as well as the case against the perpetrator. It would also mean severe disciplinary measures for you.

> **CONSOLIDATION**
>
> By now you should be aware of the importance of you and your team being able to recognise and identify signs of suspected abuse.
>
> Recall a time when you observed or heard something that raised your concerns even though, on checking it out, you realised it was not actual abuse. Describe this situation in a reflective account or in a professional discussion with your assessor and use it as portfolio evidence.
>
> You could also use a team meeting or training event to check out your team's knowledge of possible abuse in the form of a discussion based on a simple quiz or true/false exercise.

Respond to a child's disclosure of abuse

By reading the previous section you will have confirmed your good practice or increased your knowledge about how to recognise signs of possible abuse. This section relates to the techniques and strategies you should use when you respond to a disclosure of abuse.

What you need to demonstrate you can do

- Respond promptly and calmly to the child's disclosure of abuse
- Make it clear to the child that other people appropriate to the situation will have to be informed
- Give the child appropriate reassurance and support
- Communicate at the child's pace, without exerting pressure to reveal more than the child wishes to
- Record information on the disclosure accurately as soon as possible
- Follow agreed procedures for confidentiality at all times

Respond promptly and calmly to the child's disclosure of abuse

What disclosure means

As a playworker it is important that you fully understand the meaning of the term disclosure. The dictionary definition of disclosure is to expose, to reveal or to lay open. In matters of child protection, disclosure of abuse by a child or young person means that the child or young person has told you or given you clues that lead you to suspect that he or she has been or is the victim of some kind of abuse.

There are two types of disclosure:

- full disclosure – when a child or young person tells someone that he or she has experienced or is experiencing abuse
- partial disclosure – when a child or young person partly tells someone that he or she has experienced or is experiencing abuse. It may be that the child gives a hint or clues, or just some of the information.

If children feel confident they are more likely to disclose abuse

Look at the examples below and decide whether the disclosure is full or partial.

- A 13-year-old girl tells you that she is feeling sick every morning and cannot eat her breakfast.
- A 12-year-old boy shows cigarette burns to the group and, knowing that you can hear, explains that his cousin did this to him and that he has them all over his body, even in parts he would not show.
- A 12-year-old girl tells you she is pregnant and that her uncle is the father.
- A 7-year-old boy tells you that he is frightened of his stepfather and he hides in the cupboard from him.

In the first instance this is partial disclosure – the girl has told you about the symptoms but not admitted to the cause. The second instance is full disclosure – the boy has said what it was and who did it. The third instance is full disclosure. If the same girl had come to you and told you that she hadn't had a period for six weeks, it would be partial disclosure. The fourth instance is partial disclosure. If the child had told you that his stepfather chased him and hit him with a belt, it would be full disclosure.

Whatever the type of disclosure, it is a very brave thing to admit abuse. The child or young person might have already tried to tell someone else, possibly at home. The child might not have been believed, or might have been told it is his or her own fault or been ignored. It will therefore be twice as difficult the next time.

Think back to when you were a child and you did something that you had to admit to, for example, breaking or losing something of value to your family. Think how difficult it was to admit to this. Now imagine you had to tell someone something of a sexual nature. Consider whom would you tell and how would you tell them.

As a playworker you may never have a child disclose abuse to you. However, you must know how to handle this type of situation in case it does happen. A prompt, calm and sensitive approach will help the child or young person. By following the policies and procedures of the setting you will be able to support the child or young person through this very difficult period.

Responding promptly to disclosure

A prompt response is required – this means you should act without delay.

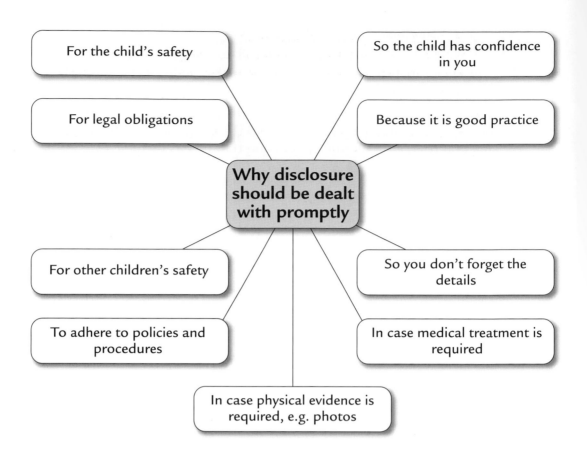

For the child's safety

For legal obligations

So the child has confidence in you

Because it is good practice

Why disclosure should be dealt with promptly

For other children's safety

To adhere to policies and procedures

So you don't forget the details

In case medical treatment is required

In case physical evidence is required, e.g. photos

The welfare and well-being of the child is vitally important and a prompt response will help ensure the child is put in no further danger.

Responding calmly to disclosure

By keeping calm you will maintain a professional attitude, even though you may feel very anxious and even frightened for the child or young person. It will help ensure that the situation is not made worse and will also help the child not to get unnecessarily upset. If you were to panic, this attitude could be passed on to the child or young person.

By remaining calm you will be able to remain objective. This will help you to think logically and to pass on information clearly and accurately, as stated in your setting's policies and procedures. It is easy to make mistakes when you panic.

Make it clear to the child that other people will have to be informed

It is your duty to inform others as appropriate. Those who will need to be informed will include the designated member of staff for child protection. This person, which might be you, must follow the guidelines regarding informing others. By telling the child that you must inform others the child:

- is aware of your role as a playworker
- will now not feel betrayed when you do bring in other people
- knows that something will be done to sort out the problem so you will build trust and respect.

Because it is your legal obligation to tell others, you will need to explain to the child exactly whom in the setting you will need to inform. You should explain that you and they will observe confidentiality and that nothing will be passed on to other children and their parents.

It is essential that children know that what they have said will not get them into any trouble, and that they were right to talk about it. This reassurance needs to be emphasised: by doing this, you are often breaking the primary control that abusers have over children.

Children may well ask that you do not tell anyone else. This is a promise you cannot make. You alone are unable to help such children and protect them. If you make a promise that you cannot keep, breaking that promise will break the child's trust. This means that you should tell abused children that in order to help them you will have to tell other people, but that these people will understand what the child is feeling, and will sort out the problem.

Some children may have mixed feelings about their abusers, and may ask what will happen to them. This type of question has to be answered truthfully, so it may be best to be vague in your answers – for example, 'I'm not really sure, but other people will look at what has happened and work out what should be done.'

By passing on information you are helping to prevent further abuse to the child and other children within the family or locality who may be at risk.

Remember to record the conversation accurately and promptly so that you do not forget or confuse the details.

Keys to good practice: Responding to disclosure of abuse

✓ Be aware of whom to discuss issues and suspicions with.
✓ Know how to maintain confidentiality and do not discuss the situation with anyone other than the designated person.
✓ Attend regular child protection training to renew and update knowledge and understanding.

It is important to remember exact wording and terminology when reporting abuse, for example, the words that the child uses for the different parts of the body, as well as any gestures the child makes towards certain parts of the body, such as pointing to the chest. It will help if you complete your paperwork as soon as possible after the disclosures. It may be needed should a prosecution take place so it must be accurate.

Give the child appropriate reassurance and support

A child or young person needs to be extremely brave to disclose abuse, so giving support and reassurance is vital. As a caring adult you need to show the child that disclosing the abuse is the right thing to do, and by supporting the child you show your approval.

Support and reassurance will help to make it as comfortable an experience as possible for the child so he or she does not feel alone and afraid. One of the best ways in which you can help children is to show that you are actively listening to what they are saying. You can do this by nodding your head, by making eye contact, and by making comments such as 'That must have been hard for you' or 'You have done the right thing in saying something.' It is also important to help children feel that they were not to blame for what has happened to them, as this is another hold that some abusers have over their victims. It is generally a good idea to let children say as much or as little as they wish, and avoid questioning them.

CASE STUDY

Harry is 10 years old, and has been hanging around asking Isabelle, the playworker, if he can help her. They sit together sharpening crayons, and he says that he likes helping like this. Isabelle says that she enjoys having someone around like this to chat to, and she is pleased that he wants to help her. They talk about school and then Harry says, 'I don't really mind school, it's better than being at home.' Isabelle says simply, 'What don't you like about being at home, then?' Harry says that he's always getting into trouble at home and that his stepdad gets cross with him. He carries on, 'Sometimes when I've done something really bad, like wet the bed, he has to get the belt out and it hurts and then that makes my mum cry.' Harry says, 'I try not to be bad, I really do, it's just that I'm not very good at being good.' Harry then starts to cry.

1 Write about how you would handle this situation. What would you say to Harry?
2 Why is it important that Harry does not feel guilty about what has happened to him?
3 How has the abuser managed to make Harry feel that he is to blame?

Communicate at the child's pace without exerting pressure

You should let the child or young person set the pace of the conversation so he or she feels more comfortable and more in control of the situation. The child or young person may not tell everything if he or she feels pressurised.

Listening carefully (active listening) will show that you are interested. It is helpful to make eye contact and to make appropriate responses to what they say. This may be by nodding your head or by a facial expression.

You should be aware that you should not press for details or ask leading questions – the child or young person will be interviewed at a later stage by a professional child protection specialist. This is also important so you do not go against legal requirements by saying or doing anything that may contaminate the evidence.

Record information on the disclosure accurately as soon as possible

Remember to record accurately and promptly so that you do not forget or confuse the details of the conversation.

Avoid contaminating the evidence

In some cases of child abuse, your record of a child's disclosure to you will be used as evidence against the abuser in a court of law. This is why it is crucial that you do not ask questions or lead the child in any way – if you did, the defence team might say that ideas were put into the child's mind.

Provide information about the possible abuse to the relevant person

If you suspect abuse, you should always inform a colleague or supervisor and follow the procedures of the setting. Most settings take their local authority guidelines and build these into their procedures. By following these procedures, you will be helping the child and also protecting yourself against accusations of maliciousness.

In cases where procedures have not been followed, abusers have sometimes not been convicted because of 'contamination of evidence'. In other cases, parents have sometimes been angered because cases have been badly handled, and it emerged afterwards that no abuse had been evident.

See page 262 for further information on providing information about the possible abuse to the relevant person according to your organisation's policies and procedures.

Ensure your information is accurate and up to date

If you have any doubts or suspicions about a child's behaviour, you should take them seriously and start evaluating whether abuse is the cause. Think carefully about what has made you suspect abuse, and then share these concerns with a colleague or supervisor – this person may also have had some background concerns about the child.

See page 257 for further guidance on ensuring your information is accurate and up to date.

Follow your organisation's procedures when responding to requests for reports and present your report to the relevant person in the required format

Your setting will have a child protection policy which will provide you with detailed information on the action to take if you suspect that a child or young person in your care is in danger of or is being abused. When you first start a job in a playwork setting the policy should have been explained and given to you to read.

If you are the responsible person (designated member of staff for child protection), it is important that you understand your role and that it is your responsibility to ensure that any staff working with you are also aware of the policy. The out-of-school care guidance in the national standards (see Standard 13) states in its focus:

> The welfare, safety and protection of children are paramount. Where the registered person and staff recognise their responsibility towards those in their care, they will be aware of their individual roles and understand the procedures they must follow if they have concerns about the welfare of a child.

The chart below shows the process that most settings follow.

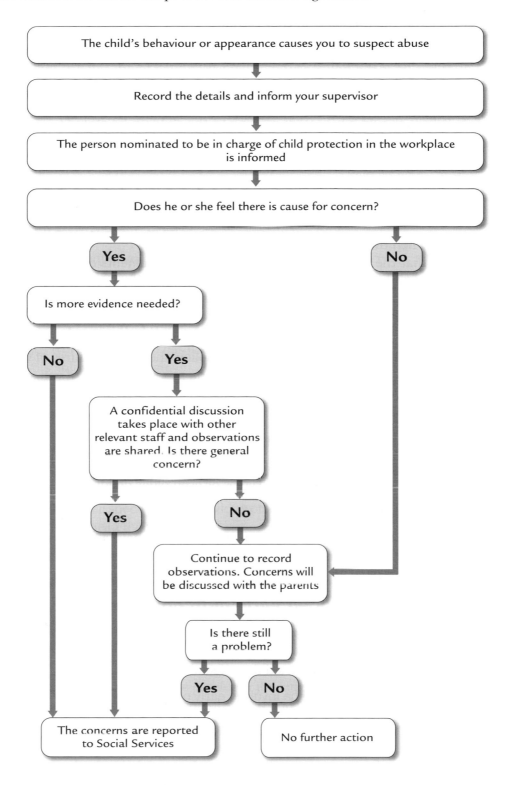

When presenting your report to the relevant person or agency, you should ensure it is in the required format and at the time requested. You should refer to your local authority or LSCB for required timings.

- concerns (note down whether these are your own, or those of someone else in your team)
- detailed descriptions of any behavioural changes or physical indicators (you could use a body map), with dates when these were noted
- details of what the child, or parents or carers have said
- action that has been taken so far (who has been contacted, what was said and who knows about the current situation).

You should include all the factual information that you have. You may then need to look at the wider context and include any predisposing factors that you are aware of and any previous monitoring or concerns that you have reported. These actual reports would be useful. You must ensure that you distinguish between directly observed signs and indicators, information from other people and opinion.

Follow agreed procedures for confidentiality at all times

It is important that as a professional person you follow the setting's guidelines and respect confidentiality. This means that you are careful whom you discuss your concerns with, where you discuss them and where you keep your notes and records. All records will need to be kept in a locked cabinet. They should only be available to those people directly concerned with the case on a need to know basis. This might include the child's key worker, the setting supervisor and the designated member of staff. It is important to follow the guidelines of the Data Protection Act.

ACTIVE KNOWLEDGE

Research the revised Data Protection Act and check this against the policies of your setting.

If you do not observe confidentiality and information is 'leaked out', you could find yourself faced with all kinds of legal problems. Your job would be in jeopardy, court proceedings could be hampered and the reputation of the setting could be damaged.

In some cases of suspected abuse, the signs of stress children show are caused not by abuse but by family upheaval or changes at school. People's lives can be ruined by gossip and false accusations. At every step of a suspected abuse case, confidentiality must be maintained. Victims of abuse have a right not only to protection, but also to their privacy. If you have reported a case of suspected abuse, do not talk about it to anyone, including colleagues, unless called upon to do so. This confidentiality must be maintained permanently, even after the case has been resolved. Any documents that are linked to the case should be securely handled and kept in a place where only those directly involved have access to them.

ACTIVE KNOWLEDGE

If you suspect a child is being abused, which of these people would you tell:

- your partner
- your colleague
- your line manager or supervisor
- a friend
- the registered person
- the admin worker
- the designated member of staff
- another child
- the child protection officer
- the midday supervisor at school?

CONSOLIDATION

Look at your setting's policies and procedures for reporting abuse to see if they comply with legal requirements. Check this out by either attending a training update or looking at the new guidelines for safeguarding children and the Common Assessment Framework on the DfES website (www.dfes.gov.uk). Update your own policies as necessary.

END OF UNIT KNOWLEDGE CHECK

1 Describe the behavioural signs you might observe if a young person has been sexually abused.

2 Name three common indicators of physical abuse.

3 If a child has been neglected what signs might you see?

4 What is the difference between a full disclosure and a partial disclosure?

5 Why should you respond calmly to a child's disclosure?

6 Why is it important to make it clear to a child who has disclosed abuse that you will have to inform others?

7 Why must you not exert pressure on the child during a disclosure?

8 When would you record the details of a disclosure?

9 Whom would you report the abuse to?

10 What legislation relates to confidentiality of information?

What you must know and understand

For the whole unit

K1: The importance of a healthy lifestyle to children's and young people's development

K2: The role that the playworker can play in encouraging and supporting a healthy lifestyle

K3: The basic stages of child development and the implications for:
- lifestyle
- nutrition
- risks to health
- common illnesses

For PW13.1

K4: Sources of information on a healthy lifestyle for children and young people and how to access these

K5: How to present information on healthy living to children and young people in an effective way

K6: How to stimulate children and young people to consider their own lifestyle and think of ways they could improve their health

K7: Levels and types of physical activity appropriate to children and young people according to their ages and stages of development

K8: Ways in which children and young people can increase their physical activity on a routine basis

K9: The importance of providing an effective role model for a healthy lifestyle

For PW13.2

K10: The types of meals and snacks which promote healthy eating

K11: Basic knowledge of food hygiene

K12: The importance of hydration to children and young people especially when they are taking part in physical play

K13: How to provide a satisfying, varied and balanced diet

K14: Refreshments that reflect cultural and specific needs

K15: How to respond to parents' wishes in regard to what their children should eat

K16: The importance of consulting children on the selection, preparation, serving and clearing away of food and drinks

K17: Examples of the use of food in wider activities

K18: The play setting's Healthy Eating Policy

K19: The play setting's procedures for preparing and storing food

---

Element PW13.1 | **Encourage and support a healthy lifestyle**

Children and young people must be aware of the importance of a healthy lifestyle if they are to develop into healthy adults. Playworkers need to engage with them to help them reflect on their present lifestyle, provide them with accurate, up-to-date information on risks to health, and create exciting opportunities for physical exercise.

What you need to demonstrate you can do

- Provide children and young people with accurate and up-to-date information on a healthy lifestyle
- Make children and young people aware of risks to their own health
- Encourage and support children and young people to consider their own lifestyles and identify ways to improve and maintain their own health
- Provide children and young people with opportunities to take part in physical activity

Provide children and young people with accurate and up-to-date information on a healthy lifestyle

Regular exercise is essential to sustain good health. The lifestyles that children establish in their early years can influence their health for the rest of their lives. Adults need to introduce ways in which children and young people can increase their physical activity on a regular basis. They also need to raise children's awareness by providing information on the benefits to them when they participate in physical activities.

Adults should ensure that children and young people are introduced to a wide range of physical activities to give the best possible chance of motivating them to establish a healthy lifestyle. One of the main ways of doing this is effective role modelling. If children and young people see adults enjoying physical pursuits they are much more likely to enjoy physical activities themselves and to maintain physical activity into later life. However, if physical play becomes too competitive some children will abandon the activity for fear that they might fail, so it is important to remember that the main focus should be on enjoyment.

Children and young people should be encouraged to choose any type of moderate or higher intensity physical activity, such as brisk walking, playing tag, jumping a rope or swimming, as long as it adds up to at least one hour a day. Children and adolescents who are just beginning to be physically active should start out slowly and gradually build to higher levels in order to prevent the risk of injury or feeling defeated from unrealistic goals. It is important that children and adolescents are encouraged to take up physical activities that interest them. This will help them establish an active lifestyle early on. Remember, if children find physical activity fun, it is likely that they will continue to exercise for years to come.

Children also need to be made aware of the benefits of healthy eating. Information on providing food that meets the nutritional needs of children and young people can be found in Section 13.2 (see page 276).

Make children and young people aware of risks to their own health

It is important to talk to children about potential risks without frightening them unnecessarily or causing them to lose confidence. You need to be aware of what the appropriate level of information is, based on their ages and stages of development. The work you do in helping children to keep themselves safe, particularly younger children, should be ongoing – regular reminders often work better than occasional activities.

Adults need to be aware of the pressures, particularly peer pressure, faced by children and young people. They may be around others who are smoking, drinking alcohol, using illegal drugs or engaging in under-age sexual activity. To help them avoid these activities they need to be fully informed of the consequences of participating.

How you present information on healthy living will influence the reaction you get from the children and young people and their level of commitment to the whole topic. You will need to raise their awareness of risks to their health. This should include information on protection from infections and avoiding substance abuse. You need to be aware that children are likely to be exposed to drugs and drug dealers at a very early age. It is important that you do not make the mistake of assuming that this is only the case if they live in disadvantaged areas of an inner city; it is just as likely in the suburban conurbations or indeed in very rural locations.

Simply telling young people not to take drugs is unlikely to be helpful and a heavy hand can be similarly futile. Playworkers are usually trusted by the young people in their care. Often they will overhear a stray comment that a skilful playworker will pick up on and use as an opportunity to reinforce the message.

There will be many opportunities to talk about potentially dangerous situations and these can be easily linked to a television programme, a book a young person is reading or a leaflet from the local health centre. It is better to make these conversations a matter of routine rather than wait until an incident occurs.

You need to be creative about how you can help children and young people identify ways of improving and maintaining their own health. For example, you could plan quizzes and competitions on ways to stay healthy, arrange visits to the local gym or involve young people in planning, preparing and cooking a healthy meal which they can then eat together at lunchtime. Playworkers must be well informed about the many risks to health and be prepared to talk openly and honestly to children and young people whenever the occasion arises.

Personal hygiene

Personal hygiene is an important element of keeping healthy. Encouraging good standards of personal hygiene is particularly important as children get older. Promoting self-care skills will help to raise their confidence and self-esteem and draw their attention to socially acceptable behaviour.

Playworkers need to be aware that there is a wide age range for the onset of puberty. Some girls will start their periods at the age of 10, while others will not be at that stage until they are closer to 14 years old. On average girls mature faster and earlier than boys.

The physical changes in their bodies are accompanied by a more adult body odour, and playworkers can help them to be aware of the need for closer attention to personal hygiene, especially after physical exercise. You will need to treat these issues sensitively but you must not avoid them as they can become a taboo subject and can result in unnecessary embarrassment or hurt feelings.

CASE STUDY

Mary, the playworker, has noticed that the children are being unkind to 11-year-old Ellie and they are calling her names and saying she smells. This is most unusual as Ellie is usually one of the most popular children in the group. Ellie is getting increasingly upset at these incidents so Mary takes Ellie to one side to talk about this. Ellie says she has baths every night, but when Mary asks she discovers that Ellie only changes her sweatshirt once a week.

1 What advice could Mary give Ellie?
2 How might a similar situation be avoided in the future?

It is sometimes hard for children to understand the need for good standards of personal hygiene as they cannot see germs. During a game, the temptation to run to the toilet and back without washing their hands is high: children do not want to 'waste' time washing their hands! It is vital that children do learn about personal hygiene, however, as this is part of developing respect for themselves and taking care of themselves.

There are several ways in which playworkers can help children learn about the importance of personal hygiene.

Being a positive role model

Children need to see you washing your hands thoroughly, and taking care of your appearance. This helps them to see that this is 'adult and mature' behaviour, and they are therefore more likely to copy it.

Activities that promote awareness of personal hygiene

It is possible to plan some activities that will help children to be aware of personal hygiene. Activities might include making perfumes and oils, or 'smell-testing' different toiletries and products. Visitors can also be invited in – a popular session with older children is a visit from beauty and skin-care advisers, who often bring free samples with them.

The use of disclosing tablets, which show where plaque is concentrated on teeth, can also be a fun activity, providing permission has been sought from parents or carers. You can also join in activities, quizzes, etc. organised by your local health promotion unit. Some manufacturers of body-care products, such as the Body Shop, offer guided tours around their factories: this can be a fun way for children to learn about personal hygiene.

Promoting independent self-care skills

As well as learning to respect and take care of their bodies, tasks in managing personal hygiene also help children to feel independent. This can boost children's

ACTIVE KNOWLEDGE

Find out where you can access up-to-date information on infections that affect young people such as meningitis, glandular fever and sexually transmitted diseases. How could the young people in your care protect themselves against these infections?

Encourage children and young people to consider their own lifestyles

Sources of information on a healthy lifestyle for children and young people should be readily available for them to access. Playworkers have a responsibility to ensure this is available, accessible and up to date in order to encourage children and young people to improve and maintain their health. It is impossible to do this alone so you need to be able to signpost effectively. Each local authority is required to create an online directory of services which is available to practitioners and the general public, so this would be an excellent starting point. If you are unsure how to access this directory, contact your local Children's Information Service and they will advise you.

Other sources of information could be suitable books, the local health education unit and the local leisure centre. You need to use a variety of media to provide information, advice and guidance on living a healthy lifestyle. These could include leaflets, books, videos, conversations, posters and, best of all, activities.

Provide children and young people with opportunities to take part in physical activity

Playworkers need to think carefully about how they provide children and young people with opportunities to participate in physical activity. It is easy to fall into the trap of thinking physical activity only takes place when they are running around outside. Many children and young people do not find 'sport' enjoyable and would much rather be left alone to sit indoors doing an activity, playing on the computer or reading a book. While there is nothing wrong in participating in these activities, there does need to be a balance with more physical opportunities. You might want to think of alternative types of activity that would be helpful in encouraging those who are not attracted to team games. These could include different forms of dance, judo, yoga or even aerobics.

There are many different types of physical activity that children can take part in

Think about it

Think about how you could encourage children to take part in physical activity. What alternative types of activity could you introduce into your setting that would be of interest to those boys and girls who do not enjoy taking part in team games?

CONSOLIDATION

Eight-year-old Emily lives in a third floor apartment with her mother and older brother. She has just started attending the out-of-school club and is settling in well. She has made a couple of friends and enjoys playing on the computer. She also spends a lot of time playing board games or watching television. She is a fussy eater and refuses to try new foods, so her main food intake while at the club consists of bread and butter and, if they are available, chips or crisps.

1 What are the main concerns with Emily's lifestyle?

2 How might you start to help Emily think about her lifestyle and ways in which she could improve her health?

Provide food and drinks to children and young people

Playworkers can influence how children and young people regard food and drinks and encourage them to develop healthy eating patterns. Staff in settings need to know how to give appropriate nutritional advice in a non-judgemental way, provide for special dietary needs and store food and drinks appropriately.

What you need to demonstrate you can do

- Provide food and drinks which are attractive and meet the nutritional needs of the children and young people
- Provide for special dietary and cultural requirements
- Prepare food and drinks in a way that meets parents' expressed wishes
- Ensure children and young people get access to food and drinks according to their needs
- Ensure the equipment, areas and methods used for storage, preparation, serving and clearing away meet legal and organisational requirements
- Encourage children and young people to consider the healthy choices in their food and drinks and the reasons
- Involve the children and young people in the selection, preparation, serving and clearing away of food and drinks

Provide food and drinks which are attractive and meet the nutritional needs of the children and young people

A balanced diet is important to ensure that children develop in a healthy way. Playworkers need to be positive role models and lead by example. It is important that children and young people learn about how nutrition can influence their health. When you give them meals and snacks you should ensure that you offer healthy options. You should encourage them to try different foods and raise their awareness of what foods are better for them. You also need to think about how food is laid out on the plate to ensure it looks attractive to children.

Promoting a balanced diet

To gain all the nutrients the body needs, children and young people have to eat a range of foods. This is because although most foods and drinks contain one or more kinds of nutrients, few foods and drinks will contain everything that the body needs. A varied diet is therefore needed to balance the body's needs – hence the term 'balanced' or 'nutritious' diet.

The five categories of nutrients are shown in the following diagram.

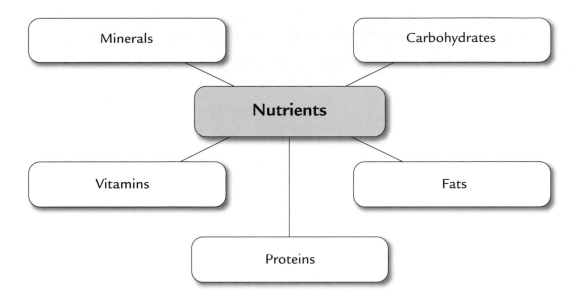

In addition to the five categories of nutrients, the body also needs water; although this is essential, it is not strictly considered a nutrient.

In order to be able to check that you are offering a balanced diet, it is useful to understand the role of the different nutrients, and also in which foods and drinks they are found. The table below shows the nutrients in common foods, and why these nutrients are needed.

Nutrient	Benefits to the body	Examples of foods
Carbohydrate	Gives energy.	Bread, pasta, flour, potatoes, yams, bananas, plantains, vegetables, sweet potatoes.
Protein	Helps the body to grow and repair cells. In children, protein is linked to growth.	Meat, eggs, fish, milk and dairy products, soya. Wheat, corn, oats, pulses (beans and peas) – these proteins need to be eaten with other foods to work well (as with beans on toast).
Fat	Gives energy and helps the body to absorb vitamins A and D.	Butter, margarine and vegetable oil as well as hidden fats in meat, fish and dairy products.
Vitamin A	Improves eyes and eyesight.	Carrots, milk, apricots, oily fish, margarine.
Vitamin B (there are a number of vitamins in the vitamin B group)	Needed for the nervous system; also helps release energy from other foods.	Bread, meat, yeast, pasta, flour, rice, noodles.

Nutrient	Benefits to the body	Examples of foods
Vitamin C	Needed for the skin and gums.	Oranges, lemons, grapefruit, blackcurrants, potatoes, kiwis.
Vitamin E	It is not fully understood how this vitamin is used.	Vegetable oils, green leafy vegetables, milk, nuts, wheatgerm.
Vitamin K	Helps blood to clot.	Most vegetables.
Vitamin D	Needed for the bones and teeth.	Milk, margarine, cheese, yoghurts and other dairy products.
Iron	Helps the blood to carry oxygen.	Red meat, broccoli, spinach, plain chocolate, egg yolk.
Calcium and phosphorus	Needed for the teeth and bones.	Milk, cheese, butter, yoghurts and other dairy products.
Fluoride	Helps to prevent tooth decay.	Water, sea fish.

As children's bodies are growing, they need foods that will give them plenty of nutrients and sufficient energy. The dietary needs of younger children and older children vary slightly. Younger children are not able to eat in large quantities: they need nutritious snacks provided for them, alongside main meals, in order that they can take in enough nutrients. Older children need plenty of protein to support their growth, with adolescent girls also needing to take in plenty of iron and calcium.

Children also have increasing energy requirements as they get older. The energy that food provides is measured in kilocalories or kilojoules. Some foods that are high in energy and favoured by children, such as crisps and sweets, are however low in other nutrients. This can mean that by filling up on these foods, children lose out on other essential nutrients. The energy requirements of children are shown in the table below.

Age	Energy (kcal)	
	Boys	Girls
4–6 years	1715	1545
7–10 years	1970	1740
11–14 years	2220	1845
15–18 years	2755	2110
Adults	2550	1940

Types of food, snacks and drinks

Wherever possible you should try to provide children with food, snacks and drinks that contain several nutrients. There are no 'set' rules as to what children can or cannot eat; the secret of a balanced diet is to eat a variety of foods that are high in nutrients. Foods that are highly processed tend to have fewer nutrients, as the manufacturing process tends to reduce the vitamin content. A frozen pizza with peppers, for example, will contain fewer nutrients than a home-made pizza, as the vitamins in the peppers will have been affected by the freezing process. This means that wherever possible you should aim to give children freshly prepared foods that contain a range of nutrients.

Meals

As well as making sure that meals are nutritious and contain a balance of nutrients, you also need to ensure they are tasty and attractive to children. Some foods are more popular than others, for example, pizzas, pasta, burgers and curries are all currently popular foods with children. Although many of these foods are often shop-bought, they can be made in settings with fresh and nutritious ingredients.

Main meals	Accompaniments	Desserts
Home-made pizza	Mixed green salad	Cheese and biscuits
Vegetable curry	Tomato salad	Fruit yoghurt
Lasagne	Rice, pepper and sweetcorn salad	Fresh fruit salad
Chicken drumsticks	Mixed bean salad	Strawberries and cream
Quiche	Grated carrot salad	Pineapple and kiwi salad
Spaghetti bolognaise	Pitta bread	Baked apples
Breaded fish	Naan bread	Rice pudding
Home-made beefburgers	Brown rice	Banana custard
Moussaka	Basmati rice	Home-made ice cream
Sausage casserole	Pasta with cheese	Fromage frais and fruit
Cauliflower and broccoli bake	New potatoes	Blackcurrant mousse
Nut roast	Mashed potatoes	Lemon mousse
Vegetarian 'meatballs'	Sweetcorn	
	Beans, peas, broccoli, carrots, cauliflower	
	Yams	
	Sweet potatoes	

Snacks

Most children need some snacks during the day as their energy requirements are quite high and they become hungry. Snacks can lead to children developing poor eating habits, however, if they are often offered foods that are high in fat, salt and sugar. Crisps, chocolates and biscuits are tasty and high in energy, but are low in nutrients. If children fill up on these type of snacks they may not be so hungry for the foods that will provide the nutrients. Gaining the taste for high-energy, low-nutrient foods may also cause children to become overweight when they are adults. Once they reach the age of about 17, the body is no longer growing and extra energy will be turned into fat. A healthy snack is therefore one that does not spoil children's appetites for their meals and that gives children some nutrients.

The following are examples of nutritious snacks:

- fresh fruits and vegetables, such as bananas, apples, oranges, kiwis, carrots
- nuts
- sandwiches
- popcorn
- yoghurt
- soups
- home-made ice creams and sorbets
- cheese and biscuits
- celery sticks filled with cheese
- cheese and pineapple sticks
- vegetables and dips.

Healthy snacks provide nutrients and don't spoil children's appetites

Drinks

As well as food, the body also needs water. Water is used in the body to support many vital functions, including digestion, flow of blood, temperature control and chemical balances. Alongside food and snacks, therefore, you should also be offering drinks. The best drink is water, although milk is also considered to be a good drink as it contains water and other nutrients such as calcium and vitamins. Fruit juices can also be provided for children, although these may be high in natural sugars. Sugary drinks are not considered to be as useful as they give children the taste for sweetness, and filling up on sugary drinks may reduce children's appetites for main meals. Sugary drinks and some fruit juices can also cause dental decay, as the sugar in them coats the teeth and turns into a weak acid.

Here are some ways to encourage children to drink water and milk:

- make sure that water is always available at mealtimes
- make sure that water is cool and fresh
- consider serving water with ice cubes
- consider serving water with thin slices of lemon or orange
- make fruit milkshakes with children
- make yoghurt drinks with children
- make hot or cold chocolate drinks.

✓ **ACTIVE KNOWLEDGE**

You have been asked to plan a picnic lunch for children going on an outing.

1 Write down the types of food that you would choose.
2 Explain how the foods you have chosen would provide children with a nutritious meal, while being easy and practical to eat.
3 What types of drinks would you provide?

Provide for special dietary and cultural requirements in line with parents' wishes

While planning food, snacks and drinks for children, you also need to be aware of any specific dietary requirements that they may have. Dietary requirements can vary considerably, so it is essential that you find out as much as possible from the parents or carers and the children.

If you are unsure whether or not a food should be given to a child, always ask – in some cases of food allergies, exposure to the allergen can be fatal. Information about children's dietary requirements should be carefully recorded, usually as each child first enters the setting, and those who prepare or give out food should be made aware of any restrictions or requirements. A notice may be put up in the kitchen to act as a constant reminder.

Dietary requirements can be put into five categories, although in some cases you might find that a child has more than one requirement, for example, a child may be diabetic and also vegetarian.

Special dietary requirements

Medical

Some children may be on a specific diet or have particular requirements because of a medical condition such as diabetes.

Allergic

Some children have allergies to specific foods, which means that they need to avoid them and any foods that might contain them. Common allergies include nuts, dairy products and strawberries. Some children may also be gluten-intolerant, which means that they have to avoid many products with cereals in them, such as wheat, barley, rye and oats.

Religious

Many religions have requirements about what food can be eaten and the way it is prepared. For example, pork and shellfish are not eaten by Jews and Muslims, and many Hindus are vegetarian.

Cultural

Children and their families may have food preferences based on their culture. This may also affect the way that food is served or eaten.

Ethical

Increasingly, people are becoming aware of how food is being produced. This means, for example, that some families will only eat organically grown food, or meat that has been 'ethically' raised and slaughtered.

Meeting religious, cultural and ethical dietary requirements

Meeting children's religious, cultural and ethical dietary requirements is of huge importance, as it is about respect. If playworkers are not prepared to meet a child's dietary requirements they are sending out a hidden message that they do not respect the child's family. You need to listen carefully to the feelings of parents and make sure that you try your utmost to meet their requirements. In cases where this might not be possible, or where you are unsure about how best to meet the requirements, you should always refer back to the parents or carers. For example, Muslims and Jews normally only use meat that has been slaughtered in a particular way, and buying in this might pose a problem for some settings. Parents or carers might therefore prefer to bring in meals for their children.

It is important not to make assumptions about dietary requirements. Some families follow some but not all of a religion's practices, for example, they may not fast, or they may not be completely vegetarian. The following table shows some of the dietary requirements of different religious groups.

Food	Muslim	Jew	Sikh	Hindu (mainly vegetarian)	Rastafarian (mainly vegetarian, although take milk products)
Lamb	Halal	Kosher	Yes	Some	Some
Pork	No	No	Rarely	Rarely	No
Beef	Halal	Kosher	No	No	Some
Chicken	Halal	Kosher	Some	Some	Some
Cheese	Some	Not with meat	Some	Some	Yes
Milk/yoghurt	Not with rennet	Not with meat; separate cooking dishes used for dairy products	Yes	Not with rennet	Yes
Eggs	Yes	No blood spots	Yes	Some	Yes
Fish	Halal	With fins, scales and backbones	Some	With fins and scales	Yes
Shellfish	Halal	No	Some	Some	No
Cocoa/tea/coffee	Yes	Yes	Yes	Yes	Yes
Fast periods	Ramadan	Yom Kippur			

Keys to good practice: Meeting children's dietary requirements

✓ Find out from parents or carers exactly what children can and cannot eat.
✓ Check the labels of all food products to make sure that the ingredients are suitable.
✓ Make sure that other staff are aware of particular children's dietary requirements.
✓ Always ask if you are unsure how to prepare food to meet religious requirements.
✓ Adapt recipes to meet dietary requirements whenever possible so that children do not always feel that they are 'different'.
✓ Do not make any assumptions about dietary requirements.

Sources of information about dietary requirements

There are many excellent sources of information about children's dietary requirements. If you are working with a child who has particular dietary requirements, it might be a good idea to find out more about these requirements, which might also mean getting ideas for recipes. Below is a list of possible sources of information:

- local library
- health promotion unit
- health visitors and dieticians
- cookbooks
- relevant websites

- videos
- parents, carers and community leaders
- specialist grocers
- local restaurants
- support groups and organisations, for example, the Diabetic Association.

Ensure children and young people get access to food and drinks according to their needs

It is very important that children and young people have access to food and drinks as appropriate to their needs throughout the day. Water (chilled if possible) should be freely available to children. This is especially important in warm weather and when children are involved in physical activities to avoid dehydration.

It would be good practice for children to have access to a refrigerator where they can store any food or drinks they bring from home. This could be separate from the kitchen area (if you have one) and exclusively for the children to use. This could then be used to generate discussions about why food should be stored in this way.

ACTIVE KNOWLEDGE

Describe how your setting provides access to food and drinks. Is the access appropriate to the needs of the children throughout the day? If not, how could it be improved?

Ensure the equipment, areas and methods used for storage, preparation, serving and clearing away meet legal and organisational requirements

Anyone who handles food carries a lot of responsibility: food poisoning is a real threat to health. It is estimated that 40 people die of food poisoning each year, and children and young people are a vulnerable group. The threat to public health posed by food poisoning means that legislation relating to food handling is very strict.

Settings should make sure that their practice conforms to the 1995 Regulations under the Food Safety Act 1990. The regulations specify that anyone handling food should be supervised, trained or instructed in the handling of food, at a level appropriate to the task they are carrying out. The level of food hygiene in a play setting that provides food should be similar to that of a restaurant. Settings that do not comply with the regulations can be closed by the environmental health team.

Principles of good food hygiene

There are three principles of good food hygiene:

- prevent bacteria from reaching the food
- stop the bacteria in the food from spreading and multiplying
- destroy the bacteria.

Food poisoning

Food poisoning occurs when the body takes in certain bacteria in the food. Food poisoning cases are usually the result of poor hygiene practices, which have either allowed bacteria to reach the food or have allowed the bacteria already in the food to spread. The most common symptoms of food poisoning are vomiting and diarrhoea.

Preventing bacteria from reaching food

Bacteria are all around us and on us! This means that very good standards of hygiene are required to stop the bacteria from reaching food. The commonest way that bacteria reaches food is on people's hands.

The diagram below shows ways to prevent bacteria from reaching food.

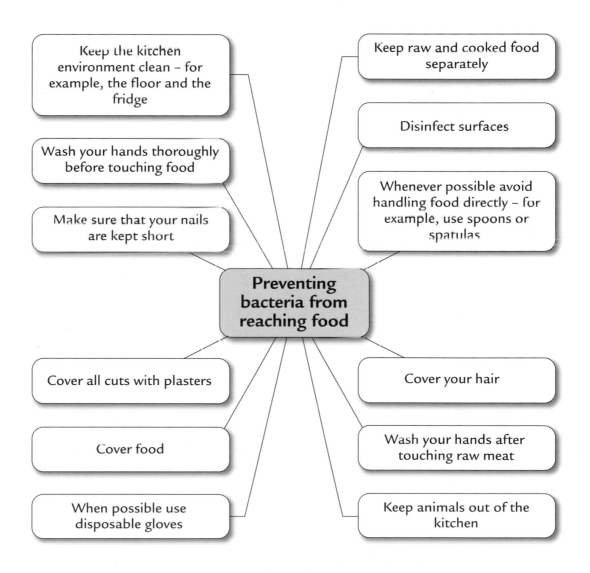

Keep the kitchen environment clean – for example, the floor and the fridge

Wash your hands thoroughly before touching food

Make sure that your nails are kept short

Keep raw and cooked food separately

Disinfect surfaces

Whenever possible avoid handling food directly – for example, use spoons or spatulas

Preventing bacteria from reaching food

Cover all cuts with plasters

Cover food

When possible use disposable gloves

Cover your hair

Wash your hands after touching raw meat

Keep animals out of the kitchen

Preventing the spread of bacteria

One factor in preventing the spread of infection is storing food safely. Fridges and freezers help this by keeping food cold. This does not completely stop bacteria from multiplying, but it does slow this down. Fridges and freezers should be regularly checked to make sure that they are at the correct temperature – fridges should be kept at 1–4 °C while freezers should be kept at -18 to -23 °C.

Bacteria grow quickly at room temperature or in a warm area, such as in the sun. The 'danger zone' is 5–63 °C. Between these temperatures bacteria multiply very rapidly.

Many raw foods – for example, chicken, meat, eggs and dairy produce – already contain bacteria when they come into the kitchen. This is why separating raw foods from cooked foods is essential. It is also important to use foods by the date recommended, and to store them as instructed.

The table below shows how to store food.

Food group	Examples of food	Storage
Dry foods	Rice, flour, pulses, baby milk, couscous	Do not allow them to become damp. Bacteria cannot grow while these foods are dry.
Perishables	Meats (raw and cooked), dairy products (such as cheese, milk and butter), eggs, fish	Keep in the fridge. The fridge temperature must not rise above 4 °C. Cooked foods must be covered, and kept in a separate place in the fridge.
Vegetables and fruit	Root vegetables, carrots, sweet potatoes, yams, apples, plums, plantains, tomatoes, etc.	These should be kept as cool as possible, and off the floor. Root vegetables such as potatoes need to be stored in the dark. Do not eat green potatoes. Fruit and vegetables lose their vitamin C if they are not eaten while fresh.

Destroying bacteria on food

The main way to destroy bacteria is to heat food up to a temperature of at least 72 °C. The food needs to remain at this temperature for several minutes to kill off the bacteria. If food is only slightly warmed through, bacteria will flourish. When reheating any food, make sure that it is piping hot.

When using microwaves to cook or heat food, follow the manufacturer's instructions as well as stirring the food to ensure that all of the food has reached 72 °C.

Serving food and washing up

As well as making sure that there is good food hygiene in the kitchen, you also need to ensure there is good hygiene when serving food and washing up. Before setting tables or handling plates and cutlery, you should always wash your hands. Children should be encouraged to wash their hands before eating. The washing up of the dishes is also important: bacteria on cups and cutlery, for example, can spread infection. All plates, cups, glasses and cutlery should be washed with hot water and washing-up liquid, and then rinsed thoroughly.

Children should be encouraged to wash hands before eating

Monitoring hygiene in the kitchen

As part of their health and safety policy, most settings will have a procedure for monitoring hygiene in the kitchen. Many settings prepare checklists to make sure that the cleanliness of the setting is checked, for example, on a monthly task sheet such as the one overleaf.

✓ ACTIVE KNOWLEDGE

1 Who in your setting is responsible for hygiene in the kitchen?
2 What types of food are prepared in your setting?
3 How do you make sure that food is stored appropriately?

Monthly Cleaning Checklist

Month: ....

The following areas must be thoroughly cleaned and checked **AT LEAST** once a month, **IN ADDITION TO** the normal daily and weekly cleaning check.

Please date and tick the box when the check or clean has been completed:

	Completed/ checked	Date
1. Tops of cupboards and cupboard doors	☐	....
2. All windowsills/doors	☐	....
3. Insides of all cupboards	☐	....
4. Fridge(s)	☐	....
5. Defrost freezer (when appropriate)	☐	....
6. Cooker	☐	....
7. Cooker hood (check filter and replace every 6 months if required)	☐	....
8. Vegetable rack	☐	....
9. Dishwasher	☐	....
10. Ensure that there is a supply of paper towels and liquid soap at the handwash sink	☐	....
11. Ensure that the First-Aid box contains Blue waterproof plasters	☐	....
12. Check deep-fat fryer and contents	☐	....
13. Microwave oven	☐	....
14. Toaster	☐	....

Signature: ....

A monthly task sheet

ACTIVE KNOWLEDGE

Find out what your setting's healthy eating policy is. If the setting does not have one, write down your ideas for a healthy eating policy and discuss them at your next team meeting.

Encourage children to consider healthy choices and involve them in the preparation of food and drink

It is important that all children and young people develop healthy attitudes towards choosing food and drink, as these play such an essential part in keeping them healthy. Playworkers can help in the following ways.

Being a positive role model

Children are influenced by the actions and behaviour of the adults around them. If they see you eating a balanced diet, they are more likely to do the same.

Children need to develop a positive attitude towards food. This means enjoying food, yet eating in moderation. It is therefore not a good idea for children to see adults who alternate between crash diets and indulgent eating. Positive role models are particularly important when working with slightly older children who are becoming more conscious of their body shape.

Cooking with children

One of the best ways in which playworkers can help children learn about food is through planning or cooking meals. Involving children in planning meals means that they can learn about what makes a balanced meal, while actually cooking foods allows them to learn about the process of cooking. For children to learn, it is important that some explanation is given during the cooking process, for example, explaining why a cake rises when it is cooked.

Cooking is one of the best ways of teaching children about food

Why not involve the children in planning the menu for a week? Alternatively, if they bring a packed meal from home, you could ask parents if the children can choose their own meal and then have a discussion about why they chose it and the health implications of their choices.

Children might enjoy preparing the following three recipes.

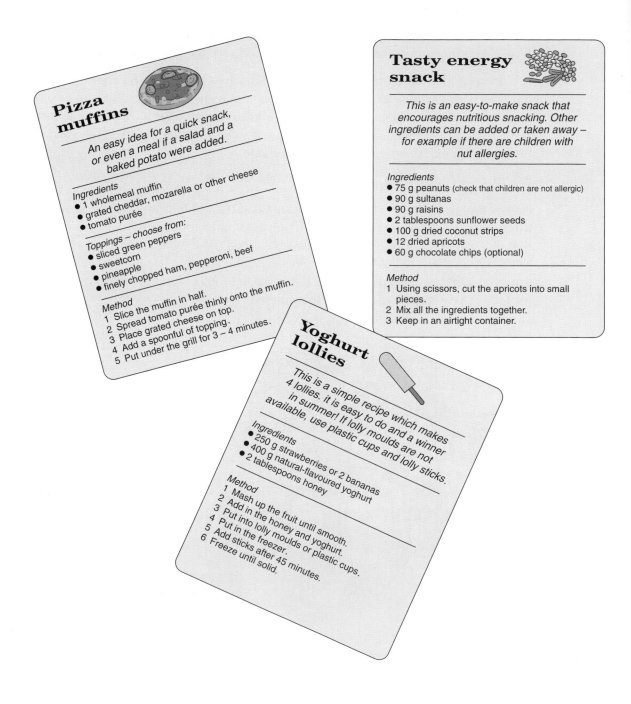

Pizza muffins

An easy idea for a quick snack, or even a meal if a salad and a baked potato were added.

Ingredients
- 1 wholemeal muffin
- grated cheddar, mozarella or other cheese
- tomato purée

Toppings – choose from:
- sliced green peppers
- sweetcorn
- pineapple
- finely chopped ham, pepperoni, beef

Method
1 Slice the muffin in half.
2 Spread tomato purée thinly onto the muffin.
3 Place grated cheese on top.
4 Add a spoonful of topping.
5 Put under the grill for 3 – 4 minutes.

Tasty energy snack

This is an easy-to-make snack that encourages nutritious snacking. Other ingredients can be added or taken away – for example if there are children with nut allergies.

Ingredients
- 75 g peanuts (check that children are not allergic)
- 90 g sultanas
- 90 g raisins
- 2 tablespoons sunflower seeds
- 100 g dried coconut strips
- 12 dried apricots
- 60 g chocolate chips (optional)

Method
1 Using scissors, cut the apricots into small pieces.
2 Mix all the ingredients together.
3 Keep in an airtight container.

Yoghurt lollies

This is a simple recipe which makes 4 lollies. it is easy to do and a winner in summer! If lolly moulds are not available, use plastic cups and lolly sticks.

Ingredients
- 250 g strawberries or 2 bananas
- 400 g natural-flavoured yoghurt
- 2 tablespoons honey

Method
1 Mash up the fruit until smooth.
2 Add in the honey and yoghurt.
3 Put into lolly moulds or plastic cups.
4 Put in the freezer.
5 Add sticks after 45 minutes.
6 Freeze until solid.

To make sure that hygiene is maintained, you should supervise children carefully and explain why good hygiene is important. This helps them to learn about food preparation and hygiene.

Learning how to cook is also a practical life skill, and as such should be offered to all children. It is important to make sure that tasks within a kitchen do not get divided in a stereotypical way, for example, girls always washing up and clearing away.

When clearing away it is good to use an antibacterial spray and to ensure all surfaces are wiped down. Leftover food should be stored appropriately or thrown away. Children and young people should be encouraged to assist with all aspects of clearing away.

Remember that cooking and learning about food does not just happen indoors. You can often capture the imagination of children who are not engaged with cooking by using the outdoors and expanding their experience of what cooking means in its most primitive state. Building a fire outdoors and cooking things like popcorn, baked potatoes or kebabs teaches children a whole new set of skills and can engage those who show little or no interest in healthy eating in a more traditional environment.

Helping children to read food labels

Food labels contain a lot of information. Helping children to read food labels can be turned into fun games, for example, labels can be taken off foods and then the children can guess which label goes with which food!

With obesity in children rising it would be a good idea to find out how much fat, sugar and salt is contained in specific foods and to discuss why those foods with excessive amounts should be avoided.

Encouraging children to taste different types of food

One way in which children can learn about foods is by tasting new foods and meals. This allows children to try out foods which they might not otherwise have as part of their ordinary diet. It is also a lovely way of involving parents and carers in settings, as they can donate favourite recipes. One play setting compiled a recipe book which they then sold to raise funds.

CONSOLIDATION

Write about a cooking activity that you have helped children to carry out.

1 How was the recipe chosen?
2 How did you use this activity as a way of helping children to learn about selecting, preparing and cooking food?

END OF UNIT KNOWLEDGE CHECK

1 Why is a healthy lifestyle important to the development of children and young people?

2 Describe two ways to present information on healthy living to children.

3 How could you make children aware of risks to their own health?

4 Identify three ways children and young people could improve their health.

5 How does your setting provide for special dietary requirements?

6 Why should children have free access to drinks at all times?

7 How could you involve children in selecting food and drinks?

8 Give two examples of how you have used food in wider activities.

9 Why do children need a basic knowledge of food hygiene?

10 How would you provide a satisfying and varied diet?

Work with parents and carers

The role that parents and carers play in the lives of their children encompasses all aspects of the developmental spectrum including:

- bonding and caring
- fun and enjoyment
- health, safety and security.

Their relationship is unique as they are the people who know their children best. They are the experts on their children; they know their likes and dislikes, their strengths and weaknesses.

Parents and carers are very important to any play setting. This unit is about establishing and developing good working relationships with the parents and carers of the children and young people who attend your setting. It is also about getting them involved in the work of the setting.

This unit is divided into two elements:

- PW14.1 Establish and develop working relationships with parents and carers
- PW14.2 Involve parents and carers in the setting.

Playwork values

The playwork values relating to this unit are shown in the table below.

Value	Details
1	The child must be the centre of the process; the opportunities provided and the organisation that supports, co-ordinates and manages these should always start with the child's needs and offer sufficient flexibility to meet these.
7	A considerate and caring attitude to individual children and their families is essential to competent playwork and should be displayed at all times.
8	Prejudice against people with disabilities or who suffer social or economic disadvantage, racism and sexism has no place in an environment which seeks to enhance development through play. Adults involved in play should always promote equality of opportunity and access for all children, and seek to develop anti-discriminatory practice and positive attitudes to those who are disadvantaged.
11	Play opportunities should always be provided within the current legislative framework relevant to children's rights, health, safety and well-being.

Standard 12: Working in partnership with parents and carers

The focus:

The relationship between the child's parents and the registered person is crucial to the child's well-being, development and progress. Children benefit most where there is a trusting and mutually supportive partnership. The registered person and staff welcome parents into the setting and there is a two-way flow of information, knowledge and expertise. (Scottish National Care Standard 1; see page 344.)

Standard 4: Physical environment

The focus:

The environment should be warm and welcoming to children, staff and parents. It should be safe and secure, with space organised to meet requirements and used appropriately to promote children's development. (Scottish National Care Standard 14; see page 344.)

What you must know and understand

For the whole unit
K1: The importance of good working relationships with parents and carers
K2: The importance of maintaining the child at the centre of the process

For PW14.1
K3: Strategies you can use to help parents and carers feel welcome and valued in the setting
K4: The importance of identifying the needs and expectations of parents and carers and how to do so
K5: Why it is important to show respect for other adults' individuality and how to do so
K6: The importance of clear communication with parents and carers
K7: The importance of being sensitive to communication difficulties with parents and carers and strategies you can use to overcome these
K8: The importance of showing that you listen to parents and carers and take their views and opinions seriously
K9: How to balance the wishes of parents and carers with the agreed procedures and policies of the setting and the rights of the child
K10: How to assure parents and carers of children who experience barriers to access that the setting is inclusive and welcomes them
K11: The importance of confidentiality and how to balance the need to respect confidential information about parents and carers with the welfare of the child
K12: Typical situations that may cause conflict with other adults and how to deal with these effectively
K13: Your organisation's complaints procedure

For PW14.2
K14: How to encourage parents and carers to become involved in the work of the setting

K15: The types of opportunities that you can create for parents and carers to become involved and the contributions they can make

K16: Legal requirements for parents and carers to become involved in activities in the setting

K17: Your organisation's policies and procedures for involving parents in activities

K18: The importance of parents and carers understanding and supporting the values and policies of the setting, including those for inclusion

K19: The types of guidance, information and support parents and carers may need to be involved in the setting

The partnership with parents and carers

The role of a playworker includes establishing and maintaining relationships with the parents and carers so that you can work in partnership with them. You both have the same ultimate aim – the well-being of the child.

Parents and carers are usually the child's first carers. From them the children acquire:

- their name
- their place within the family
- their social background.

The child's culture and religion usually emerge from their social background. Children's early experiences and opportunities in life impact on all aspects of their lives including their personality.

The main responsibility for a child lies with the parents and carers. The Children Act 1989 saw the introduction of new legislation relating to the care of children. The main aim of the Act was to form a balance (similar to a see-saw). On one side is the child with his or her needs and rights; on the other side are the parents with their rights and responsibilities. By forming a balance between the two the well-being of the child is protected.

Needs and Rights   Rights and Responsibilities

Later legislation, including the green paper Every Child Matters and the Children Act 2004, reinforces the earlier Act. The legislation focuses on the child being at the centre of playwork practice and stresses that the welfare and well-being of the child is paramount.

Your setting will have a policy regarding working with parents and carers which may be similar to the one below.

Carlton Kids Out-of-school Club

Partnership with parents and carers

The Carlton Kids Out-of-school Club recognises and believes partnerships formed with parents and carers are vital to the existence and growth of the club. The club's aim is to broaden its relationships with parents and carers by maintaining the following policies and procedures.

- Parents and carers will be kept informed about how their children have settled at the club, their involvement in opportunities, their personal achievements and any accidents or incidents that have occurred.
- Parents' and carers' views regarding improving the policies and procedures will be welcome at all times.
- Parents' and carers' concerns will be dealt with in the strictest confidence.
- Parents and carers will be asked to give written and signed consent when children are taken out on trips.
- Parents and carers will be kept informed of any changes regarding the club.

The play leader will be happy to meet with parents prior to taking up registration to discuss their children's needs, club policies, opening times and fees. There will also be an opportunity to meet the team and the other children.

The policy should also refer to the terms of the Children Act 1989, the inspection criteria it follows and parental rights to access information relating to the inspection report.

The importance of good working relationships with parents and carers

Good relationships with parents and carers are important to all settings. If parents and carers do not feel comfortable and confident about the service you provide they will not allow their children to attend.

Keys to good practice: Maintaining good relationships with parents and carers

✓ Develop understanding and trust.
✓ Be polite and courteous.
✓ Ensure that good lines of communication exist.
✓ Encourage participation in the activities of the setting.
✓ Help them to feel welcome and valued.
✓ Set a good example (be a good role model) for the children.
✓ Try to boost the self-esteem and confidence of the parents.
✓ Find out how to meet the children's needs.
✓ Enhance your understanding of the children.
✓ Provide consistency and stability for the children.
✓ Make yourself approachable to the children and the parents and carers.

Good communication between parent and playworker is important

Maintaining the child at the centre of the process

The child must always be at the centre of the process. Partnership arrangements will work well if you have the same common aim, which should always be the well-being of the child. The needs, the security and the welfare of the child should be addressed. If children are content and happy in your setting then the parents will usually continue to send their children. A consistent approach is always useful.

Establish and develop working relationships with parents and carers

Parents and carers play a crucial role in children's lives and hopefully provide the love and stability that is so essential to children. By developing and maintaining a working relationship with parents and carers you will be able to enhance your interactions with them and their children.

What you need to demonstrate you can do

- Initiate relationships with parents and carers in a way that helps them to feel welcome and valued in the setting
- Respect the individuality of parents and carers
- Identify the needs and expectations of parents and carers who use the setting and seek to meet these as much as possible
- Provide clear and accurate information to parents and carers which meets their needs
- Respect the wishes of parents and carers within the agreed procedures, values and children's rights
- Respect confidential information about parents and carers as long as the children's welfare is maintained
- Handle any disagreements with parents and carers tactfully and in a way that is likely to maintain good relationships between parents and carers and the organisation
- Respond promptly and positively to complaints and suggestions and follow organisational procedures for carrying these through

Initiate relationships with parents and carers in a way that helps them to feel welcome

Strategies you can use to help parents and carers feel welcome and valued in the setting

A good starting point when thinking about parents and carers is to consider how you can make them feel welcome. Parents and carers who feel relaxed about coming into the setting are more likely to talk to you and to feel confident about leaving their children in your care.

There are many aspects to making people feel welcome, but at heart what matters is to make them feel wanted. If you ignore a parent or keep a carer waiting, you give the message that they are not valued or wanted. In contrast, if you greet a parent or ask a carer whether he or she needs any help, you send out a positive message.

Greeting a parent or carer sends out a positive message

It is important that you make an effort to find out the preferred name of parents and carers and greet them by this and ensure that it is pronounced correctly. Remember that in other languages the word may have a totally different meaning if pronounced differently and you may in fact be insulting them.

Keys to good practice: Helping parents and carers to feel welcome

✓ Greet them positively by their preferred names.
✓ Tell them about what their children have done, remembering to focus on the positive aspects.
✓ Invite them to sit in during sessions.
✓ Ask them for feedback and encourage them to ask questions.
✓ Acknowledge their ideas and comments.
✓ Listen attentively to their concerns and feelings.
✓ Take an interest in them as people.
✓ Create a friendly atmosphere.
✓ Ensure that they are introduced to all staff, including new members of staff.
✓ Be willing to reassure them.

Remember that first impressions count and if you want a parent or carer to use the facility they need to feel welcome with you, the other workers and the setting.

Respect the individuality of parents and carers

The importance of showing respect for other adults' individuality

One of the key factors in building good relationships with parents and carers and making them feel welcome is valuing and respecting them. More information on this topic can be found in Unit PW8, page 123.

Recognising your own values and prejudices

Everyone has values and prejudices. These are learnt during childhood and through life experiences. Values and prejudices tend to affect people without them realising it. People tend to get on better with other people who have similar attitudes and lifestyles to themselves.

To show true respect and to value others, it is important to be aware of your own values and prejudices and then to consider whether these are likely to affect the way you might relate to others.

Identify the needs and expectations of parents and carers and seek to meet these

Parents and carers will have preconceived ideas about the type of care that they require for their child. These ideas are based on a wide variety of factors relating to their own care practices and experiences and the ideal situation that they want for their child.

To set aside time to talk to parents and carers about such matters including diet, special hair and skin care, family names, language, medical conditions, etc. will give them an opportunity to talk about and identify any needs. It is important to discuss these needs with them so that they are aware of the type of care and provision that you offer. It will be easy for you to meet some of the needs relating to the child, but there may be times when you are unable to meet all of the parental wishes. It is important to remind parents and carers that you are a play facility and that your ethos is about providing a child-centred environment with a range of play opportunities that can be freely chosen by the child and that are enjoyable and fun.

You will need to acknowledge that the parents' wishes and requirements may change. To ensure that you keep abreast of developments, trends and influences, you will need to re-assess their requirements on a regular basis. You could use the methods described in Units PW10 and PW11 regarding feedback from parents and carers (see pages 178 and 218). It is important to remember that if you ask for information about their needs and feedback on your service, you acknowledge and address any issues they raise.

CASE STUDY

Mia attends your after-school club and has just moved up into another class at school. Her mother calls in to see you as she is concerned that you do not sit with Mia and make her do her homework.

1 What would you say to Mia's mother?

CASE STUDY

Ben's father collects him once a week in between his appointments for his job. He requests that Ben be ready to go when he arrives as he has very limited time available.

1 What would you do about this request?

Your facility will have policies and procedures regarding diversity and you should always promote these in all that you say and do. The following is an example of the policy of an after-school club.

Provide clear and accurate information to parents and carers

You may need to provide parents and carers with a range of information once their children attend a play setting. More information on this topic can be found in Unit PW8, page 124.

Respect the wishes of parents and carers

Balancing the wishes of parents and carers with the agreed procedures and policies of the setting and the rights of the child

There will be many occasions when you need to consult with parents and carers and listen to their wishes. For example, you might plan a trip to the swimming pool but find that a parent or carer would prefer their child not to attend for religious or health reasons.

At such times you might need to remind yourself that it is the parents or carers, not you, who have legal responsibility for the children. If you fail to respect their wishes, you are in effect sending a message that you do not value them.

However, there may be times when parents' and carers' wishes may be in conflict with the policies and procedures of your setting and the rights of the child. For example, if a parent requests that you keep his or her child totally away from another child or other children, or tells you not to give the child anything to eat as a punishment. In instances such as these it is good practice to discuss the issue and explain the reasoning, ensuring that you relate this to your policies and procedures and/or legislation.

CASE STUDY

Katie, aged 4, had a slight accident yesterday. When her mother arrived to collect her, you explained that Katie had been totally absorbed in her play so had left it too late to go to the toilet and had wet her pants. As they left the setting you heard Katie's mother telling her off for wetting her pants. Today when Katie's father arrives to drop her off, he tells you that if Katie wets her pants today you are to tell her off and make her wash out her pants.

1 Would you:
- agree to his requests
- explain that yesterday's incident was because she was playing so intently and enjoying her play so much that she forgot to go to the toilet
- tell him you do not have any washing facilities for washing clothes
- explain that children often wet their pants when they are absorbed in play and that you have a selection of new pants for these occasions
- offer to remind her occasionally to see if she needs the toilet
- firmly refer to your policies and procedures
- ask if this is a regular occurrence or just a one-off incident and see if there is any way you can work together to help Katie?

2 You may find that you will choose several of the options above.

CASE STUDY

When Amy's mother drops her off in the morning she says to you that she is worried about Amy and she is restricting the E numbers in her diet. She has packed her a more healthy option for lunch and asks whether she could just have water to drink.

During the day some team games are organised and Amy joins in. Afterwards Jenny, one of the playworkers, makes the children a drink of orange. One of the other playworkers asks Jenny whether Amy should be drinking orange. Jenny simply laughs and says that Amy's mother tends to be a bit of a fusspot, and that Amy wants a drink.

1 Why is Jenny's attitude wrong?
2 How might the parent feel when she finds out that her instructions have not been respected?
3 How would you have handled this situation?

Assuring parents and carers of children who experience barriers to access that their individual needs will be met

Each setting will have a special needs policy which should be given to and explained to parents and carers when they enquire about the facility. Settings may have different titles for these policies but they will all relate to children who experience barriers to access. An example is shown on the next page.

Carlton Kids Out-of-school Club

Special Needs Policy

Carlton Kids Out-of-school Club works within an equal opportunities framework. It recognises that everyone has a contribution to make to society and has the right to equal treatment regardless of their ability. The club is committed to including all children with special needs.

The children will be:

- treated as valued members of the club
- supported and equally involved while their needs and abilities will be respected
- given the opportunity to participate in all activities
- encouraged to interact, socialise, form friendships and have fun.

The club will:

- meet with parents/carers to discuss the children's needs and ways of meeting these needs
- provide one-to-one support where appropriate
- provide a range of activities and play opportunities in accordance with the ages and abilities of the children
- make adaptations where possible so that the children can participate in group activities
- regularly review staff training in special needs
- make regular users aware of the needs of all children in order to overcome fears or prejudice.

For it to be effective, a policy should be consistently implemented by all members of the playwork team.

Make time for one-to-one support where needed

The setting should portray positive images, with equipment and materials that meet diverse needs and that show and celebrate diversity. All staff should have attended diversity training and be willing and confident to challenge all forms of discriminatory practice. They should act as positive role models for the children and young people in their care.

Parents and carers should be invited to make several visits before their child attends a setting. They should be assured that their children's needs will be addressed sensitively and consistently in a way that shows respect and values the parents' wishes.

Respect confidential information about parents and carers

Recent legislation regarding confidentiality of information and access to information in the form of the Data Protection Act and the Freedom of Information Act sets out strict guidelines regarding the confidentiality issues when receiving, storing and transmitting information. These guidelines should be observed within the play setting. Every play setting should have a policy regarding confidentiality based on these guidelines and also on the Children Act. All staff should be aware of and should follow this policy.

The importance of respecting confidentiality

Parents and carers often divulge information that is confidential. They do this to help staff understand the needs of their children, or to explain the reasons behind their child's behaviour. Often the information they give you will be personal and in some cases painful for them. Unless the child's welfare is at stake, therefore, this information must remain confidential and be passed on only to those who really need to know.

If you are given information that you feel indicates that a child's welfare is at stake, seek help either from your line manager or from social services. Occasionally, you may be given information about parents and carers from other professionals, such as a social worker. This type of information is equally confidential, and again should not be passed on to anyone else.

Keys to good practice: Respecting confidentiality

✓ When parents or carers are sharing information which is personal, find a quiet and private area so that others cannot overhear.

Handle any disagreements with parents and carers tactfully

Most play settings that maintain good relationships with their parents and carers rarely have disagreements with them. However, there may be times when misunderstandings occur. More information on this topic can be found in Unit PW8, page 127.

Respond promptly and positively to complaints and suggestions

Responding to complaints and suggestions

Unit PW10 looks at the importance of gaining feedback in order to improve individual performance and the organisation's practice (see page 178). Some feedback will be provided by parents and carers, and it is essential that you listen to it and respond well. Parents and carers will sometimes have a different perspective from your own. By listening carefully to their suggestions, you might find ways of improving your service for the future.

Always listen carefully to feedback from parents and carers

Complaints are often harder to handle than suggestions – it is not easy to take on board criticisms. Try hard to see any complaint from the parent's or carer's perspective. Remember that they will often have come into the setting having rehearsed in their own mind what they are going to say. This may make them seem aggressive, when in fact they are apprehensive. If you can see that there has been some mistake, misunderstanding or poor practice, apologise and explain that you will ensure that this will not happen again. Most parents and carers react well if they feel that what they are saying is being taken seriously. In some cases, you might need to refer a complaint to your line manager, or tell the parent or carer that you will report back once you have found out more.

Your organisation's complaints procedure

If misunderstandings and disagreements are of a more serious nature and you are unable to resolve them amicably then you will need to follow the setting's policies and procedures.

Each play setting will have a complaints procedure that will be available to parents and carers. The procedure will be in line with the Children Act and Ofsted guidelines and will state the steps a parent should follow if they have a complaint about your service.

Your policy should look similar to the one below.

Homestead Out-of-school Club: Complaints Procedure

Making complaints known

A parent who is uneasy about any of the out-of-school club's policies should first talk over any worries with the officer in charge. If this does not have a satisfactory outcome or if the problem occurs again, the parent should put the concerns or the complaint in writing and request a meeting with the officer in charge. Both parties should have a friend or partner present if required, and an agreed written record of the discussion should be made. A copy of the written record should be available to both parties. Most complaints should be resolved at this initial stage.

If the matter is still not settled to the parent's satisfaction, the parent should again contact the officer in charge. If no agreement can be reached, it might be helpful to acquire the services of an external mediator. A mediator has no legal powers but may help to clarify the situation. The mediator will help to define the problem, review the action taken so far and suggest further ways in which it might be resolved. The mediator will keep all discussions confidential, will meet with the out-of-school club if requested and will keep a written record of all meetings that are held. Copies of the written record will be given to all parties concerned.

The role of the registering authority

In some cases it will be necessary to bring in Ofsted, the registering authority, who have a duty to ensure that specified requirements are adhered to. The out-of-school club works in partnership with Ofsted to encourage high standards. The registering authority will become involved if a child appears to be at risk or if there is a possible breach of registration requirements. In these cases, both the parents and the out-of-school club will be informed and the officer in charge will work with Ofsted to ensure that a proper investigation of the complaint is followed by appropriate action.

Some settings provide a form which will help the parents and carers give the required details of the complaint. They will also provide the address of the local Ofsted office so that complaints can be addressed as quickly as possible.

PORTFOLIO EVIDENCE

Think of a time when a parent or carer complained about an aspect of the service that you provide. Think about how you responded and how the conflict was resolved. If you write this up or recall this in a professional discussion with your assessor, it will be a good source of evidence for your portfolio.

CONSOLIDATION

You may think that your setting is welcoming and friendly but what do others think? You could send out a survey or questionnaire asking parents whether they feel they are welcome and valued in the setting. They could also be asked for their ideas on how to make the setting friendlier.

nent PW14.2 Involve parents and carers in the setting

Parents and carers play crucial roles in children's lives. They provide – or do not provide – the love and stability that are so essential to children. Most know their children better than anyone else and can often pick up on their joys and sorrows with a single look. If you see yourself as being in partnership with parents, you should be able to learn more about the children with whom you are working and how to meet their needs.

There are other benefits, too, for play settings that are able to develop positive relationships with parents and carers. Such settings often find that they receive enormous support in return and in some cases this helps them to attract new children, resources and funding.

What you need to demonstrate you can do

- Encourage parents and carers to involve themselves in the work of the setting
- Find opportunities to involve parents and carers that are appropriate to their needs and skills
- Make sure that parents and carers meet legal and organisational requirements for the activities they will be involved in
- Make sure that parents and carers understand and support the values and policies of the setting
- Provide parents and carers with the information they will need to take part in activities, including ground rules and procedures
- Monitor parents' and carers' involvement in the setting and provide them with any guidance or support they need

Encourage parents and carers to involve themselves in the work of the setting

If you provide an atmosphere within your setting where parents and carers feel welcome, where they are respected and valued as important people both in the lives of their children and in the provision of the setting, you will find that parents and carers will be more willing to become involved in certain aspects of the work of the setting. The lifestyles of people vary and some people will have more time and energy to put into the setting than others. This is not to say that they care more or less about their children but that they may have more personal commitments and less time available. It is important to remember that a non-judgemental attitude will always enhance relationships.

Parents should be involved in the work of the setting

If you provide a good range of opportunities in which parents and carers can be encouraged to become involved, they will be more likely to offer to help.

Find opportunities to involve parents and carers that are appropriate to their needs and skills

The types of opportunities that you can create for parents and carers

There are many different ways in which parents and carers can become involved in the setting. These may range from providing resources for the collage box to becoming a member of the management committee. A lot will depend upon the type of setting that you operate and the management structure that you have.

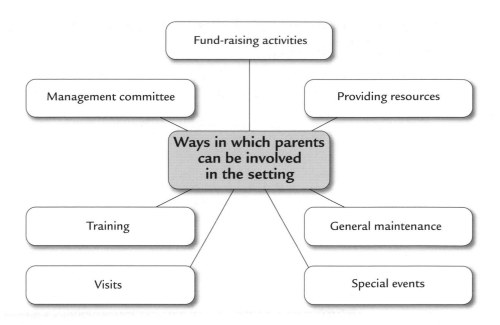

Parents can be involved in different ways

CASE STUDY

It is coming up to the Chinese New Year and you decide to hold a session in which you provide information about and celebrate the festival.

1 How could you involve the parents and carers in this?
2 What about a carer who works full-time and has a lot of family commitments?
3 How could you find out what they would like to do and what skills they may wish to share?

Make sure that parents and carers meet legal and organisational requirements for the activities they will be involved in

Your organisation's policies and procedures for involving parents in activities

The legal requirements for parents and carers to become involved in activities in the setting are not always clear. However, your setting may have a policy in place which you follow. The Children Act sets out guidelines about the supervision of children and young people and also about the responsibility of playworkers to safeguard them, including who has access to them and their records.

When accompanying children on an outing, parents would be expected to follow guidelines such as the following:

- never leave children alone
- stay with those children who have been allocated to you
- have a meeting point in case anyone gets lost

- ensure you know what to do in the case of an accident
- keep in mobile phone contact with staff
- ensure you are back at the meeting point at the specified time at the end of the day.

If a parent or carer is a regular helper, it would be advisable to follow the setting's policy with regard to volunteers. For example, it might be the policy of the setting for volunteers to have a discussion with the play leader about how to behave in the setting which would then form the basis of an agreement. If a parent has offered to help with a one-off activity, which will only last an hour or so, he or she may not necessarily need to go through the whole volunteer procedure.

The introduction of the Criminal Record Bureau checks (CRB checks) means that anyone who is to be left alone with children and young people will need to have had CRB clearance. If it is unlikely that you would leave a parent or carer alone with the children, and therefore a CRB check has not been carried out, you must ensure supervision. It is important that all staff are vigilant about ensuring that helpers are not left alone with the children. It may also be good practice to remind your team not to discuss other children and to abide by the Data Protection Act with regard to confidentiality of records.

Make sure that parents and carers understand and support the values and policies of the setting

If parents and carers are to be involved in the work of the setting, it is important that they feel part of the team. As with volunteers, you will need to spend time discussing with them the policies and procedures that you abide by. They will require guidance, information and support. They should be made to feel welcome and you should have realistic expectations as to what they can and are willing to do. You should also be aware that different parents will have different skills and knowledge, and that some will have more experience and confidence than others.

Remember that other people's values and beliefs may vary from those of the setting so it is important to take time to go over the policies and procedures that relate to diversity and inclusion. You can find more information about this in Unit PW6 (see page 9). A mentor scheme may be useful in some circumstances. This will enable parents and carers to feel supported and they will know where to go to get advice and help.

CASE STUDY

Jack's father has volunteered to spend the day working in the setting and hopes to enlist the help of the children and young people. He has agreed to do some gardening around the new, all-weather play surface.

1 What information about your policies and procedures would you give him?
2 What would you do if he did not agree with the policy about respecting diversity and inclusion and said that he thought those children should be in special settings?
3 Would you still let him help?
4 How could you help him to overcome this discrimination?

Monitor parents' and carers' involvement in the setting and provide them with any guidance or support they need

Once a parent or carer becomes involved in the setting, it is good practice to monitor their involvement. This will enable you to feed back on the positive aspects you or others may have seen and to address any issues as they arise. Although you may have gone through all of your policies and procedures, you must remember that many parents and carers are not trained in childcare and so may need reminding of the procedures. They may address things differently, they may not be aware of terminology used in the setting or they may have difficulty allowing the children and young people to take risks and do things for themselves. To show patience but to sensitively address any areas for development will allow parents or carers to think about and change their behaviour.

Keys to good practice: Involving parents and carers in the setting

✓ Make parents and carers feel valued and welcome.
✓ Be realistic in what you ask them to do.
✓ Remember that it is unlikely they are trained in working with children and young people.
✓ Observe the setting's policy with regard to supervising them.
✓ Check that they understand what is expected of them.
✓ If you have to challenge them about something, do it sensitively.
✓ Remember to thank them – manners cost nothing.

CASE STUDY

Cordell says that his father is attending night school to learn about music. You talk to Cordell and he tells you about all the musical instruments that his father can play. The next time his father comes to collect Cordell you discuss music with him. He says he will come in to one of the sessions with his musical instruments to show to the children.

1 What would you say to him?
2 Would you have any guidelines for him?

It is good practice to monitor parents' involvement

ACTIVE KNOWLEDGE

Check your setting's policies and see if you have one about parental involvement. If you have, discuss it at your next team meeting to see if it needs updating. If you don't have a policy, discuss what should be included in one and present this to your management committee.

CONSOLIDATION

Think about the parental involvement at your setting and of ways that you can increase this. You could make a poster or flyer to send out to parents asking for their help and listing the types of help that would be appreciated.

END OF UNIT KNOWLEDGE CHECK

1 Why is it important to have good working relationships with parents and carers?

2 Give three examples of what you could do to make parents and carers feel welcome in your setting.

3 How would you handle a situation in which a parent's wishes were in conflict with the policies and procedures of your setting?

4 Why is it important to respect confidential information about parents and carers?

5 How can you encourage parents and carers to be involved in the setting?

6 Why is it important that parents and carers who come to help are aware of the values and policies of the setting?

7 Give three examples of things you would tell a parent who had volunteered to help on a day's outing.

8 Why should parents have a copy of your complaints procedure?

Administer playwork provision

Unit PW15

This unit is about implementing access procedures and maintaining records about children and young people. Access in this case means admission procedures and general entry to the play setting. The unit is appropriate for all settings whose main purpose is providing children and young people with opportunities for freely chosen, self-directed play.

This unit is divided into two sections:

● PW15.1 Implement access procedures
● PW15.2 Record and report key information.

Playwork values

The playwork values relating to this unit are shown in the table below.

Value	Details
1	The child must be the centre of the process; the opportunities provided and the organisation which supports, co-ordinates and manages these should always start with the child's needs and offer sufficient flexibility to meet these.
3	Whereas play may sometimes be enriched by the playworker's participation, adults should always be sensitive to children's needs and never try to control a child's play so long as it remains within safe and acceptable boundaries.
11	Play opportunities should always be provided within the current legislative framework relevant to children's rights, health, safety and well-being.

Ofsted national standards

Standard 9: Equal opportunities

The focus:

Children need to feel valued and to be free from discrimination. Where the registered person and staff are committed to equality they recognise that children's attitudes towards others are established in these early years. They understand relevant legislation and plan to help children learn about equality and justice through their play. The provision is carefully organised and monitored to ensure all children have access to the full range of activities. Family members and staff should work together to share information, for example, about cultures, home languages, play activities and children's specific needs. (Scottish National Care Standard 8; see page 344.)

What you must know and understand

For the whole unit

K1: Playwork assumptions and values relevant to this unit

K2: The importance of effective administration to the running of a play setting

K3: The basic provisions of the data protection act relevant to your work

For PW15.1

K4: Why it is important to implement access procedures correctly

K5: The requirements of disability and equal opportunities legislation in regard to access

K6: The provisions of the Children Act in relation to play provision and record keeping

K7: Why it is important to deal with enquiries promptly and courteously

K8: The types of enquiry which are likely to be made and how to deal with these

K9: Enquiries which may need to be passed on

K10: The information which needs to be collected about children and their families and why

K11: Why it is important to record information clearly and fully

K12: Organisational procedures for processing and communicating this type of information

K13: The importance of applying access procedures correctly

For PW15.2

K14: Why it is important to keep records complete, legible and up to date

K15: Why it is important to store records securely but in a way which enables them to be found quickly

K16: Methods of organising and storing records

K17: The importance of confidentiality

K18: Agreements on confidentiality which have been made with parents and carers

K19: Organisational requirements covering confidentiality

K20: The types of information which may need to be passed on to authorised people in the organisation and why requests should be dealt with promptly

---

Element PW15.1 **Implement access procedures**

An important administrative task in any setting is to provide information to prospective parents, carers and children, and to complete registration with them if they wish to take up a place. This section looks at the types of information and procedures that are needed within this task.

What you need to demonstrate you can do

- Answer enquiries about the access of children and young people
- Collect the necessary information about children, young people and their families
- Record information clearly and fully
- Pass the information on, following organisational procedures
- Provide clear and accurate information to people enquiring about future places
- Ensure that access procedures are followed

Answer enquiries about the access of children and young people

Most parents and carers will want to find out about a setting before registering their child. For many parents and carers the way that a setting responds to their first phone call or visit can be a deciding factor in whether they wish their child to attend the setting. Settings that respond to enquiries promptly and warmly are therefore more likely to fill places.

A good first contact between the setting and parents helps to establish a positive working relationship. It also makes the setting look efficient and professional. This is important, especially to a setting that has just started up and needs to attract new children in order to keep going.

In order to be able to respond to parents' questions promptly and accurately, you need to have absorbed basic information about the way your setting operates. If you are unsure about any area of information, ask a colleague or line manager. If you are responding to a telephone enquiry and cannot answer a question, ask if you can return the call once you have the information. Then ring back promptly with the answer or to explain why the information is not available.

A good telephone manner is important when answering queries

If a parent or carer arrives for an impromptu visit, welcome them warmly. If possible, show them around. If it is not possible to spend time answering their enquiries – for example, because you were just about to go out on a trip – explain why and arrange another time that will be convenient to them.

The table below shows some of the common questions that parents and carers ask. Parents will also ask questions specific to the needs of their children, for example, a child who enjoys art and painting may wish to be in a setting where there are plenty of creative activities going on.

Area of information	Types of questions that are asked
Cost	How much does it cost per session to send a child?
	Is there any reduction for more than one child?
	What does the price include?
	Is there a cancellation fee?
	What happens if a child cannot attend due to sickness?
Session times and availability	What are the session times?
	What sessions are available?
	Is there any flexibility about sessions?
Food, drink and snacks	Are these included in the price?
	Can the setting cater for children with specific dietary requirements, such as a gluten-free or vegetarian diet?
	What does a typical menu look like?
Activities	What type of activities are provided?
	Are all activities free?
	Is any special equipment or clothing required?
Settling in/transport arrangements	Is there a collection service from schools or from the local area?
	How are children made to feel welcome?
	Are the children divided into age groups?
	How many other children are in the child's age group?
	Are there any other children from the child's school?
	Who looks after children once they have arrived?

During the course of a conversation with a parent or carer it may become apparent that you will not be able to offer a place. For example, the setting may be full, or it may become clear that the setting will not meet the requirements of the parent or child. Be honest about what your setting can and cannot provide. Invite the parent or carer to leave you a contact number in case a place becomes available or you think of another setting that might be suitable. This type of gesture helps build a good reputation for your play setting.

ACTIVE KNOWLEDGE

Look at the types of questions that parents and carers commonly ask in the table on the previous page.

Write a short answer to each of these questions, based on your own setting's procedures.

Collect the necessary information about children, young people and their families

It is important to keep basic information about children and their families on file in the setting. This will be needed in the event of an emergency, for example, or to provide proof to an auditor of the number of children attending the setting. The information is also useful in helping a setting to meet children's particular needs, such as dietary or medical requirements. This information should be collected before the child starts at the setting to ensure that the needs of the child are met without delay.

Most settings collect this information either by sending out a form or by filling in a form with the parents or primary carers. Filling in the form with parents or primary carers can be particularly useful because it allows parents to discuss issues as they are covered on the form, for example, the medication that children may need in a setting. This can help to build a relationship with parents and will provide more detailed information about the child's habits and needs. Filling in the form with or for parents can also help those parents who find form-filling difficult because their vision is impaired, for instance, or because they have difficulty in reading.

It is helpful if parents are told why the information is needed, and that it will remain confidential. Under the Data Protection Act 1998, they have the right to check any stored information.

You can also use this opportunity to explain to parents how the setting is run, and give them any additional information that they might need. Some settings produce handbooks or starter packs.

Filling in forms with parents gives them the opportunity to discuss issues as they arise on the form

The table below outlines the type of information that is generally collected when a child takes up a place at a setting.

Information	Reason for its collection
Address of parents/carers	To send letters or to contact parents/carers in an emergency.
Full name of child	To make sure that it is correctly spelt. It will be needed in case of an emergency.
Date of birth	To help find a child's medical records in an emergency. The age of the child is also important in meeting registration requirements.
Emergency contact numbers and addresses	To contact parents/carers quickly in the event of an emergency.
Doctor's name and address	To access a child's medical records in the event of an emergency.
Health	In case of an emergency, and also to make sure that any particular needs can be met. For example, an allergy to bee stings would mean that staff would be extra-vigilant and would seek medical assistance if the child were stung.
Dietary requirements	To make sure that all foods and drinks are suitable for the health, cultural or religious needs of children.

Why you need to keep records: the Children Act (1989) and the Data Protection Act

The Children Act (1989) was introduced to ensure that childcare settings were regulated and safe. This has meant that settings have had to apply to be registered. As part of the registration requirements, settings that fall under the Act must keep certain records. It is interesting to note that even settings that do not have to comply with the Act still keep similar records as these are seen to be good practice. The list below shows some of the records settings need to keep:

- daily attendance register
- current information on children
- accident/incident book
- records on staff/volunteers
- insurance details.

Remember that the Ofsted inspector will look at the type of information collected, and where and how records are stored. The officer will also check compliance with the Data Protection Act.

The basic principles for holding information within the guidelines of the Data Protection Act are listed below.

- Information must be collected and used fairly and inside the law.
- It must only be held and used for the reasons given to the parent.
- It can only be used for those registered purposes and only be disclosed to those people. You cannot give the information away or sell it.
- The information held must be adequate (enough), relevant and not excessive (too much) when compared with the purpose it is required for. So you must have enough detail but not too much for the job that you are doing.
- Information must be accurate and be kept up to date. There is a duty to keep it up to date, for example, to change an address when people move.
- Information must not be kept longer than is necessary for the registered purpose. You can keep information for certain lengths of time but not indefinitely.
- The information must be kept safe and secure. This includes keeping the information backed up and away from any unauthorised access. It would be wrong to leave records open to be viewed by just anyone.
- The files may not be transferred.

Record information clearly and fully

If you are responsible for recording information about the child, be sure to do this accurately and legibly. Although many settings have one main form, there might also be other documents to be filled in. Common additional forms include:

- forms giving permission for children to go on outings
- forms giving permission to have children's photographs taken and shown in the setting
- forms to entitle parents to bursaries or subsidised places.

Permission is needed before children's photographs can be taken and shown in a setting

Once information has been collected, you may have to transfer details on to other day-to-day documents such as the register, the list of children who have snacks, or the list of children who need to have inhalers near them. Information must be transferred carefully and accurately or children might not have their needs met.

Pass the information on, following organisational procedures

The information gathered must be carefully stored and passed on to others as necessary. The manager or senior team member in the setting will need to know at all times how many children are in the setting, their ages and their needs.

Every setting has its own way of passing on such information. In smaller settings, the manager will want to meet the prospective parents and the child if possible; in larger settings, it might be the responsibility of the group leader to do this. Whatever the procedure, most settings pass on information quickly to avoid potential problems.

Efficient access and registration procedures will:

- ensure accurate information
- help meet children's and parents' needs
- help build positive relationships with parents
- prevent confusion in the setting
- aid the smooth running of the setting
- meet legislation and registration requirements.

Provide clear and accurate information to people enquiring about future places

You may receive enquiries about future places if no places are currently available, or if one playscheme is ending and parents wish to find out whether another will be running.

Give honest and accurate information to parents so they can make their childcare arrangements based on what has been said to them. Sometimes you may not be able to give a complete answer, for example, if the committee that organises the playscheme has not yet been appointed. In such cases you should refer the enquiry to a colleague or write down the names and contact details of the interested parents and pass these on to your line manager. The parents can then be informed of future developments.

ADMISSION FORM

Please use capitals

1. Full name of child: ....

2. Date of birth: .... Age: ....

3. Proposed date of admission: ....
   For each session required please state the approximate arrival and departure times:

   Monday ....

   Tuesday ....

   Wednesday ....

   Thursday ....

   Friday ....

4. Name of parent/guardian: ....

5. Home address/telephone number: Work address/telephone number:

   ....

   ....

   ....

   ....

6. Position of child in family: (e.g. 2nd of 3 etc.) ....

7. Name/address of Health Visitor ....

   ....

   ....

8. Has your child had all the usual inoculations including whooping cough?

   Yes ☐   No ☐

A registration form

Ensure that access procedures are followed

Every setting should have an admissions policy which is available to anyone who requires it. It should state clearly how children will be prioritised for a place at the setting, especially if there is a waiting list. It may be that your setting accepts children in strict chronological order according to when they were registered to attend the setting, or you may think other criteria should apply. For example, siblings of children already attending or children from a particular age range might take priority.

Whatever criteria you choose, you need to be sure the policy is used in a completely fair and equitable manner when allocating available places. If the setting's procedures are not followed there is a strong chance that complaints will occur and it will be so much harder to convince parents that favouritism has not taken place.

Settings should be mindful of the requirements of Ofsted Standard 9 (see page 315), the Children Act, equal opportunities legislation and the Disability Discrimination Act (DDA) when setting criteria for admission. The DDA makes it unlawful for a service provider to discriminate against a disabled person by refusing to provide any service which it provides to other members of the public.

Keys to good practice: Ensuring access procedures are followed

✓ Always follow the setting's procedures.
✓ Be aware of the requirements of the national standards.
✓ Treat all children and adults with equal concern.
✓ Be aware of relevant anti-discriminatory good practice.
✓ Promote equal opportunities with regard to admission and access to resources and activities.

CONSOLIDATION

Look at the admissions policy for your setting.

1 What are the access procedures?

2 How will knowledge of the admission policy help parents or carers?

3 How is this information kept up to date?

Record and report key information

In order that settings may run smoothly, it is important that good records are kept and maintained. This section looks at the types of records that most settings need to keep and ways of maintaining them.

What you need to demonstrate you can do

- Make sure information is complete, legible and up to date
- Store information securely but conveniently
- Restrict access to information appropriately
- Provide information promptly when necessary

Make sure information is complete, legible and up to date

Types of records

Records are vital in all settings. There is a legal obligation to maintain some records, such as an accident book, while others allow the setting to make plans and monitor their performance.

ACTIVE KNOWLEDGE

1 What type of records does your setting keep?
2 Who has overall responsibility for making sure that these records are kept up to date?

The table below lists the types of records that are usually kept in most settings.

Type of record	Reason
Accident books	It is a requirement of the Health and Safety at Work Act 1974 that employers keep a record of all accidents to their employees that take place in their setting. Play settings often keep separate books – one for the children and one for employees. The accident books must be accessible and available for inspection.
Attendance registers	These are needed for several reasons. In case of an emergency they give the number of children in the setting at that time. Some settings are funded according to the number of children 'on roll': attendance registers provide evidence of the numbers on particular days.
Emergency contact details	These are needed in the event of an emergency. Many settings ask for several contacts in case one is not available.
Outing consent forms	Consent forms are needed when children are taken out on trips and outings. Some settings ask parents to sign one for every outing.

Type of record	Reason
Health and dietary needs	Records are kept of children's particular needs in relation to their health or diet. This enables staff to make sure that any activities, food and drinks that they are planning are appropriate. It also allows them to take the correct course of action if they see that a child is looking unwell.
Records of medicine administered	Where settings are willing to administer medicines to children, it is important that records are kept of the type of medicine that is brought into the setting, who it belongs to, and how it is to be administered. Parents have to sign the records to show that they have given their consent for medicine to be given to the child. Staff must keep a record of what has been given and at what time.
Information about children and their families	Most settings fill in a general form when a child first enters a setting. This form includes details about the child and the family, such as their address and full name. This form must be kept up to date, as some details may change, for example, a child's name might be changed or the family might move.
Inventory of equipment	Many settings keep a list of the equipment and the resources that they have. This allows them to check from time to time that equipment is still in good order and has not gone missing. Inventories must be kept up to date in case there is an insurance claim, when they can be used as evidence.
Insurance details	Up-to-date records of insurance details are important. Some, such as public liability, must be displayed in a setting. Common insurance policies include public liability and employers' liability, buildings insurance and contents insurance.
Staff/volunteers records	Employers need to keep records about the staff. This should include a copy of their job descriptions, application forms or curricula vitae and details about their pay, including National Insurance contributions and income tax. Staff also need to be approved by the Criminal Records Bureau (CRB), and staff and volunteers in settings need to have police clearance.
Work rotas and logs	Most settings find it useful to keep a work rota or log so that they can pay staff accurately and check that rotas are fair.

Other information that should be maintained

You will also need to keep the following information.

- The name and contact details of the person responsible for the setting (the registered person).
- A record of visitors: this should be in the form of a visitors' book indicating the name, purpose of visit and time in and time out. This is important both for knowing who is on the premises in case of an emergency such as a fire, and as a record of everyone who has visited the setting. This will be required for inspection by the Ofsted inspector.
- Infectious, notifiable diseases: there are a number of diseases that must be reported to the Communicable Disease Surveillance Centre at the Health Protection Agency, for example, dysentery, food poisoning, tuberculosis or meningitis. If you are not sure how to do this, contact your local Children's Information Service (CIS) for advice.
- A record of risk assessments carried out: this will be required for inspection by the Ofsted inspector.
- A record of fire drills carried out: this will be required for inspection by the Ofsted inspector.
- Insurance certificates: these need to be displayed, and will be required for inspection by the Ofsted inspector.

The Ofsted Childcare Register

The Childcare Bill of 2005 announced the creation of an Ofsted Childcare Register for provision for school age children. This builds on existing legislation concerning people who are suitable to work in childcare as well as health and safety. It stipulates child:adult ratios and what are considered suitable qualifications for people working in the various fields of childcare. It is compulsory for all childcare providers for children under 8 to join the Ofsted Childcare Register. Registration is voluntary for providers caring for children from 8 to 14.

If a setting is on the register, parents using that setting can access childcare tax credits. They will not be able to do this if the setting is not on the register.

Keeping records up to date, legible and accurate

Many records are essential to a setting, not just because they help the setting to run smoothly but also because there is a legal requirement to keep them. This means that they need to be kept up to date, and be legible and accurate. To do this, you need to be very disciplined and organised. You will be wise to note down information in the correct place soon after it has been given, or write a note to yourself as a reminder to do so later.

Some records need updating rather than adding to, such as the list of emergency contact numbers. At least once a year, parents should be asked to check the information on file to make sure it is still correct. In the same way, staff files might need to be checked periodically so that the information stored is still accurate.

To keep the records up to date, some people build in a regular daily time slot when they know that they will be able to concentrate on the administration without being disturbed. It is not uncommon to find playworkers doing this after the end of sessions.

Store information securely but conveniently

Filing systems

It is helpful to have a systematic filing system. If documents are put away in order they can be retrieved quickly when you need to give information to an authorised person or agency.

There are many ways of storing information. Some people use large files, while others store the majority of information in filing cabinets. Whatever system you use, make sure that you label everything clearly and logically so that others can find information if you are not available. This will be essential in an emergency situation, when a child's or a staff member's folder will be required immediately.

The filing system should distinguish between information that needs to be secure and information that needs to be easily accessible to others in the setting. Staff files, for example, will need to be locked away, whereas the week's work rota will need to be displayed. Some information, such as children's records, might be kept unlocked during the sessions, but locked when the setting is closed.

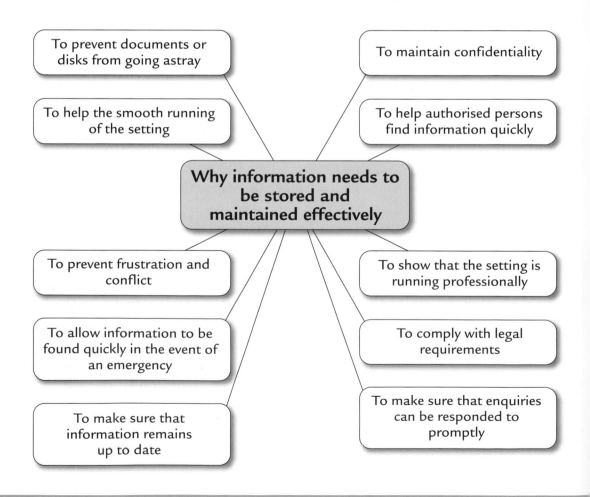

It can be helpful to put a 'contents' list on the front of the filing cabinet drawer or at the front of a file so others can find information easily. This enables people to check quickly whether the information they are looking for is available.

The diagram on the previous page shows the reasons why information needs to be stored and maintained effectively.

An organised filing system helps you and others to find information quickly and easily

Restrict access to information appropriately

Restrictions on access mean that information is more likely to be kept confidential, and if there is a breach of confidentiality it is easier to discover the source. If you are responsible for maintaining records, it is important that you understand who can have access to them. This will often vary according to the type of information that is being stored.

All playworkers within a setting will probably need access to attendance registers and information about children, but this is likely to be restricted for volunteers or students working within the setting. In the same way, only the manager and the person responsible for personnel may have access to staff files, although most settings have a policy whereby they allow staff to have access to their own files.

If you are asked to provide information and you are unsure whether the person asking for it should have access to it, refer to your line manager or another senior colleague. To prevent unauthorised people having access to information, always lock away information and make sure that the key is kept in a secure place. If several types of records are being stored together, it may be best to take out the records that the person is authorised to look at, rather than allow him or her to retrieve the information and perhaps stumble across other information that is sensitive and confidential.

ACTIVE KNOWLEDGE

Look at the following list of records that might be kept in a setting:

- attendance register
- emergency contact numbers
- staff employment details
- accident book
- telephone numbers of staff.

For each type of record, write a list of people within your setting who have free access to this information.

Access to information

The Data Information Act 1984 was brought in to protect people. Personal information that was held on computer could not be passed on without the person's knowledge. This Act applied only to information that was held on computers, not on paper. The Access to Personal Files Act 1987 extended it to paper-based records kept by local authorities. The Access to Health Records Act 1990 further extended the law, this time to include health providers. A new Data Protection Act passed in 1998 updated the law and provided for all records about clients, whether on paper or held electronically.

Under the law, anyone who is storing personal information about others on computer must register with the Data Protection Register. Anyone who is registered must abide by the following code.

- Individuals have the right to know what data is being held about them, and the right to correct it if it is inaccurate.
- Individuals may refuse to provide information.
- Data must be lawfully collected and processed fairly.
- Data cannot be passed on or used for other purposes without permission.
- Data must be accurate and kept up to date.
- Data can only be collected and stored for the purpose that has been registered.
- Data should not be kept longer than necessary.
- Data must be kept secure, so that confidentiality is protected.

CASE STUDY

Mary is convinced that she is being underpaid in comparison with other playworkers at the setting. She does not want to ask the others how much they are getting paid, but is very keen to find out. She decides to look at the staff files to see what everyone else is being paid.

She wanders into the office where you are working, and asks you if you have a key to a filing cabinet to check something out. When you ask her what she needs, she says that she wants to look at her own employee file.

1 **Explain how you would handle this situation without breaching any confidentiality.**

Provide information promptly when necessary

If you are responsible for storing some types of information, you might on occasion be asked to provide it for your line manager or others such as auditors, registration officers and the emergency services. Being able to provide the information quickly is important, not least because it shows that the setting is being run professionally and efficiently. In extreme cases, such as where a child has a medical condition, it might even be life-saving. The diagram below shows some of the reasons why information might be requested from authorised people.

To provide evidence of attendance

To help a line manager make a decision or resolve a dispute

To answer a query from a prospective client

To check dietary or medical requirements

Reasons why information might be requested

To provide statistics for a fund-raising bid

To check that quality standards are being met

To help an investigation from social services, the police or the health and safety executive

To check access arrangements where children are estranged from one parent

To provide information for a survey for another organisation

To show auditors where money has been received and spent

CONSOLIDATION

Choose an example of one type of record that you are responsible for maintaining and storing.

1 Why is this information needed?

2 How do you make sure that it is kept up to date?

3 Who has access to this information?

4 How do you ensure that this information is easily retrievable?

END OF UNIT KNOWLEDGE CHECK

1 Why is it important to keep accurate records?

2 Name three Acts of Parliament that influence administration in a setting and briefly describe their impact.

3 Outline three areas of information which may be requested by parents.

4 Why is it important that information is gathered about children?

5 Outline three types of records that have to be maintained.

6 Give three reasons why records must be stored and maintained effectively.

7 What is the Data Protection Act and how does it affect your setting?

8 Give two methods of organising and storing records.

Further reading

A Taxonomy of Play Types, Bob Hughes (2002), available at
www.playeducation.com

Best Play, Children's Play Council (2002), available at www.ncb.org.uk/cpc

Evolutionary Playwork and Reflective Analytic Practice, Bob Hughes (2001),
Routledge

First claim – Desirable Processes, Play Wales, Baltic House, Mount Stuart
Square, Cardiff bay, Cardiff CF10 5HE Tel 02920 486050

Growing up: from eight years to young adulthood, Jennie Lindon (1996), National
Children's Bureau

Involving Volunteers in Children's Play, Donne Buck (1987), Volunteer Centre UK

Parachute Play, Meynell (1993), Meynell Games Publications

Partnership with Parents, Phillipa Russell, National Children's Bureau

Play, Catherine Garvey (1990), Harvard University Press

Play Environments – a question of quality, Bob Hughes (1996), available at
www.playeducation.com

Playwork – Theory and Practice, Fraser Brown (ed) (2002), Open University Press

Risk and Safety in Play, Dave Potter (1997), E F Spon Publishers Ltd

Resource books for parents of children and young people with disabilities,
10–18-years-old, Council for Disabled Children

The Ambiguity of Play, Brian Sutton-Smith (2001), Harvard University Press

The Busker's Guide to Playwork, Shelly Newstead, available at
www.commonthreads.co.uk

The Play Cycle, Gordon Sturrock and Penny Else (2003), available on cd-rom
via www.commonthreads.co.uk

Your Child from 5 to 11, Jennie Lindon (1993), National Children's Bureau

Useful addresses

Every effort has been made to ensure that all details were up to date at the time of publication.

Many of the details below are for each organisation's head office, which should be able to provide local contact numbers.

ADD/ADHD Family Support Group
1a The High Street
Dilton Marsh
Nr Westbury
Wilts BA13 4DL

Barnardo's
Tanners Lane
Barkingside
Ilford
Essex IG6 1QC
Tel: 020 8550 8822
Web: www.barnardos.org.uk

Allergy UK
3 White Oak Square
London Road
Swanley
Kent BR8 7AG
Allergy Helpline: 01322 619 898
Fax: 01322 663 480
Email: info@allergyuk.org
Web: www.allergyuk.org

British Council of Disabled People
Litchurch Plaza
Litchurch Lane
Derby DE24 8AA
Tel: 01332 295 551
Minicom: 01332 295 581
Fax: 01332 295 580
Web: www.bcodp.org.uk

British Deaf Association (BDA)
69 Wilson Street
London EC2A 2BB
Email: london@signcommunity.org.uk
Videophone IP: 81.138.165.105
Textphone: 020 7588 3529
Tel: 020 7588 3520
Fax: 020 7588 3527
Web: www.bda.org.uk

British Red Cross Society (BRCS)
UK Office
44 Moorfields
London EC2Y 9AL
Tel: 0870 170 7000
Web: www.redcross.org.uk

Child Accident Prevention Trust
4th Floor, Cloister Court
22-26 Farringdon Lane
London
EC1R 3AJ

ChildLine
Studd Street
London N1 0QW
Helpline: 0800 1111
Web: www.childline.org.uk

ChildLine Scotland
18. Albian Street
Glasgow G1 1LH
Tel: 0870 336 2910
Fax: 0870 336 2911
Web: www.childline.org.uk/Scotland

ChildLine Scotland (North and North East)
2 Paynernook Road
Aberdeen AB11 SRW
Tel: 0870 336 2900

The Children's Society
Edward Rudolf House
Margery Street
London WC1X 0JL
Tel: 0845 300 1128
Web: www.the-childrens-society.org.uk

Commission for Racial Equality
St Dunstan's House
201-211 Borough High Street
London SE1 1GZ
Tel: 020 7939 0000
Fax: 020 7939 0004
Email: info@cre.gov.uk
Web: www.cre.gov.uk

CRUSE Bereavement Care
126 Sheen Road
Richmond
Surrey TW9 1UR
Tel: 020 8939 9530
Helpline: 0870 167 1677
Web: www.crusebereavementcare.org.uk

EPOCH (End Physical Punishment Of Children)
77 Holloway Road
London N7 8JZ
Tel: 020 7700 0627
Associated web: www.stophitting.com

Kidscape
2 Grosvenor Gardens
London SW1W 0DH
Tel: 020 7730 3300
Fax: 020 7730 7081
Email: webinfo@kidscape.org.uk
Web: www.kidscape.org.uk

MIND (National Association for Mental Health)
15–19 Broadway
London E15 4BQ
Tel: 020 8519 2122
Fax: 020 8519 21725
Email: contact@mind.org.uk
Web: www.mind.org.uk

National Childminding Association (NCMA)
Royal Court
81 Tweedy Road
Bromley
Kent BR1 1TG
Tel: 0845 880 0044

Scottish Childminding Association (SCMA)
Suite 3
7 Melville Terrace
Stirling FK8 2ND

National Deaf Children's Society
15 Dufferin Street
London EC1Y 8UR
Tel: 020 7490 8656
Email: ndcs@ndcs.org.uk
Web: www.ndcs.org.uk

National Drugs Helpline
Helpline: 0800 776600
Email: helpline@ndh.org.uk
Web: www.ndh.org.uk

NSPCC (National Society for the Prevention of Cruelty to Children)
42 Curtain Road
London EC2A 3NH
Tel: 020 7825 2500
Fax: 020 7825 2525
Helpline: 0808 800 5000
Textphone: 0800 056 0566
Web: www.nspcc.org.uk

National Toy and Leisure Libraries
68 Churchway
London NW1 1LT
Tel: 020 7255 4600
Fax: 020 7255 4602
Email: admin@playmatters.co.uk
Web: www.natll.org.uk

Royal Society for the Prevention of Accidents (RoSPA)
Edgbaston Park
353 Bristol Road
Edgbaston
Birmingham B5 7ST
Tel: 0121 248 2000
Email: help@rospa.co.uk
Web: www.rospa.co.uk

SCOPE
6 Market Road
London N7 9PW
Helpline: 0808 800 333
Email: cphelpline@scope.org.uk
Web: www.scope.org.uk

Scottish Executive Education Department
Web: www.scotland.gov.uk

St. John Ambulance
27 St John's Lane
London EC1M 4BU
Tel: 08700 10 49 50
Email: info@sja.org.uk
Web: www.sja.org.uk

4 Children
Tel: 020 7512 2112
Fax: 020 7537 6012
Email: Info@4Children.org.uk

Glossary of terms

Anti-discriminatory practice	– being aware of and removing potential barriers that might cause discrimination either intentionally or unintentionally.
Applicants	– people who are interested in working in a setting.
Bullying	– aggression deliberately and/or persistently directed against a particular target or victim.
Child-centred play environment	– a place where children can play freely and in safety.
Children's and young people's rights	– entitlement under law and the United Nations Convention on the Rights of the Child – in particular that children and young people have a right to play and free time, to say what they think and be listened to about decisions that affect them.
Collating information	– bringing different sources of information together.
Conflict	– times when children disagree during their play.
Constructive criticism	– feedback given in a positive way designed to improve performance.
Disclosure	– a term sometimes used when children report or indicate that they are being abused.
Feedback	– information given by others.
Financial transaction	– when money is transferred from one person or organisation to another.
Formal feedback	– information given in an organised way.
Inclusion	– ensuring that play provision is open and accessible to all so that all children and young people, including the disabled and those from other minority groups, can participate.
Informal feedback	– information given in a spontaneous way.
Interagency working	– work involving more than one agency or organisation.

Index

Page numbers in italics refer to diagrams and illustrations.

Appendix: Scottish National Care Standards for SVQs

Standard 1: Being welcomed and valued

Each child or young person will be welcomed, and will be valued as an individual.

Standard 2: A safe environment

The needs of each child or young person are met by the service in a safe environment, in line with all relevant legislation.

Standard 3: Health and wellbeing

Each child or young person will be nurtured by staff who will promote his or her general wellbeing, health, nutrition and safety.

Standard 4: Engaging with children

Each child or young person will be supported by staff who interact effectively and enthusiastically with him or her.

Standard 5: Quality of experience

Each child or young person can experience and choose from a balanced range of activities.

Standard 6: Support and development

Each child or young person receives support from staff who respond to his or her individual needs.

Standard 8: Equality and fairness

You will be treated equally and fairly.

Standard 12: Confidence in staff

Each child or young person receives support and care from staff who are competent and confident and who have gone through a careful selection procedure.

Standard 13: Improving the service

You can be confident that the service will evaluate what it does and make improvements.

Standard 14: Well-managed service

You can be confident that you are using a service that is well managed.